ABUSE BETWEEN YOUNG PEOPLE

Awareness of peer-on-peer abuse is on the rise and is a matter of increasing international concern. *Abuse Between Young People: A Contextual Account* is the first book to offer a contextualised narrative of peer-on-peer abuse that moves beyond recognising an association between environments and individual choice, and illustrates the ways in which such interplay occurs.

Using both sociological and feminist perspectives, Firmin reshapes the way that peer-on-peer abuse is perceived and investigates the effect of gendered social context on the nature of abuse between young people. This text also uses an in-depth case study to explore associations between abusive incidents and young people's homes, peer groups, schools and neighbourhoods, in addition to broader societal influences such as pornography and politics. National and international policies are woven into each chapter, along with insights from parenting programmes, the troubled families' agenda, and bullying and community safety policies.

Abuse Between Young People presents a clear insight into the various contexts that affect the nature of peer-on-peer abuse, providing a thorough analysis into the debates on this issue. In so doing, Firmin creates a vital contextual approach to safeguarding young people affected by this issue. It is invaluable reading for students and researchers in social work, education, criminology, sociology and psychology, as well as practitioners and policymakers concerned with the protection of young people.

Carlene Firmin, MBE, is a Principal Research Fellow at 'The International Centre: Researching Child Sexual Exploitation, Violence and Trafficking' at the University of Bedfordshire, UK.

ABUSE BETWEEN YOUNG PEOPLE

A Contextual Account

Carlene Firmin

Routledge
Taylor & Francis Group

LONDON AND NEW YORK

First published 2018
by Routledge
2 Park Square, Milton Park, Abingdon, Oxon OX14 4RN

and by Routledge
711 Third Avenue, New York, NY 10017

Routledge is an imprint of the Taylor & Francis Group, an informa business

British Library Cataloguing-in-Publication Data
A catalogue record for this book is available from the British Library

Library of Congress Cataloguing-in-Publication Data
Names: Firmin, Carlene, author.
Title: Abuse between young people : a contextual account /
    Carlene Firmin.
Description: Abingdon, Oxon ; New York, NY : Routledge, 2018.
Identifiers: LCCN 2017034103 | ISBN 9781138932227 (hardback : alk. paper) |
    ISBN 9781138932234 (pbk. : alk. paper)
Subjects: LCSH: Violence in adolescence. | Abused teenagers. |
    Sexually abused teenagers. | Interpersonal conflict in adolescence. |
    Youth and violence. | Child welfare.
Classification: LCC RJ506.V56 F55 2018 | DDC 616.85/836—dc23
LC record available at https://lccn.loc.gov/2017034103

ISBN: 978-1-138-93222-7 (hbk)
ISBN: 978-1-138-93223-4 (pbk)
ISBN: 978-1-315-67938-9 (ebk)

Typeset in Bembo
by Apex CoVantage, LLC

CONTENTS

SECTION I

Setting the scene

Peer-on-peer abuse and contextual investigation

1

INTRODUCTION

Over the past decade public concern, political debate and research evidence on abuse between young people has increased. National inquiries into institutional abuse in Australia and the UK have surfaced evidence of young people being sexually abused by peers in children's homes and schools. Approaches to preventing teenage relationship abuse have been developed in the UK, US and Australia (De La Rue, et al., 2014; Home Office, 2013; Our Watch, 2016) in response to a burgeoning concern that a significant number of young people, particularly young women, experience physical, emotional and sexual abuse from partners before they turn 18. An upsurge in identified cases of child sexual exploitation perpetrated by adults has raised awareness of peer-on-peer sexual exploitation (Barnardo's, 2013; Firmin, 2013; Pitts, 2013), and street-based violence between young men continues to be an issue of global concern to the UN and multiple state departments (HM Government, 2016; Office of National Statistics, 2013; UNGEI, 2015).

There isn't, strictly speaking, one research community that has influenced this increasing prioritisation of policy and practice responses to peer-on-peer abuse. For example, some researchers study the phenomenon of harmful sexual behaviour, others violence against women and girls, and others serious youth violence. Some are criminologists, others psychologists, social work academics and even geographers. These discrete research communities have been guided by different definitions of abuse between young people and explored particular dynamics of these abusive behaviours. For this book, they are drawn together under the definition of:

Physical, sexual, emotional and financial abuse, and coercive control, exercised within young people's relationships

While some academics have helpfully drawn these academic disciplines together through edited collections on 'peer-victimisation' (Barter & Berridge, 2011;

Hagell & Jeyarajah-Dent, 2006), much about what this evidence base has to collectively offer in advancing our understanding of peer-on-peer abuse is yet to be explored. One such under-investigated aspect of the evidence base is its communal narrative on the influence of the social contexts and situations in which abusive behaviours escalate. From schools and other educational settings, public spaces such as transport hubs, parks and shopping centres, through to peer and familial relationships, research routinely suggests a relationship between the social-cultural contexts in which peer-on-peer abuse occurs and the behaviour itself. And it is this element of the evidence base, the nature and interactions of the contexts associated with peer-on-peer abuse, that this book endeavours to explore.

The contextual dynamics of peer-on-peer abuse

Contexts associated with peer-on-peer abuse have been clearly and consistently identified (Barter, et al., 2009; Cowie, 2011; Firmin, 2013; Letourneau & Borduin, 2008; Warr, 2002). Whether researchers have been concerned with sexual exploitation, youth violence or teenage relationship abuse, these same contextual relationships have emerged. Predominantly, research and policy responses have focused on the relationship between young people's families and their experiences of peer-on-peer abuse. Experiences of familial abuse, exposure to domestic abuse and criminality within families are some of the factors within young people's homes that are considered to increase young people's vulnerability to abusing, or being abused by, their peers. Peer relationships and peer group dynamics, including those that are informed by harmful gender norms, violence and aggression, have been found to motivate and normalise young people's abuse of their peers and partners. Many of these harmful peer relationships have been developed in school, community or neighbourhood contexts and are played out in online and offline spaces. Young people's exposure to violence and criminality in these public contexts, and their lack of protection and safety in these spaces, has motivated weapon carrying amongst young people, normalised abusive and exploitative social rules, and created contexts conducive with peer-on-peer abuse. These social-cultural contexts set the stage, and increase the vulnerability, for peer-on-peer abuse occurring, but the nature and implications of this require greater consideration.

Firstly – in what ways do these different environmental and relational factors interplay with one another? How does the fact that a young person lives in an abusive home relate to their experiences of violence or harmful gender norms in their peer relationships? Likewise, when young people live in safe and supportive families, to what extent does this safeguard them from the association between street-based victimisation and experiences of peer-on-peer abuse? Understanding the relationship between contexts associated with peer-on-peer abuse has the potential to better inform how the social-cultural dynamics of the issue are responded to in practice – and this also has implications for how young people's behaviours and choices are understood.

'Choice' is often central to how young people's experiences of peer-on-peer abuse have been conceptualised and how responses to their experiences have been critiqued. Inquiries into sexual exploitation have admonished practices which held young people 'responsible' for making 'choices' to be in abusive situations and relationships (Berelowitz, et al., 2013; Coffey, 2014; Jay, 2014). The age at which young people are held criminally responsible for their actions and the contextual dynamics that might mitigate their culpability have also been disputed and discussed (Aynsley, et al., 2016; Criminal Justice Joint Inspection, 2013; Crown Prosecution Service, 2012). These debates have surfaced the ways in which context constrains or creates choices for young people affected by peer-on-peer abuse. By bringing contextual dynamics to the fore, and exploring the relationships between contexts, a social account of choice is enabled and the importance of embedding such accounts into policy and practice is illustrated.

By understanding choice in a social way the relationship between young people's agency and dependency also becomes a feature of a contextual account of peer-on-peer abuse. When contexts, rather than individual decisions, are the primary focus, consideration has to be given to young people's dependency, as well as agency, in all of these social spaces. Who are young people dependent upon for their safety when they are at school, using local transport services, socialising with peers or spending time in their local park? This question is critical once these contexts are recognised as ones in which young people encounter peer-on-peer abuse. While they are social agents in these spaces – and making choices as outlined previously – their sense of agency and individual freedoms will be informed by a dependency on others who create and shape the contexts in which they spend their time.

In focusing on the environments and relationships associated with peer-on-peer abuse interplays between contexts, the social dimensions of choice and the relationship between young people's agency and dependency is illuminated throughout this book. Not only does such an approach further how peer-on-peer abuse is understood but it also provides a foundation upon which to assess, critique and advance existing policy and practice responses to the issue.

Policy and practice responses to peer-on-peer abuse: a contextual assessment

The need to improve safeguarding responses to young people at risk of abuse during adolescence is a matter of national and international debate, and has been for many years (Hanson & Holmes, 2015; House of Commons Education Committee, 2012; Ofsted, 2011; United Nations, 2015). In relation to peer-on-peer abuse, the UK government, like many others, has introduced a range of policies, funding streams and guidance documents to advance local responses to different forms of peer-on-peer abuse – such as serious youth violence (Home Office, 2011), teenage relationship abuse (Home Office, 2013) and peer-on-peer sexual exploitation (HM Government, 2016). These issue-specific activities build, and are dependent, upon the statutory frameworks in place to safeguard children and young people.

As such there is a relationship between the need to advance general practices to safeguard young people during adolescence and policies and procedures that have been developed to more specifically respond to peer-on-peer abuse. Research, inquiries and campaigns have pointed to the insufficiencies of policy and practice frameworks concerned with both peer-on-peer abuse specifically, and safeguarding young people more broadly. The contextual account of peer-on-peer abuse presented in this book contributes to and, to an extent, furthers this discussion in three key ways.

As the social and contextual dynamics of peer-on-peer abuse have emerged in the evidence base, researchers have highlighted the limitations posed by 1:1 assessment, intervention and support put in place to respond. They argue that accounts of abuse and violence which focus on the deficits and behavioural characteristics of individuals affected by peer-on-peer abuse fail to address the social factors that may be driving abusive incidents. Similar criticisms have also been levelled at child protection systems more broadly – particularly those that focus on intervening with families, rather than the social factors that undermine the ability of families to safeguard their children (Featherstone, et al., 2016; Firmin, et al., 2016; Parton, 2014). While this book presents the individual characteristics of young people who have abused, or been abused by, their peers, these characteristics are put into context and considered in this light. By doing so it further evidences the limitations of policy frameworks which only intervene with individuals affected by social issues, and makes a case for contextualising child protection and safeguarding frameworks broadly and developing contextual responses to peer-on-peer abuse more specifically.

Related to the aforementioned point, this book provides a detailed account of education, public and peer contexts associated with peer-on-peer abuse – all of which have been acknowledged in policy responses to peer-on-peer abuse but are not accommodated by wider child protection frameworks. Policy responses to gang-associated violence and exploitation have identified alternative education provisions, residential children's homes and violent neighbourhoods as sites in which young people have been abused by peers (HM Government, 2016). Residential children's homes have also been linked to young people's experiences of sexual exploitation, including peer-on-peer exploitation, along with schools, hotels, transport hubs and public businesses such as fast food restaurants and take-away shops (D'Arcy & Thomas, 2016; Hughes-Jones & Roberts, 2015).[1] It is important to note, however, that much of this policy development has emerged from policing and criminal justice government departments rather than those concerned with safeguarding and child protection. In fact, statutory child protection frameworks in the UK and similar policy contexts do not explicitly incorporate interventions and partnerships with services that operate in and manage public and social environments. A contextual account of peer-on-peer abuse has implications for this significant limitation within child protection practices and makes a case for extending child protection processes and partnerships to services that are better placed to engage with the peer groups and school and public environments associated with peer-on-peer abuse.

Finally, in bringing together discrete areas of research (into harmful sexual behaviour, serious youth violence, peer-on-peer sexual exploitation and teenage relationship abuse), the contextual narrative offered in this book furthers the need for holistic policy frameworks for responding to the interconnected nature of different forms of peer-on-peer abuse. To date, responses to peer-on-peer abuse have straddled issue-specific policy frameworks that don't necessarily talk to one another, or general child protection frameworks that don't engage with the contextual dynamics of the issue. For example, when a young woman is physically abused by her partner, who is associated with a gang and has been victimised by peers himself, and is then sexually exploited by him, there is not one policy framework in place to address this issue. Wider child protection frameworks would not be able to accommodate the contextual associations established in the research to date, and discrete policy agendas focus on the distinct elements of different manifestations of peer-on-peer abuse but not necessarily where they interconnect or are shared. The contextual account presented in this book is achieved via a holistic narrative of different forms of peer-on-peer abuse. It focuses on contextual elements of peer-on-peer abuse that are shared across different manifestations of abuse and provides a foundation for advancing holistic and child protection responses that are better equipped to safeguarding adolescents.

Structure and approach of the book

This book builds a contextual account of peer-on-peer abuse, and the implications for policy and practice, by using international research, media and policy accounts, supplemented with unpublished evidence from reviews of nine cases in which young people were raped or murdered by their peers. Case review evidence is used to illustrate and further the contextual information already documented in published research and is used to assess and query existing policy and practice responses. Case review evidence is largely presented thematically, interwoven with secondary literature to exemplify the relationship between contextual dynamics and individual choices at the point of an abusive incident. However, it is also used to build a vignette that runs throughout the book. The vignette is developed from the nine cases that were reviewed and offers the reader a contextual account of a peer-on-peer abuse incident to personalise the data presented in the book.

The international research, case review evidence and contextual vignette of peer-on-peer abuse are presented in this book across three sections. The first section, including this chapter and the two that follow, set the scene for the book. It documents the behaviours involved in peer-on-peer abuse and the individuals affected, illustrating the scale of the challenge faced by policymakers and the need to understand these characteristics through a contextual lens. Having presented the importance of a contextual account, the theoretical framework for building the required narrative is presented and the methodological approach taken to exploring the evidence is outlined. By the end of Section I the reader will have a clear understanding of the need for a contextual account of peer-on-peer abuse and the approach taken in the book to achieve this.

The second section of the book is dedicated to the contexts associated with peer-on-peer abuse. Spread across four chapters, the family and peer relationships of young people affected by peer-on-peer abuse and the educational, public and social contexts in which these relationships formed are considered. By examining each context in detail, the relationship between them begins to emerge. Taken collectively, this section puts into context the behaviours young people display and the choices that they make when they are abused by, or abuse, their peers.

The third and final section of the book outlines the implications of contextual interplay, social accounts of choice and the recognition of contextual dependency and agency on policy and practice frameworks concerned with peer-on-peer abuse. Across the four chapters of Section III the implications of the contextual account offered in Section II are explored and recommendations for policy and practice are developed. The final chapter of Section III provides the foundations for building a sufficient safeguarding response to young people affected by peer-on-peer abuse specifically, and extra-familial risk more generally, and in doing so builds upon wider calls to improve the safety and well-being of adolescents across the world.

Ultimately, when we interrogate the environments in which peer-on-peer abuse escalates, we are forced to ask questions of ourselves and of the services charged with duties to keep young people safe. In this book, safeguarding emerges as an issue, and a responsibility, for all those who manage and/or inform the nature of the environments in which peer-on-peer abuse manifests. While responding to young people's experiences of sexual, emotional and physical abuse may appear to be primarily the duty of children's services and the police, the contextual nature of the phenomenon draws a wider set of agencies and individuals into the safeguarding frame. From those who manage and use the buses upon which young people experience robbery and violence, to those who attend or manage the schools in which young people are bullied, preventing, identifying and responding to peer-on-peer abuse is presented as a social responsibility. Developing approaches to accommodate the contextual implications of this book are in their infancy. However, through this book I have provided a theoretical foundation upon which approaches can be developed, tested and adapted which address these implications. In doing so this book contributes to the creation of a contextual approach to safeguarding – one equipped to keep young people safe in *every* social environment in which they encounter significant harm.

Note

1 Less attention has been paid by policymakers to the contextual dynamics of teenage relationship abuse and the behaviours of young people who display harmful sexual behaviours.

2

THE CHALLENGE WE FACE

The nature of peer-on-peer abuse and those affected

From sexual harassment in school corridors, muggings on public transport and online threats via social media, through to inter-gang rapes, sexual exploitation in peer groups and physical assaults in their intimate relationships, young people are harmed by their peers in a myriad of ways. Far from being isolated incidents that hit media headlines, a 2012 survey of 1,065 13–14 year olds in England found that just over half (52.5%) had at least one experience of victimisation, perpetration or witnessing relationship abuse. It is estimated that children aged 10 to 15 in England and Wales experienced 821,000 incidents of crime in 2013, of which 465,000 (57%) were violent incidents and 79 per cent of these were perpetrated by someone who was also 10–15 years old (ONS, 2015). Far from being a phenomenon to have emerged over the past few years, nearly two thirds (65.9%) of adult survivors of contact child sexual abuse have reported that they were abused by another young person when they were younger and not by an adult.

While this may seem like a large number of young people, the UK, like other European countries, has far lower reported rates of peer-on-peer abuse than in other parts of the world, including North America, Latin America, Israel and Nicaragua. According to the World Health Organisation (2002), at the turn of the millennium 199,000 young people[1] were killed by other young people globally – at a rate of 9.2 per 100,000. For every young person killed by a peer worldwide an estimated 20 to 40 are injured to the point of requiring hospital treatment. Comparatively, global figures of young women's experiences of sexual violence are similar to that of the UK, with the same World Health Organisation report finding that a third of adolescent girls around the world have experienced sexual violence.

This chapter documents the nature of the abusive behaviours and the characteristics of individual young people behind these statistics. In doing so it demonstrates the interconnected and sometimes overlapping nature of forms of peer-on-peer abuse which, to date, have largely been explored and responded to independently of one another. It also identifies that while some young people who have abused, and/ or have been abused by, their peers have particular experiences or characteristics in common, there is no single feature that unites them all. As a result, the behaviours and individual characteristics documented here may be better understood in relation to the contexts in which they form and interact – contexts which the remainder of this book explores.

Defining peer-on-peer abuse

There isn't one collective research community or policy agenda dedicated to furthering understandings of and responses to peer-on-peer abuse. Instead, as indicated in Chapter 1, research into teenage relationship abuse and intimate partner violence, child sexual exploitation, serious youth- and gang-related violence, young people with harmful sexual behaviour, multiple perpetrator rape and bullying all contain subsets of evidence on peer-on-peer abuse that help shape how the phenomenon has been understood and responded to (Figure 2.1).

The UK government has developed distinct policy responses to each of these discrete research areas. In 2008 and 2011, for example, the UK government published strategies to tackle gang-related and serious youth violence; in 2011 a separate policy unit within government developed a strategy for responding to violence against women and girls (which included teenage relationship abuse and multiple perpetrator rape); and in 2009 and 2017 a wholly distinct government department published guidance on responding to child sexual exploitation (DCSF, 2009; DfE, 2017). Education policy departments have provided advice on responding to bullying within schools (DfE, 2014) and, in the absence of a government strategy on the issue, health guidelines have been developed on young people who display harmful sexual behaviours (NICE, 2016). Following suit, local strategic partnerships across England and Wales have developed individual strategies for addressing these distinct policy areas, conceptualising them as different forms of abuse.

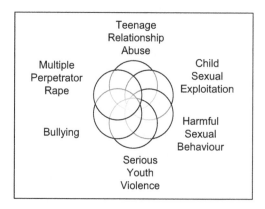

FIGURE 2.1 Subsets of peer-on-peer abuse

Each of these research and policy areas utilises its own definitions; many are either too broad or too narrow to capture all manifestations of peer-on-peer abuse. For example, research on, and policy responses to, child sexual exploitation engage with incidents of adult-on-child, as well as child-on-child, abuse. Comparatively the study of young people who display harmful sexual behaviour, and the developing policy response to this issue, is concerned with incidents of sibling abuse and the abuse of much younger children by those in adolescence, as well as peer-on-peer sexual abuse. Finally, the policy response to serious youth violence, and research conducted in this area, often extends to people up to the age of 25 and is therefore not only targeted at individuals legally defined in UK policy as children (under age 18).

The aforementioned approach to defining, studying and responding to young people's experiences of violence and abuse often focuses on particular aspects of an incident in order to categorise it appropriately. For example, let's consider an offence of 'rape'. Legally, rape is defined as:

- (A) intentionally penetrates the vagina, anus or mouth of another person (B) with his penis;
- (B) does not consent to the penetration, and
- (A) does not reasonably believe that (B) consents
  Penetration of the mouth is included.
  Rape is still a crime of basic intent, and drunkenness is no defence.

(Sexual Offences Act, 2003; Section 1)

To categorise this incident further using the aforementioned research and policy demarcations, supplementary questions may be asked such as: Was an exploitative exchange involved in the sexual act – in which case it could be defined as a rape in the context of child sexual exploitation? Was anyone involved in the incident gang-affiliated – in which case it could be perceived as a gang-associated rape? Did it involve the use of a knife – if so it could be considered an act of serious youth violence? Were the young people involved in an intimate relationship – if so the same act could also be an example of teenage relationship abuse?

We may feel that there is much which is qualitatively different about the various situations outlined previously. Siloed approaches to research and policy development often bring these distinctions to the fore and are focused on developing different responses to accommodate for these distinct dynamics. However, as much as research into, and case reviews of, peer-on-peer abuse demonstrate some differences between incidents of peer-on-peer sexual exploitation and teenage relationship abuse, for example, they also evidence that there is much in common between these distinctly defined expressions of abuse. For example, research into young people with harmful sexual behaviour, particularly those who sexually harm similar-age peers, has found that the individuals involved often have similar profiles and life experiences to young people who are known for other forms of anti-social or violent behaviour (Beckett & Gerhold, 2003; Letourneau & Borduin, 2008). Likewise, testimonies from young women affected by gangs and serious youth violence chart a relationship between abuse they experience in their intimate relationships and their association with violent youth groups:

> One time him and 10 of his mates turned up, kicked my door in and all battered me for something I'd said to him, and did I get help, did I fuck; what would be the point of that?
>
> *(Firmin, 2011:42)*

> When the doors were closed, when there were no visitors around, anyone to see, he was a monster, yeah he turned into a monster over the years. Threatened me with a sword. He beat me up when I got pregnant with [child], tried to force me to have an abortion, so I ended the relationship . . . . It's normal, like . . . say if I told someone I had to call the police on my baby-father because he pulled a knife out, this is true, it happened, they would go, 'oh' – not at the fact that he pulled a knife out on me, but because I called the police. That's how normal it is.
>
> *(Beckett, et al., 2013:20)*

These examples give voice to the findings from large-scale surveys which imply that young people may experience different, and overlapping, forms of peer-on-peer abuse at any one time regardless of the definition/s employed by researchers and policymakers to describe that experience. Physical, emotional and sexual abuse often intersect in cases of serious youth violence (Beckett, et al., 2013), teenage relationship abuse (Barter, et al., 2009) or harmful sexual behaviour (Hackett, 2014). A young woman who is being physically and emotionally abused by her partner may be required to carry weapons for him and his friends who are also gang-affiliated and will be threatened with sexual violence if she does not. In a case such as this the abuse that the young woman experiences in her relationship directly informs, and enables, the ability of her partner and his friends to coerce her into weapon carrying. Likewise, threats of sexual violence serve to normalise the abuse she experiences in her relationship and expands her experiences of coercion from her intimate relationship to her wider peer network. Her experiences of peer-on-peer abuse are overlapping, and no single definition, policy area or research agenda outlined earlier in this chapter can, on their own, provide evidence or guidance to afford her sufficient protection.

In recognition of the relationship between different forms of peer-on-peer abuse, some scholars have produced edited collections that explore 'peer-violence' (Barter & Berridge, 2011) or 'interpersonal violence' (Hagell & Jeyarajah-Dent, 2006) in the round. Likewise over the past 12 months, policymakers in the UK have moved beyond policies which address specific forms of abuse towards strategies for addressing vulnerability, victimisation and/or violence more broadly (HM Government, 2016). The UK government has sought to broaden their response to sexual exploitation and developed a strategy for addressing all forms of exploitation – including the use of young people to traffic drugs across the country or those who are groomed into gang involvement. Locally, police forces across the UK are developing vulnerability, harm and risk action plans to coordinate their responses to different violent offences. Likewise, since 2009 multi-agency strategic partnerships in England and Wales set about to create working groups concerned with sexual exploitation – in the past 12 months a number of these have broadened their agendas to respond to adolescent vulnerability more generally or to explore the links between young people who go missing, have been sexually exploited and/or are at risk of gang-related violence. While limited, moves have also been made to ensure holistic international policy frameworks for preventing all forms of violence and abuse against children (World Health Organisation, 2014). In keeping with this direction of travel, this book brings together evidence on different forms of peer-on-peer abuse to explore the phenomenon holistically – the behaviours involved, the young people affected and the contexts to which such incidents are associated. The approach is one that should engender a policy and practice response to address the shared, and often contextual, dynamics of abuse.

The nature of the behaviours

Peer-on-peer abuse, in its various manifestations, involves physical, emotional and/or sexual abuse between young people – expressions of abuse that have often been explored discretely.

From punching, kicking and strangulation through to weapon-enabled violence, including murder, the media and academia have documented the ways that young people have physically abused their peers and partners in England (BBC, 2008; Barter, 2014; Berelowitz, et al., 2012; Gadd, et al., 2013; Hackett, 2014; Pitts, 2008; The Guardian, 2009). Young people themselves have described their experiences of being physically victimised by and victimising their peers:

> But then I've had some pretty bad injuries from both my exes and their mates: fractured eye socket, I've had me jaw broke, broken collar bone, broken hands, broken legs. R broke both of my legs six months into being with me, because we was at a party and his friends given me a hug, and as he's done that he's touched me bum, like on purpose.
>
> *(Firmin, 2011:44)*

> I came out of XXXX (Young Offender Institution) and there were these six boys on the XXXX estate who wanted to fight me because of something I was supposed to have said when I was inside. You have to fight; otherwise you'd look scared and it would get worse and they would think they could do what they like with you. They have to know that it won't be easy.
>
> *(Pitts, 2008:46)*

Large-scale surveys have demonstrated the extent to which individual accounts documented in research and media reports illustrate the experiences of significant numbers of young people in the UK and internationally. A 2014 survey conducted across five European countries, including the UK, found that between a half and two thirds of young women and between a third and two thirds of young men (aged 14 to 17 years old) surveyed reported experiencing intimate partner abuse (Barter, 2014). In a survey of young people in the UK five years prior (Barter, et al., 2009), the rates of relationship-based physical abuse reported by young women was comparable to those in the US (Halpern, et al., 2001; Hickman, et al., 2004).

Young people's experiences of physical abuse often feature elements of emotionally abusive behaviours (Barter, et al., 2009; Chung, 2005; Pitts, 2008). Over recent years the use of social media to facilitate emotional abuse has been ever-present in public and academic discourse (Berelowitz, et al., 2012; Ringrose, et al., 2011). High-profile cases of suicide that have occurred following online bullying (Herald Express, 2013; Mail Online, 2015b) and threats to post sexually explicit videos or photographic images of young people online, dubbed 'revenge porn' by politicians (Crown Prosecution Service, 2014), have led to calls for new legislation to address emotional abuse facilitated via the worldwide web. While these forms of emotional abuse are by no means the exclusive domain of young people, they punctuate and enable experiences of peer-on-peer abuse in ways that would not have been possible 10 years ago. Studies have reported the persistently present nature of the online space and how this impacts young people when being bullied and/or sexually harassed:

> R: Well, I know lots of times I've been asked and sometimes I will say 'No' and they will say, 'Okay' and they will be like nice to you and then they will ask again and then they will put pressure on you and stuff like this and I will just be like, 'I'm sorry, I don't want to' and they will say 'Why' and I will say 'I just don't want to', and they will say, like 'There's nothing wrong, like all you need to do is just suck on it' and I will be like, 'But I don't want to do that' and just keep going and they put the angry face on BBM and dedicate their status to you in a negative way.
>
> *(Ringrose, et al., 2011:38)*

Research has documented ways in which young people have ridiculed their peers, threatened them with social isolation or engaged in other bullying behaviours to cause distress and harm as well as sustain controlling and coercive peer and intimate relations (Barter, et al., 2009; Warr, 2002). The European study noted earlier (Barter, 2014) found that between 31 per cent and 59 per cent of young women and 19 per cent and 41 per cent of young men experienced some form of emotional abuse from a partner, including being threatened with violence, being shouted at, put down and made to feel bad about themselves. In addition to facilitating physical abuse, emotional abuse can also enable peer-on-peer sexual abuse.

Internationally, the World Health Organisation estimates that at least one in three adolescent girls will experience some form of sexual abuse from a partner (World

Health Organisation, 2002) – a figure in keeping with surveys of schoolgirls in England (Barter, 2014; Barter, et al., 2009). As noted previously, a 2011 survey of adult survivors of child sexual abuse found that close to two thirds had been abused by a peer and not an adult (Radford, et al., 2011). Interestingly, participants in this study were less likely to have disclosed their experiences when sexually harmed by a peer as opposed to an adult – in four out of five of cases (82.7%) they hadn't told anybody about what had happened to them.

Simon Hackett has helpfully outlined a continuum across which peer-on-peer sexually abusive behaviours can be conceptualised:

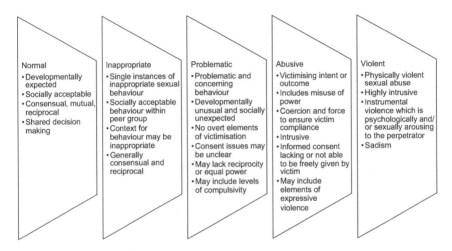

FIGURE 2.2 Hackett's continuum of children and young people's sexual behaviours

International studies have identified manifestations of sexual behaviours displayed by young people towards peers that cut across Hackett's continuum (Barter, et al., 2009; Connolly, et al., 2000; Franklin, 2013; Hackett, 2014; Melrose & Pearce, 2013). When viewed together this body of research suggests that sexually abusive behaviours between young people can involve harassment, exploitation, bullying, rape and the posting of images/video online within young people's intimate relationships, peer group settings and other less-established peer relationships (Barter, et al., 2009; Connolly, et al., 2000; Gadd, et al., 2013).

In sum, research, media reports and policy documents have acknowledged that young people experience sexual, physical and emotional abuse from peers, in their intimate relationships and friendships. While research and policy have often explored different manifestations of these experiences under distinct definitions of youth violence, relationship abuse, sexual exploitation, etc., the collective messages in this evidence base present the interconnected and overlapping nature of many of these behaviours. But what is known about the young people who are involved in, experience or instigate these instances of peer-on-peer abuse?

The individuals involved and affected

Research has somewhat inconclusively found that:

- Young people who are abused by, or who abuse, their peers have varied life stories
- Some young people are more likely to be abused by, or abuse, their peers than others

Young people with a history of abuse, those who are in the care of the state, young people who go missing and those who are involved in offending behaviour and/ or who have specific psychological traits are considered to be more vulnerable to being abused by (Barnardo's, 2011a; Berelowitz, et al., 2012; Khan, et al., 2013), and/ or abusing (Gadd, et al., 2013; Hackett, et al., 2013; Losel & Bender, 2006), their peers. However, the age and gender of those involved tend to be the most consistent characteristics shared by those affected by the phenomenon and are explored here first before this chapter then presents the wider vulnerabilities of those affected by peer-on-peer abuse.

Gender and age

Across the world young men are more likely than young women to abuse their peers (be they partners, friends or acquaintances) (Losel & Bender, 2006). A total of 77 per cent of violent incidents experienced by 10–15 year olds, and recorded in the 2013 crime survey for England and Wales, were perpetrated by males (who were also mainly 10–15 years old). Self-report studies often find that young women more frequently report using physical violence against a partner (Barter, et al., 2009; Hickman, 2004), but are also more likely to report that they used physical violence in self-defence, whereas young men report it as being used to exert control (Hickman, et al., 2004). Studies of young people who commit serious acts of interpersonal violence, including murder and manslaughter, also report that young men commit the vast majority of offences (Hagell & Jeyarajah-Dent, 2006) – one study that reviewed the profiles of young people convicted of murder and manslaughter in the Netherlands found that 90 per cent were young men (Nieuwbeerta & van der Laan, 2006). Research into young people in the UK and the US who have sexually harmed peers reinforces these gendered patterns, predominantly focusing on young men and their abuse of similar-age young women, younger children and, on occasion, adults and/or other young men (Hackett, 2014).

Compared with perpetration, the gender of those who are victimised by their peers tends to vary relevant to the form of abuse being experienced. Teenage relationship abuse – at least that which occurs in heteronormative contexts – largely involves the abuse of young women. According to academics in the UK, abuse in young people's intimate relationships is 'indisputably differentiated by gender' (Barter, et al., 2009:179). Despite young men and young women both reporting experiences of physical and emotional abuse in their relationships (Fox, et al., 2013), it is young women who more consistently report that these experiences have a negative impact on their well-being (Barter, et al., 2009; Connolly, et al., 2000). Young men, comparatively, report being 'unaffected or, at the very worst, annoyed' (Barter, et al., 2009:180) by their experiences of partner abuse. Young women are also more likely to report sexual abuse in their relationships than young men, and are more likely to be identified as victims of peer-on-peer sexual exploitation in the UK (Firmin, 2013; MOPAC, 2015; McNaughton Nicholls, 2014). These gendered patterns have been replicated in studies from the US, the Caribbean, Australia and Brazil (Prange and Neher, 2014; Powell, 2010; UNICEF, 2014).[2]

Aside from intimate partner abuse and sexual violence, however, available data suggest that boys and young men disproportionately experience peer-on-peer physical violence and abuse (Anderson, 1999; ONS, 2015; Squires & Goldsmith, 2011; Stanko, 1994). Young men in street gangs, sports clubs and other male-dominated spaces report higher rates of physical violence from their male peers than young women (Aisenberg & Herrenkohl, 2008; Allenye, et al., 2014; Anderson, 1999; Centre for Social Justice, 2009; Young & Hallsworth, 2011; Pitts, 2008). Of the 185 young people recorded as murdered in London over a 10-year period, 164 were young men, largely killed by other young men. This disproportionality is replicated around the world where young men make up the majority of those who experience robbery, are killed or are seriously harmed on the streets (ONS, 2015; UNICEF, 2014); and are considered as being the principal 'perpetrators' and 'victims' of youth homicide (World Health Organisation, 2002:13).

Literature on 'sexting' and bullying all indicate that, like physical abuse, emotional abuse is a gendered affair (Maxwell & Aggleton, 2010; Ringrose, et al., 2011). Global research has documented a myriad of ways in which young people utilise gendered stereotypes and other inequalities to emotionally abuse their peers. Young women's sexuality is policed by peers who draw upon narratives of 'slags' and 'whores' to blame them for their experiences of sexual coercion or bullying (Cowie, 2011; Ringrose & Renold, 2011). Likewise, young men's behaviours are scrutinised by peers for signs of emotional sensitivity that indicate they are 'weak' and an easy target for further bullying behaviours (Allenye, et al., 2014; Anderson, 1999; Beckett, et al., 2013; Messerschmidt, 2012b).

But, as noted previously, gender is not the only consistent identifying feature of those impacted by, or involved in, peer-on-peer abuse. Although children of any age can be abused by other young people, and harmful sexual behaviour, for example, has been identified in children much younger than age 10 (Hackett, 2014), experiences of peer-on-peer abuse have largely been connected to a period associated with adolescent development within particular Western cultural contexts. The onset of young people's involvement in acts of serious youth violence and gang association has been linked with the transition into secondary education – aged 11 and upwards (Squires & Goldsmith, 2011; Warr, 2002). UK research identifies young people who have been sexually exploited by peers from the age of 10 upwards, although some reports have identified victims as young as 7 or 8 (Barnardo's, 2013).

Teenage relationship abuse and acts of gang-related and serious youth violence are largely documented as involving young people aged 11–15, with a clustering of those aged 13 and above (Barnardo's, 2013; Beckett, et al., 2014; Berelowitz, et al., 2012; Cockbain, et al., 2014). In most cases, peer-on-peer abuse seems to occur at an age when young people socialise and form relationships with reduced adult supervision and, at a time when they are increasingly responsible for managing their own safety in extra-familial contexts (Coleman, 2011; Skelton & Valentine, 1998; Hagell & Jeyarajah-Dent, 2006; Warr, 2002). In countries where young people enter into intimate relationships at a younger or older age, or socialise on the streets with their peers at other ages, it is likely these patterns will shift.

While abuse between young people appears to follow the same gendered patterns as that which occurs between adults (Barter, et al., 2009; Corr, et al., 2012), age-related differences between adult-on-adult and child-on-child abuse have emerged. It has been reported that young people are more likely to sexually abuse their peers in groups than older people (Lambine, 2013; Warr, 2002). Abuse between young people appears to occur more frequently in public localities (Connolly, et al., 2000; Finkelhor, et al., 2009; Squires & Goldsmith, 2011), compared with abuse in adult relationships, which has largely been constructed as a 'private' space phenomenon (ONS, 2015). Such age-specific patterns point to a potential relationship between the characteristics of those who experience peer-on-peer abuse and the environments in which the abuse occurs – a relationship that is central to this book and is explored throughout its chapters.

Despite the consistencies in terms of the ages and gendered identities of those involved in peer-on-peer abuse, these patterns still only apply to a minority of young people globally. Many young people of the same age and gender as those affected by peer-on-peer abuse have not abused or been abused by their peers. We therefore have to explore why these consistencies exist for those who have been affected by peer-on-peer abuse, and what this means for how we understand the phenomenon. It may be that particular biographical experiences (such as being taken into care) or psychological factors (such as having a conduct disorder) of some young people intersect with certain age/gender characteristics to create risks of involvement in peer-on-peer abuse. Perhaps it is the presence of these additional vulnerabilities which provide an explanation of why some young men abuse their peers, why some young women facilitate this, and why some young women and some young men are abused by them in the consistent fashion identified thus far.

Additional vulnerabilities

A number of individual experiences, behaviours and psychological factors are considered to increase the likelihood that a young person will abuse, or be abused by, their peers. The extent to which these factors have an evidenced influence on the behaviours of young people involved in peer-on-peer abuse cases, however, is variable, with correlation rather than causation typifying most associations.

Some which appear most consistently in the literature and are therefore explored in this chapter are:

- Being looked after by the state rather than living with the biological family
- Experiencing physical, sexual or emotional abuse within the family
- Having a history of offending behaviour
- Having a diagnosed learning disability or conduct disorder
- Going missing from home, care and education

Young people who are living in care are considered to be more vulnerable to being abused by their peers and to abusing others (Barter, 2006, Beckett, 2013, Gadd, et al., 2013). While being placed into care may be necessary for a young person's safety and well-being, the process can also affect their sense of identity, disrupt relationships, leave them feeling isolated, and for some create a sense of loss similar to that of bereavement (Beckett, 2013; Coy, 2009; Shuker, 2013a). All of these factors are said to create vulnerabilities to being abused or abusing others. A young person's desire to belong, having been removed from the environment in which they had previous embedded connections and attachments, can be exploited by others and therefore contribute to the abuse they experience (Beckett, 2013). Likewise, the same desire could result in young people who engage in abusive behaviours alongside their peers in order to demonstrate loyalty to them and strengthen their sense of belonging to the group.

The reasons that young people are placed into care can also create an association between their 'care status' and their experiences of peer-on-peer abuse. Having been physically, sexually or emotionally abused, or neglected during childhood is also said to increase young people's vulnerability to sexual exploitation and partner abuse (Berelowitz, et al., 2012; Hackett, et al., 2013; Wood, et al., 2011). Studies into young people who have killed others in England and Wales (Boswell, 2006) and in the Netherlands (Nieuwbeerta & van der Laan, 2006) state that most of these young people have 'disturbed backgrounds' which feature experiences of abuse (Boswell, 2006, 131). Children and young people who sexually harm their peers have been found to have histories of abuse in early childhood (Hackett, 2014; Vizard, 2007). Life narratives of young men who abuse their partners have also surfaced similar findings:

> Participants . . . revealed a range of personal vulnerabilities, a considerable number describing mental health problems, learning difficulties and attention deficits, amidst illicit drug use, excessive alcohol consumption, and multiple forms of social disadvantage. These social disadvantages included homelessness and other acute forms of housing instability, living in homes where parents were involved in crime or addicted to drugs, the absence of stable parental care, being subject to imprisonment and institutional care, exclusion from school, low levels of education and underemployment. Witnessing violence at home or between family members was evident in most participants' accounts.
>
> *(Gadd, et al., 2013:29)*

Young people's experiences of care and familial child abuse can also affect their mental state and emotional well-being. Whether as a result of these experiences or not, young people who abuse, and/or are abused by their peers, are said to disproportionately possess an array of cognitive characteristics associated with socially challenging behaviours, including 'impulsiveness, hyperactivity, attention problems, emotional instability, developmental delays, language deficits and relatively low overall intelligence' (Losel & Bender, 2006:50). Case reviews of young people with harmful sexual behaviour suggested that in 38 per cent of cases where a disability status was recorded the young person involved in sexually harming others had a learning disability (Hackett, et al., 2013). A recent study into gang-associated young women in England found that just in excess of a quarter included in their sample had a 'suspected diagnosable health problem' and that 40 per cent had shown signs of behavioural problems before they were 12 years old (Khan, et al., 2013).

Beyond the psychological and experiential characteristics attached to those considered more vulnerable to peer-on-peer abuse, a list of behaviours are said to indicate that someone is at greater risk of abusing, and/or being abused by, their peers (Barnardo's, 2011a; Berelowitz, et al., 2013; Gadd, et al., 2013; Hackett, et al., 2013; Khan, et al., 2013). Two of these behaviours are going missing from home, school or care, and prior involvement in offending behaviour. In terms of going missing, most studies recognise that this can occur both as a consequence and as a cause of abusive experiences. Going missing is considered to be the risk factor most strongly associated with a risk of sexual exploitation, and increasingly in relation to gang association (HM Government, 2016; Khan, et al., 2013). Likewise, young people within youth justice services in England are considered to be at increased risk of sexual exploitation and serious youth violence (Cockbain, et al., 2014; Khan, et al., 2013). A study of 700 young people who had displayed harmful sexual behaviour found that, of the 650 where data were available, 42 per cent had a previous caution or criminal conviction (Hackett, et al., 2013).

However, as with the case with young people who go missing, offending behaviour can occur as a result of abusive experiences or the escalation towards it. While common, prior offending is not a prerequisite for young people who commit even the most serious acts of interpersonal violence (Nieuwbeerta & van der Laan, 2006).

In fact, none of the individual characteristics outlined previously are consistently associated with *all* young people involved in or affected by peer-on-peer abuse. If a history of abuse led young people to abuse their peers, this would result in the vast majority of abusers being young women (Herrera & Stuewig, 2011), and yet the converse appears to be true. While a number of young people who are abused by, or abuse their peers, have a history that involves chronic experiences of abuse, others do not (Hackett, et al., 2013; Hackett, 2014; Hagell & Jeyarajah-Dent, 2006).

Much of the strength of association between a child's individual characteristics and their experiences appears to be dependent upon wider circumstances.

Scholars have also urged caution when assessing the likelihood of a young person being abused or abusing others, related to particular psychological or cognitive characteristics (Hackett, et al., 2013; Henry, 2008; Losel & Bender, 2006). They argue that, by focusing on these individual characteristics, research has the potential to pathologise behaviours which are actually 'social' (Losel & Bender, 2006; Warr, 2002). Furthermore, consider the identified relationship between being in care and experiences of peer-on-peer abuse. Some young people are safer once they are placed into care and are supported to form healthy attachments that were not available to them in abusive home environments. While a disproportionate number of young people in care have been abused (either by their peers or by adults), the vast majority were living at home when that abuse actually began (Berelowitz, et al., 2012; Melrose & Pearce, 2013). In fact, most young people involved in peer-on-peer abuse are living with their families when these experiences begin (Catch 22, 2013; Hackett, 2014) (a matter to be considered in greater detail in Chapter 5). Therefore, while it may be true that for some young people being in care is an individual risk factor associated with peer-on-peer abuse, for the majority an absence of a 'looked-after' experience is not sufficient to guard against involvement in peer-on-peer abuse.

It seems that despite a wealth of evidence which suggests that certain personal factors are influential to some, sometimes a significant number of those involved, there is nothing about these young people's life stories that unite their journey towards abusing, or being abused by, their peers. What's more, considering these in isolation of the contexts/situations in which abuse occurs significantly limits our ability to understand why these particular characteristics feature in the evidence base at all. Young people who aren't living in care, who don't have an extensive offending history and/or who don't have histories of intra-familial abuse have also been affected by peer-on-peer abuse. Comparably, research finds far more consistency in the documented gender and age of young people abused by, or who have abused, their peers than in the other individual characteristics documented in this chapter (Barter, et al., 2009; Beckett, et al., 2013; Losel & Bender, 2006; Squires & Goldsmith, 2011; Stanko, 1994). And yet, while gendered and age-specific patterns have emerged in the literature, these patterns are not representative of the experiences of *all* young people of a similar age and gender. Ultimately, peer-on-peer abuse is far from a determined outcome for young people who fit this individual profile (Cowie, 2011; Hackett, 2014).

The extent to which these concerns are valid is a question explored through the contextual account offered by this book. By foregrounding context in an account of peer-on-peer abuse, the social, rather than individual, dynamics of issue can be better understood and an assessment can be made as to whether this advances our ability to address it. While the individual characteristics of those affected may be of some relevance to the development of policy and practice responses, their significance may be best measured through a more situational or contextual lens (Letourneau & Borduin, 2008).

A collective message about context

In exploring the individual charactersitics of those affected by, or experiencing, peer-on-peer abuse, and the nature of behaviours involved, messages begin to emerge regarding the significance of the contexts and relationships to which these characteristics and behaviours are associated. Media reports and studies into peer-on-peer abuse have consistently documented abuse within young people's intimate relationships, friendships groups, urban street gangs and in the process of peer inter-action within public/social settings, including schools, sports clubs, transport hubs and shopping centres (Aisenberg & Herrenkohl, 2008; BBC, 2013; Catch 22, 2013; EVAW, 2010a; GirlGuiding UK, 2014; Young & Hallsworth, 2011; Franklin, 2004; Pedersen, 2014; Ringrose, et al., 2011; Wikström, et al., 2012; World Health Organisation, 2002).

The contexts documented are the social situations, relationships and environments in which young people spend time with their peers. Young people who abuse their peers as opposed to much younger children are more likely to do so in public spaces and schools than in a private residence (Beckett & Gerhold, 2003; Finkelhor, et al., 2009; Hackett, 2014). Many young men who are murdered in gang-related attacks and other forms of serious youth violence are killed on the streets. A number of high-profile cases in England have, for example, featured young men being chased through transport hubs or onto/off buses before being killed by their peers (BBC, 2015a; BBC, 2013; BBC, 2011). School has been repeatedly identified as a site of sexual harassment for young women, with international reports stating it is the place where young women are most likely to experience sexual violence (EVAW, 2010a; Women and Equalities Committee, 2016a).

The public nature of many of these settings is associated with the ages of those involved. Peer-on-peer abuse occurs at a time when young people in many countries spend increasing amounts of time away from the family home, in school and their local neighbourhood, socialising with peers. In addition, young people aged 10 to 17, in the main, don't live with their partners or peers, and therefore their relationships often are formed, develop and play out in social and public spaces – both online and offline (Ashurst & McAlinden, 2015; Aynsley, et al., 2016; Coleman, 2011; Connolly, et al., 2000; Corr, et al., 2012; Skelton & Valentine, 1998; Warr, 2002; Wikström, et al., 2012).

Despite these clear and consistent messages about the contexts of abuse in the UK, we have seen a proliferation of risk assessments and risk indicator checklists for young people affected by sexual exploitation and relationship abuse which focus on the types of individual histories, behaviours and characteristics of those affected that have been documented in this chapter. Such checklists invariably reference a young person's care status, whether or not they have a history of being abused, and whether they are involved in offending (Berelowitz, et al., 2012; Home Office, 2011; Losel & Bender, 2006; SafeLives, 2015). Potentially it is both research agendas that have prioritised the documentation of individual characteristics and individualised policy agendas that have led us down a path in which our national, and sometimes global, debates about peer-on-peer abuse neglect the relationship between individual characteristics, behaviours and environmental influences associated with peer-on-peer abuse. In the age of individualism it may make some more comfortable to think of the individual triggers that lead to abusive behaviours or experiences. It is also arguably easier to gather statistics on the individuals involved in incidents of abuse (and use these as an evidence base for assessment) than it is to explore the environments in which abuse flourished.

In response to these challenges, and as a direct refutation of individualised responses to peer-on-peer abuse, scholars and practitioners have increasingly critiqued the limitations posed by individual accounts of a phenomenon that appears inextricably connected to the environments in which it occurs. In 2008, Letourneau and Borduin recognised that in the US:

> The extant research literature indicates that multiple characteristics of individual youths and their social systems (family, peers, school) are linked with juvenile sexual offending . . . and these characteristics can be viewed within a socio-ecological framework that views youths as embedded within increasingly complex systems, including family, peers, and school.
>
> *(Letourneau & Borduin, 2008:2)*

In Australia Connolly et al. (2000), Powell (2010) and Chung (2005) identified context as critical to young people's experiences of relationship abuse, with Chung articulating that:

> The individualistic discourse supports young women's rights to choose to stay or leave a relationship. However, it also dictates that should she remain in an abusive relationship that it is her choice to do so as she is an individual of free will, with the social context (gendered power relations) not taken into account. In total, this leaves gendered power relations relatively intact as they are invisible within an individualistic discourse which further masks the effects of gender inequality
>
> *(Chung, 2005:435)*

Five years later in the UK, a range of academics (Brodie, 2013; Firmin and Curtis, 2015; Pearce, 2013) were questioning the validity of contextless accounts regarding sexual exploitation, including Melrose (2013), who claimed that the individualisation of the issue does not:

> identify the specific social processes that create the conditions for exploitation nor facilitate an understanding of what might be wrong with a society in which sex appears as a best option for those who are vulnerable and/or financially impoverished.
>
> *(Melrose, 2013:17)*

Given these accounts, and the wider research base of which they are an illustration, it seems that rather than seeking to identify which individual characteristics should score most highly on a risk assessment checklist, we should instead be asking: In which social conditions do the individual characteristics explored in this chapter become vulnerabilities associated with peer-on-peer abuse?

Using an international evidence base, underpinned by illustrations from case reviews, this book seeks to do just that. Reviews of peer-on-peer abuse cases in the UK are used to illustrate the interplay between social contexts, behaviours and individual characteristics when young people are abused by, or abuse, a peer. In doing so this book provides a contextual account of peer-on-peer abuse and the homes, peer groups, schools and neighbourhoods in which it occurs. Such an approach will provide answers to questions that this chapter alone has failed to do – in what environments do individual vulnerabilities, or an absence of them, lead to peer-on-peer abuse?

Notes

1 The World Health Organisation uses the term 'young person' to refer to an individual aged 10–29 years of age and therefore counts a broader spectrum of people than those incorporated into the definition of peer-on-peer abuse used in this book.

2 It is also important to note that there is increasing evidence regarding the sexual abuse of young men by their male peers (largely although not exclusively with gang contexts), and the grooming of young men to be abusive by older peers (Beckett, et al., 2013; Cockbain, et al., 2014) – although these experiences are still thought to disproportionately affect young women.

3

DEFINITIONS, THEORY AND METHODOLOGY

This book provides a contextual scaffold upon which to hang the individual characteristics, behaviours and experiences of those involved in peer-on-peer abuse (documented in the previous chapter) and, in doing so, shine a light on the social conditions of the phenomenon. This is achieved by employing specific definitions, theoretical frameworks and case study evidence to explore and supplement existing evidence on the nature and scale of peer-on-peer abuse. This chapter outlines the approach taken in the book to achieve this, the limitations of the approach and the unique contribution it makes to international conceptualisations of, and responses to, peer-on-peer abuse.

Purpose

The previous chapters introduced the contextual dynamics of peer-on-peer abuse and outlined the limitations of only accounting for the phenomena with reference to the individual characteristics of those involved. The purpose of this book is to explore the relationship between these two factors (individual and context) and in doing so explore the decisions and behaviours of young people who are abused by, and/or who abuse, their peers. We know that the environments that young people spend their time in influence their behaviours and attitudes. Whether it's being exposed to violence on their local streets or being sexually harassed in school, young people have described the ways in which they have tried to survive abusive environments by making constrained, risky and often harmful 'choices':

> Then they get caught in town by other gang members and they're like 'Ah, she chills with such and such a people' and then obviously they have to do something to them . . . . I don't think they know how serious it can get when

they're doing it. Cos they've not grown up around it. The girls round here, they're involved but it's not a choice thing.

(Beckett, et al., 2013:39)

Far from being accounts only documented in academic texts or government policies, young people's experiences of the contexts in which peer-on-peer abuse occurs has also been documented in national media reports:

I said, 'no', and he pulled me in, shut the door and started to sexually assault me . . . . Parents believe that you are safe in school and that nothing bad is going to happen, but this changes your whole outlook as to what school is.

(BBC, 2015d)

Yet our evidence suggests that only a significant minority of young people abuse their peers in response to these experiences, and so contextual experiences far from determine that peer-on-peer abuse will occur. Therefore, we need to approach this phenomenon by understanding the *relationship* amongst environment, individual characteristics and the choices that young people make; and importantly, the relationship*s* between the multiple environments in which young people spend their time. For example, while two young people, A and B, may both spend their time in the same abusive school environment, the harmful norms they are exposed to in this context may be challenged or reinforced by the social norms and relationships in the homes, peer groups and/or neighbourhoods to which they are associated. Young person A's friendship group could provide a set of social rules that encourage and enable safe, pro-social and equal relationships, whereas young person B's friends adopt the same abusive norms as those which permeate their school environment and in doing so create a social context conducive with peer-on-peer abuse. It is this complex, multi-way network of norms, relationships, contexts and choices that require consideration if we are to understand what enables young people to display safe behaviours in abusive environments and develop an appropriate response.

When researching the impact of serious youth violence on women and girls in 2010, I met Kendra in a young offenders' institution. She was 16 years old, the youngest of five siblings and the only girl in her family. Throughout her childhood Kendra watched her older brothers physically and emotionally abuse their partners. She also witnessed the exploitation of girls in her local school and on the streets in her neighbourhood. Kendra was clear – she wasn't going to be abused. Instead, Kendra adopted a persona akin to that of her brothers and the young men in her local area – she became an abuser:

I'm scared that I've forgotten how to feel things. I don't cry anymore. One of my boys got killed and I couldn't even cry at the funeral. You learn not to care cos there's no point. If you care too much it makes you weak and that's why most girls don't last in this way of life, cos they can't take it. Hold another girl down while your boys do stuff to her; gun-butt someone in the face with blood everywhere; you have to just think – whatever. If you care you're finished.

Kendra's account vocalises two things about the evidenced drivers of peer-on-peer abuse: young people's behaviours are influenced by the environments in which they develop (Connolly, et al., 2000; Letourneau & Borduin, 2008), and young people make choices when surviving, navigating or growing in those environments (Young & Hallsworth, 2011; Pearce, 2013).

It is clear that the norms in Kendra's school, family and neighbourhood influenced her decision to abuse others, yet there may have been other young women, exposed to the same levels of abuse, who chose not to abuse others. If we want to understand peer-on-peer abuse, therefore, we need to understand the relationships that exist between the individual choices that young people make, their individual characteristics and the environments in which they display certain behaviours.

Although there is an emerging evidence base on the contextual dynamics of peer-on-peer abuse, research, policy and public debate on the issue is yet to consistently consider the role of context in informing power, choice and agency. Instead, a focus on assessing and intervening with the individualised characteristics and behaviours of those affected persists and is not always presented alongside the contextual dynamics which make these individual factors important. An exploration of group dynamics related to peer-on-peer abuse is particularly limited (Latchford, et al., 2016). Except for multiple-perpetrator rape literature and some studies into youth violence, much of the research landscape fails to state whether there are differences between the nature of abuse perpetrated by groups or individuals or differences in the profiles of the young people involved – and importantly, what the implications may be for how we respond to or prevent peer-on-peer abuse. The implied, but significantly under-explored, evidence on peer group influence indicates that while assessment tools and established practices are predominantly built upon an individual's pathway to abuse, the dynamics of a peer group could actually be what is most strongly associated with some young people's experiences of, or involvement in, peer-on-peer abuse. If this were the case there would be implications for how practitioners identify the risks associated with peer-on-peer abuse and the best way to protect young people from their involvement in the issue.

Without an ability to understand how, through interactions with young people, contextual dynamics can create vulnerabilities for peer-on-peer abuse, few responses have been developed which are intended to create the social conditions which prevent or disrupt abuse. Some authors who have located abuse within the environments in which it happens have provided the building blocks for contextual accounts of peer-on-peer abuse that is required (e.g. Barter & Berridge, 2011; Beckett, et al., 2013; Firmin, 2013; Hackett, 2014; Letourneau & Borduin, 2008; Melrose, 2013; Pitts, 2008; Shuker, 2013a; Pearce, 2013) – an account this book intends to provide.

Definitions

As introduced in Chapter 1, for this book, peer-on-peer abuse is defined in a manner that can accommodate the different contextual and situational ways in which young people experience violence and abuse:

> *Physical, sexual and emotional abuse in young people's relationships, including their intimate relationships, friendships and wider peer associations*

This incorporates young people displaying harmful sexual behaviour, young people sexually exploiting, or being exploited by, peers, abuse in young people's intimate relationships and behaviours which have been defined as serious youth violence (all explored in the previous chapter).

By 'young people' this book is concerned with abuse between those aged 10 to 17, that is, young people above the age of criminal responsibility for abusive acts in England and Wales but still legislatively considered to be children. It is important to note that this age range leaves a potentially large age gap between those who are abused and those who abuse them – for example, a 10-year-old being abused by a 17-year-old. However, research into peer-on-peer abuse used for this book is largely concerned with incidents of abuse that feature an age gap of five years or less between those involved. Furthermore, the case file data used to provide illustrative evidence of peer-on-peer abuse (the methodology for which is outlined later in this chapter) involves age gaps no larger than three years between the person who was abused and the person/people who abuse them.

While the social dynamics of peer-on-peer abuse are of particular interest in this book, as the remainder of this chapter explains, it is the rules at play within specific social spaces and relationships that are examined. The social norms within homes, schools and public spaces in local neighbourhoods, as well as peer groups and family networks, are of particular importance to the account provided by this book rather than wider, and arguably more abstract, accounts of abusive norms at a societal level.

Theory

Theoretical concepts developed by Pierre Bourdieu provide a helpful framework for exploring the interplay between individual characteristics/experiences, social environments and individual behaviours/decisions. His perspective, referred to as 'constructivist structuralism' by many, claims that individuals are structured by the social environments of which they are a part and through their participation in these environments also structure them. In short, there is a two-way interplay between individual behaviours/attitudes and social rules/structures. For Bourdieu, reality is created within this interplay, and it is therefore impossible to consider a context in the absence of the individuals within it and vice versa. In the case of Kendra, introduced earlier in this chapter, her decisions were informed by the nature of her social interactions at home, school and in her local neighbourhood while her behaviours also served to inform the nature of those environments.

Bourdieu offered a number of concepts to explain his position that these can be used to further explore the interplay between Kendra and the different environments in which she spent her time.

Social field: These are the rules in operation within a given social environment – for example, the social rules of Kendra's school, neighbourhood and home environments.

Capital: These were the resources that Kendra had and could draw upon when entering different social fields. She had economic capital (financial resources), social capital (her networks such as her peers on the road and her brothers) and cultural capital (her access to the relevant language/terminology and other social cues that operated in each environment). Drawing upon all three provided Kendra with her symbolic capital – her reputation/rep – in any given social field that she entered.

Habitus: This was Kendra's feel for the rules in any given social field. Kendra could draw upon her various forms of capital to play the rules of any given social field in order to achieve social status, and her ability to do this was expressed through her behaviours.

Symbolic violence: According to Bourdieu, individuals play the rules in any given social field in pursuit of social status. Therefore, upon entering a social field such as her neighbourhood, Kendra would draw upon her capital – for example, the social capital she got from association with her brothers and other violent peers – to achieve status in that violent field. Her pursuit of status would mean that Kendra would engage with these rules even if it was to her detriment – for example, engagement required her to abuse others or risk being caught by the police. The engagement of social rules even when to one's detriment was referred to by Bourdieu as 'symbolic violence'.

Some scholars have critiqued Bourdieu's approach to describing human interaction with the social world as too deterministic (Butler, 1999). If individuals comply with the rules of the environments they are in, even when to their own detriment, then where is the space for them to act differently? However, others argue that, according to Bourdieu's theory, social norms are 'entrenched but not unsurpassable' (McNay, 2004). Bourdieu argued that individuals were social agents with a 'generative capacity' to do things differently and were not subjects or puppets of 'social fields' (Bourdieu, 1992). Individuals like Kendra are capable of behaving differently to that which they have become accustomed upon entering an alternative social field and engaging with a different set of rules. Therefore, if Kendra entered a neighbourhood or school environment where the social rules promoted healthy and non-abusive relationships between her peers, she would have been better placed to generate a different set of behaviours, act in safe ways and not cause harm to others. Importantly, because individuals need to actively engage with social rules, rather than just observe a different way of behaving, Kendra needed to spend time practicing a new way of socialising and forming healthy relationships rather than just being told about them. In this sense, change could be found in a shift in the social conditions of Kendra's decisions rather than a simple intervention with Kendra.

Bourdieu's account of the social world, and Kendra's engagement in it, is largely inconsistent with the direction of practice interventions. For the most part, practitioners in the UK would have been trained to assess Kendra and work with her to change her behaviour – rather than trying to alter the social rules of the neighbourhood and school in which she was forming peer relationships. When interventions have been built to focus on individuals (Letourneau & Borduin, 2008; Parton, 2014), thinking about broadening approaches so as to impact the nature of social spaces can feel a bit out of reach. It is for this reason that followers of Bourdieu have argued that his account of how to change human behaviour presents a 'pessimistic but not determined' view of the world – and arguably the current power of intervention (Lawler, 2004; McRobbie, 2004; Powell, 2010).

Social fields and adolescence

In the UK, US, Australia and other Western social contexts, young people move through a socially constructed period of adolescence – largely defined from the age of 13 through 18 (Coleman, 2011). During this time individuals spend longer days in school environments, use transport services on their own and socialise in other offline and online public and social spaces such as parks, shopping centres and youth clubs, where they can form friendships and relationships beyond those provided by their families (Ashurst & McAlinden, 2015; Coleman, 2011; Connolly, et al., 2000; Gardner & Steinberg, 2005). During this process young people engage with a range of rules, alongside their peers, members of the public and professionals with whom they share these social spaces.

During the same period young people also remain dependent upon, and engaged with, their families and carers. Most are financially dependent upon their parents/carers, will rely on them for food and shelter, and will have loving and supportive relationships with family members. When with their families/carers, and spending time in the family home, young people will also engage with the social rules of that space and the expectations of relationships, respect and intimacy in that setting (Coleman, 2011; Catch 22, 2013; Warr, 2002).

The nature and range of social fields in which young people are forming relationships, developing their individual identities and making decisions are particular to adolescence – for two key reasons. Firstly, the range of social fields in which young people are engaged broadens compared with those that are prominent during early childhood. When they are younger, individuals spend most of their time under adult supervision – largely with their parents – and once they are 5 years old, with teachers, play leaders and others who run activities in which their parents/carers may have enrolled them. During this time the social norms of their families/carers are of primary importance, not only because of the amount of time children spend in this social field, but also because their carers will also select most of the people with whom these children spend their time. Secondly, during adolescence some social fields beyond the family become increasingly influential and can outweigh the influence of family norms when informing the decisions that young people make (an idea which is explored and extrapolated throughout this book). Evidence of both the broadened range of social fields that are important to individuals during adolescence and the increased weighting of these extra-familial social fields require consideration when providing a contextual account of peer-on-peer abuse. Rather than considering the relationship between broad societal norms and young people's experiences of peer-on-peer abuse, this book considers the relationship between the rules at play in specific social fields of importance to young people when they abuse, or are abused by, peers.

Building upon the potential for Bourdieu's theory to illustrate the particular contextual dynamics of the adolescent experience, scholars who have used Bourdieu in exploring experiences of abuse (e.g. Powell, 2010) and notions of childhood (e.g. Jenks, 2005) are particularly helpful. Taken together, these approaches provide further guidance for creating a framework through which to illuminate the contextual dynamics of peer-on-peer abuse and the implications for policy and practice.

Social fields and abuse

In her work on consent between young adults in Australia, Anastasia Powell (2008, 2010) found that young people engaged in intimate relationships by 'embodying' (i.e. practicing) a set of social rules. These social rules were played out in their friendship networks and the places in which they spent their time, and for some were reinforced by social cues they were exposed to at home, in school/college or in wider societal interactions. So entrenched were the rules at play that young people expressed adherence to them through behavioural cues as well as the things that they said. Young women stated that when they didn't want to engage in sexual activity with partners they would pretend to have a headache or not physically react to their partners' touch to demonstrate their feelings rather than saying 'no' to attempts at sexual contact. Likewise, young men demonstrated an awareness of these behavioural cues, and stated that they knew when their partners didn't want to have sex with them and that they also demonstrated their feelings through behaviour as well as words. Through interviews, Powell identified that a reliance on behavioural cues enabled non-consensual sexual contact – with young adults knowing that non-consent was communicated through behaviour but verbal cues were still relied upon to justify the fact that 'well if they didn't say no' then sexual contact was permissible. For both young women and young men in Powell's study, their behaviours were in keeping with wider societal rules associated with gender that 'position an active, desiring male sexuality against a passive, receptive female sexuality . . . [which creates] an uneven playing field for the negotiation of sexual encounters' (Powell, 2010:173). In keeping with Bourdieu's account of the social world, abusive behaviours between young people in Australia were informed by an interplay between social rules and individual choice. Given the influence of wider societal norms, which set the rules of sexual encounters, Powell argues that sexual violence can only be addressed through attempts to change the social rules of gender, relationships and consent running alongside individual interventions with those who perpetrate abuse.

Social fields and childhood

Like Powell, Chris Jenks (2005) drew upon Bourdieu to explore the relationship between structure and agency in the lives of young people. Using Bourdieu's argument of an interplay between the rules of social fields and human behaviours, Jenks used the concept of 'development through dependency' to discuss the nature of 'childhood'. For Jenks, individuals develop attitudes, which in turn inform their behaviours and choices, through their interaction with societal norms and expectations. The idea of 'child development' therefore describes the process through which individuals engage with social norms, practiced through their relationships with peers, parents and other social actors. This process will differ across the various social spaces operating across the world, but in drawing directly upon Bourdieu's concepts, Jenks argues:

> Instead of asking, 'Why is my child a heroin addict? What went wrong in his or her development', we should, from a sociological perspective, be asking, 'What is it about this free, liberal, advanced, technological democracy that makes heroin a desirable, alternative possible course of action?' Development through dependency then becomes an instrument in the process of social and cultural reproduction.
>
> *(Jenks, 2005:40)*

For Jenks, individuals are dependent upon social structures and the relationships that operate within them. Like Powell, Jenks concludes that alternative action, an opportunity to act differently, requires an individual to be engaged with a new set of social and cultural rules/codes/expectations. We have to consider, and respond to, the nature of the social fabric with which individuals are engaged in order to understand and alter their behaviours. It is not enough to analyse and intervene with individuals to alter their course of action – they are engaged in an interplay with the rules of the social fields of which they are a part. Therefore, for both Powell and Jenks the rules of social fields warrant attention when seeking to change human behaviour.

A conceptual framework for exploring peer-on-peer abuse

Drawing together the arguments of Jenks and Powell provides a foundation for exploring the contextual dynamics of, and responses to, abuse between young people. Powell provides a contextual account of abusive behaviours and norms, while Jenks offers a contextual narrative for childhood development and the relationship between individual children, the decisions they make and wider societal expectations. Applying both positions to the life story of Kendra and wider evidence on adolescent development and social fields, we are directed to ask:

- What were the social rules at play in her home, peer group, school and neighbourhood that informed the nature of the abusive relationships that developed within them?
- What was it about the social rules at play in these environments, upon which Kendra was dependent for her development, which made her abusive behaviours a viable course of action?

Following this direction of travel, and building upon the work of both Powell and Jenks, this book looks at the lives of young people like Kendra to identify the interplay between the rules at play in a range of social fields associated with adolescent development, and young people's dependency on those spaces/relationships which made abusive behaviours a viable outcome. To achieve this I have built a five-stage conceptual framework (Figure 3.1), informed by Powell's and Jenks' application of

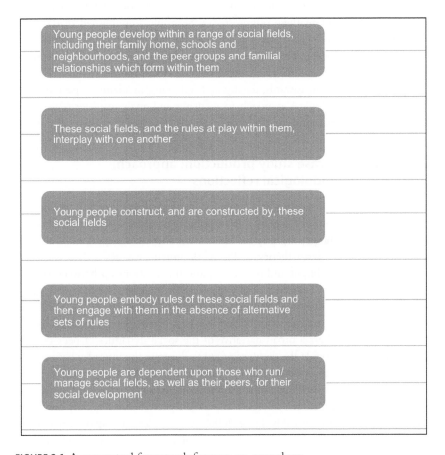

FIGURE 3.1 A conceptual framework for peer-on-peer abuse

Bourdieu, which recognises a reflexive interplay between individual choice/action (agency) and contextual rules or constraints (structures) with which young people are engaged.

This framework provides a contextual lens through which to examine evidence of the nature of peer-on-peer abuse. It draws attention to the social fields associated with incidents of peer-on-peer abuse, young people's engagement in the social rules of those fields, and the roles played by other actors in those social fields – be they other young people, parents, professionals or members of the public. It asks the same question that Jenks poses – what is it about societal norms, and young people's engagement with them, that makes peer-on-peer abuse a viable option? And as Powell argues, what social rules warrant intervention in order to change the norms that underpin young people's abusive behaviour? These questions are approached throughout the remainder of this book through two sources of evidence. Firstly, published materials – research, policy and media accounts – that document the nature of peer-on-peer abuse are presented through a contextual lens, bolstered by wider studies which detail the nature of the social environments under consideration, namely homes, peer groups, schools and neighbourhoods and the engagement of online interactions in these offline spaces. Secondly, unpublished material – a review of nine cases of peer-on-peer abuse in England in which young people raped or murdered their peers. This material provides depth to the breadth offered by the wider evidence base through practical illustrations of the contextual dynamics at play in the escalation towards, during and following incidents of peer-on-peer abuse. The methodological approach to securing and analysing case review evidence, and ethical reflections on this process, are documented in the next discussion.

Case review and case study production: approach, ethics and methodological reflections

As introduced in the two previous chapters, international research, governmental policies and media reports suggest a relationship between the nature of the social spaces in which young people spend their time and their experiences of peer-on-peer abuse. The social theory of Pierre Bourdieu provides a theoretical lens through which to highlight and further explore this relationship between context and human behaviour. However, simply applying the conceptual framework introduced previously to the pre-existing research and policy landscape is insufficient to provide the contextual account of peer-on-peer abuse that is required. To date the evidence base offers a broad narrative of the social dynamics of peer-on-peer abuse but is yet to provide the depth required to illustrate the interplay between the choices made by young people and the norms at play in the social fields to which they are associated. A small number of studies have used life narratives (i.e. Messerschmidt, 2012b) to illustrate this aspect of peer-on-peer abuse. Not only have these approaches provided 'depth' (Flyvbjerg, 2006) to our understanding of peer-on-peer abuse, but also they give an account of the interplay between context and choice at the point of an abusive incident.

Case reviews: a route to explore interplay

Like life narratives, case files held by professional agencies (such as the police and children's social care) hold information about specific incidents of peer-on-peer abuse and the behaviours that led up to them (and, on occasion, motives). While not intended to formally record contextual and relational information about the nature of peer-on-peer abuse, in order to investigate a case where a young person has abused a peer, professionals need to gather information about young people's peers and family relationships and their behaviours in school, at home and sometimes in their local neighbourhood. While these incidents are being investigated by the police, other professionals, including those in children's social care, health and education, work together to assess and support those involved in an incident. As a result, files contain information about the way that practitioners responded to young people affected by peer-on-peer abuse and the outcomes of these interventions. Professional case files, therefore, can be used to build case studies on incidents of peer-on-peer abuse.

In the same way that life narratives of actual incidents identify a relationship between context and individual action/choice, case studies have the potential to add depth to the broader evidence base on the contextual nature and scale of peer-on-peer abuse and existing responses. To realise this potential I designed a case review methodology, in consultation with a large police force in England, to identify whether case files could be turned into case studies of peer-on-peer abuse and whether these case studies would illuminate the contextual factors of the phenomenon.

Methodology design

There were two fundamental stages to building the case review methodology used for this study.

The first stage was to assess whether case file materials had the potential to illuminate the relationship between context and individual action. While social care records and assessments are primarily focused on children and families (HM Government, 2015), consultation with a police force confirmed that police investigations gather evidence from a wide range of partners to build a broader picture on the nature of offences, the motive for them, and peer, as well as familial, relationships that may have featured. To investigate a case the police would need to build a picture of the factors that influenced the behaviours and decisions involved and that many incidents would have occurred in school or neighbourhood spaces as indicated in the two previous chapters. Police investigations would also contain 'third-party' material – information from a wide range of agencies that were also in contact with the young people involved in any case, including children's social care, health, youth offending, education and wider youth service provisions.

Having established that police investigation files were likely to contain information about contextual factors associated with peer-on-peer abuse, the second stage was to design a case review template (see the Appendix). The template was required to extract information from investigation files to turn the case file material into an anonymised and contextual case study of peer-on-peer abuse. Each case study needed to document: the nature of the incident and escalation towards it; the characteristics of the individual young people involved in the case and the families/ homes, peer groups, schools and neighbourhood localities where they spent their time; and the nature and outcome of the practitioner response. To achieve this the template was designed in three sections. Section 1 documented the nature of the incident. Section 2 documented individual and contextual characteristics. Section 3 documented how the incident was identified, how practitioners responded and what the outcomes were of these interventions.

Developing a case study template was beneficial for a number of reasons. Firstly, individual police investigation files were likely to record different levels of information and to have involved different services. For case studies to be compared and analysed as a collective evidence base, a sense of uniformity between them was required. A template approach provided the route to ensuring uniformity across the case studies that were developed. Secondly, a template enabled multiple sources of information to be collated and stored in one place in an anonymised form. Original materials featured in any police investigation would be in paper and online formats and would contain information that made each case identifiable. By transfering information from investigation files onto templates, each case study would be anonymised at the point of access, and evidence for a case could be held on one document as opposed to potentially hundreds of sources. Finally, using a template ensured a directed focus on information that would be extracted from each investigation file and could provide a measure for managing researcher bias. Rather than collecting information which may have, for a number of reasons, 'stood out' to the person reading the file, the template structure directed the reader to collect all information relevant to a contextual account and not unduly weight evidence based on the interest of a reader.

Methodology application

Having identified a route, approach and resource to build a contextual narrative of peer-on-peer abuse from 2011 through 2014, I used the case review template to build nine case studies of peer-on-peer abuse. The objective of this process was to illustrate, illuminate and build upon international research into different forms of peer-on-peer abuse which, as Chapter 2 demonstrated, suggests a relationship between young people involved in abusive incidents and the environments in which they spend their time. By producing an account of specific cases, the process was intended to test, bring to life and ultimately offer depth to a broad account of the contextual nature of peer-on-peer abuse. By accessing practitioner files the process would also identify the nature of the professional response to incidents of peer-on-peer abuse and explore the capacity of practitioner approaches to engage with the contextual factors of incidents.

I worked with one large police force who expressed an interest in developing their responses to peer-on-peer abuse. Working with this force provided me with an opportune sample, and for the purposes of expediency it was decided that, given their relatively large size and engagement in the work, investigation files would be randomly sampled from them as a single service, once certain selection criteria had been applied.

The study used the definition of peer-on-peer abuse introduced in earlier chapters of this book to identify investigation files:

> *Physical, sexual, emotional and financial abuse, and coercive control, exercised within young people's relationships*

This broad definition encompassed a number of different manifestations of peer-on-peer abuse explored in research and addressed in policy documents – including peer-on-peer sexual exploitation, teenage relationship abuse, young people who display harmful sexual behaviours towards peers and other forms of serious youth violence. In terms of police investigation, a range of offences fit within this definition – from assault, stalking and sexual harassment through to grievous bodily harm, rape and murder, if in the context of peer relationships between young people.

Working on advice from the participating police force it was recommended that murder investigations (in the context of both intimate and non-intimate peer relationships) and multiple-perpetrator rape investigations would have involved in-depth evidence collection, from multiple services, that would provide a route to build the contextual accounts required. While these offences are some of the most severe expressions of violence, case studies were not being built as illustrations of all forms of peer-on-peer abuse. Instead they were being developed to explore the contextual dynamics of peer-on-peer abuse, and the files that would provide the best detail for this purpose were the more detailed and extensive investigations.

Case selection

Having agreed to the broad parameters for identifying cases, I worked with a police analyst to select and sample investigations for inclusion in the study. Selection criteria were developed with four components. The first component was concerned with identifying the relationships involved in the abusive incident. An objective of the study was to illuminate the contextual, including relational, factors involved in peer-on-peer abuse. Therefore, investigations were included in which a 'relationship' between some of the young people involved was important. Offences characterised as 'multiple-perpetrator rape' (with an identified relationship between the suspects), 'domestic abuse' (where the incident occurred within an intimate relationship) or 'serious youth violence' (where there was a peer relationship/friendship/acquaintance between those involved) were selected. It was agreed that, if any cases were sampled that didn't involve some form of established relationship between some of those involved, they would be discounted from the study.

The second component was the ages of the young people featured in the investigations. In England, individuals are defined as children up until their eighteenth birthday and are considered criminally responsible for their actions from the age of 10. Children also transfer from primary to secondary education at the age of 11 and will often start to travel to school alone (or with peers) and spend more time independently from their family from this age onwards. These elements provide a set of socially constructed parameters for adolescence in England. Given the research messages about the ages of those involved in peer-on-peer abuse, the social fields of importance to this age group, and the statutory duties of professionals to safeguard young people up until their eighteenth birthday, cases were selected that featured young people aged 10 to 17. An age parameter of 10 to 17 was particularly important when considering the response of professionals to peer-on-peer abuse: these boundaries demarcate the extent to which others are responsible for keeping individuals safe (up to age 17) and the age at which young people can be held responsible for their actions (from the age of 10).

The third component of the selection criteria relates to gender. As Powell's use of Bourdieu (explored previously) has implied, gendered social norms inform the rules at play within the social fields in which young people spend their time. In addition, research into peer-on-peer abuse specifically implies that the phenomenon affects young women and young men differently (i.e. Barter, et al., 2009). To consider the gendered nature of contextual factors, an approach to sampling was adopted that would ensure the victimisation of both young men and young women, and their victimisation of others, would be considered.

The fourth component of the selection criteria related to dates when the incidents, and investigations, occurred. A five-year time span from 2007 to 2012 was recommended by the participating force. This would ensure that the investigations used had been closed by the time of analysis and the researcher could identify whether practitioner approaches changed/developed over time or remained static. By the time that analysis would be completed, outcomes could also be tracked.

From these criteria a cohort of cases were identified by a police analyst in the participating force, as presented in Table 3.1.

Investigation files were sampled from the available selection documented in Table 3.1. Of the 47 rape investigations that involved a female suspect, the twenty-third was selected because it was numerically in the middle of the available selection. There were 805 remaining rape investigations and every 160th case was selected for inclusion, yielding three gang-associated cases and two non-gang–associated cases. The third of the seven domestic abuse files was selected, being numerically in the middle, because it wasn't a gang-associated case and involved a female complainant. The other two murder cases were selected from the 10 serious youth violence investigations that featured at least one female suspect (the fourth and eighth cases); one of these was gang-associated and one was not.

A total of nine cases were selected for inclusion in the study – three were murder investigations and six were multiple-perpetrator rape cases. I had agreed with the participating police force that if, following initial analysis, the data set was

TABLE 3.1 Cases sampled for the study

Offences (January 2007 – December 2012)	Total number[1]	Gang-associated	Female complainant 10- to 17-year-olds	Female suspect 10- to 17-year-olds	Male complainant 10- to 17-year-olds	Male suspect 10- to 17-year-olds
Multiple-perpetrator rape	806	8.6% (n = 69)	96.80% (n = 780)	5.80% (n = 47)	1.74% (n = 14)	76.80% (n = 619)
Murder; teenage relationship abuse	7	14.2% (n = 1)	85.7% (n = 6)	14.2% (n = 1)	14.2% (n = 1)	85.7% (n = 6)
Murder; serious youth violence	87	39.1% (n = 34)	11.5% (n = 10)	20.7% (n = 10)	89.6% (n = 78)	95.4% (n = 83)

insufficient to draw thematic conclusions, then additional cases would be selected from the initial sample. However, each investigation yielded extensive data and was sufficient for the purposes of this exploratory study.

Investigation file contents

Each investigation file contained a varied range of documents, including:

- Police reports for each young person, including any records of them going missing, committing offences and/or living at addresses where there had been reports of domestic abuse incidents between their parents/carers
- Witness and suspect statements related to the incidents themselves
- CCTV footage, social media and phone records which evidenced movements and conversations in the lead-up to the incidents, during the incidents and in the days and weeks following the incidents
- Minutes from multi-agency meetings, including strategy and child protection meetings held to plan responses to the incident in question or agree to interventions for those young people involved
- School reports, children's social care and youth-offending assessments for young people involved in the incidents
- Emails from the police, Crown Prosecution Services, children's social care, schools and youth-offending teams where the incidents, the young people involved or the professional response were discussed

When information from these sources was used to complete a case review template for each investigation, the contexts and individuals featured in the nine studies produced totalled:

- 145 young people (aged 11–17)
- 160 households

- 21 peer groups
- 30 schools/colleges/alternative education providers
- nine neighbourhoods/local authorities with specific localities, including parks, transport hubs and bus stops, high streets, take-away shops, stairwells, alleyways, streets and open green spaces

Of the 145 young people, 76 were suspects, nine were complainants, 45 were witnesses and the remaining 15 were classified as 'other' (generally young people related to complainants or suspects who had some association to the investigation). The language of complainant, suspect and witness was used throughout the study and is referenced in this book as well. It was the primary terminology used in investigation files. More importantly, this approach provided a conceptual space to recognise the victimisation of suspects in the cases and avoided prescribing a static victim status to any individuals involved (Melrose, 2013).

Process of data collection and analysis

Information from each of the nine investigation files was transferred to the case review template outlined previously in this chapter. All data collection and transfer occurred on police force premises. Documents were reviewed investigation by investigation. As each document was reviewed, its title and a brief description were recorded on a spreadsheet (a document log). Each young person in the investigations was allocated a code, as were the names of schools and any public places featured. Information on the nature of the offence, the individual characteristics of the young people involved, the nature of their family and home environments, peer relationships, school environments and the public spaces in which they spent their time was recorded in the case review template.

When all nine templates were completed, the evidence held within them was transferred into two SPSS files for quantitative analysis and the templates themselves were uploaded onto NVivo for qualitative analysis. An analytical framework was designed to facilitate this process. The framework was built around the contexts of concern for the study – seeking to draw out the relationship between environments and individual behaviour in each case and the extent to which practitioners responded to this interplay.

Two SPSS files were created – one to analyse information on case studies as a whole (n = 9) and the other to analyse information on the 145 individuals and the social fields (160 households, 21 peer groups, 30 school and nine neighbourhoods) that featured in each case. Nodes were created in NVivo (122) and variables in SPSS (74 for the cases and 121 related to the individuals and contexts in each case) to explore the nature of each context, how contexts interplayed with one another and with individual young people's behaviour. For example, nodes and variables were created to capture evidence of criminality in each social field in each investigation file. SPSS data were used to count the number of young people who engaged in, or were exposed to, criminal activity in each context (home, peer group, school and neighbourhood), along with the number of responses to criminality that were recorded in these systems. NVivo data was used to provide a qualitative exemplification of those findings. Findings were then organised for each individual, in each case study, as outlined in Table 3.2.

When a table had been created for each young person in each case review, all tables were linked together and, combined with an overview of the incident and practitioner response to it, provided the data to produce a contextual case study as illustrated in Table 3.3.

For each police investigation a case study was produced, and along with supplementary and explanatory qualitative and quantitative data, provided a practical illustration of the contextual dynamics of peer-on-peer abuse which

TABLE 3.2 Example of contextual framework for organising and analysing case file data

Case study 03	Suspect 1	Response
Home 1	Exposure to domestic abuse	None
Peer group 1	Sexually offend together Share abusive images Commit robberies together	Bail conditions forbid contact
School 1	Sexual harassment identified by students Complaints regarding bullying	Suspects excluded – no other action taken
Neighbourhood 1	Young men experience robbery in local parks and on buses	No action taken in association with investigation

TABLE 3.3 Table used to make a contextual case study record

Incident overview Points of escalation	Nature	Professional response
Individual characteristics of young people involved		
Families and home environments		
Peer groups and relationships		
School environments		
Neighbourhood and public spaces		

illuminated wider research into this issue. In building these case studies and identifying themes across them, I was able to evidence the ways in which social fields, particularly those that were extra-familial, have informed young people's behaviours when they abuse, or are abused by, their peers. Likewise, young people's behaviours, and the decisions that they made, contributed to the nature of the social fields in which they spent their time. Importantly, the professional responses to each case rarely engaged with the extra-familial or relational dynamics of peer-on-peer abuse and instead focused on assessing and addressing the individual and familial characteristics of the young people in each case. Like the wider critiques of individualised child protection practices, the safeguarding response in each case focused on individual vulnerability factors and the need to address these in order to prevent abuse. For this book, the case studies that I have produced provide the depth required to offer a contextual account of peer-on-peer abuse – highlighting and furthering the international evidence base and increasing the need for policymakers to accommodate the contextual dynamics of this issue.

Reflection regarding ethics of study, limitations and learning yielded from the process

A number of ethical considerations were made to successfully complete this study, and they remain relevant to all publications that feature the evidence base that I have produced.

From a practical perspective the study received approval from a two-stage research ethics review process at the University of Bedfordshire in addition to the ethical approvals process of the participating police service. To gain these approvals a number of issues required attention, including consent, data security, the anonymity of the young people, families and professionals featured in the files, the limitations of confidentiality, researcher welfare and the parameters of data protection. Relevant security procedures were followed – investigation files were only accessed on police premises and only anonymised information was transferred onto password-protected case review templates. To ensure the anonymity of those in the files, no case study has ever been published in full, and only combined statistical evidence, thematic accounts and vignettes created from composite themes drawn from the nine cases as a collective are used to communicate the study findings.

Because material used to build case studies came from investigation files, I was not accessing information about the safety and well-being of children that wasn't already held by professionals. However, on four occasions I identified safeguarding concerns that emerged through a contextual analysis of the investigations file that did not appear to have been addressed through the original professional response. For example, in providing evidence to an investigation when their friend was murdered by her boyfriend, a number of young women made disclosures related to sexual exploitation and peer violence. However, the investigation was primarily focused on the murder, and case file materials did not evidence whether this wider network of sexual exploitation within the associated peer group had been addressed. On each of these occasions I raised concerns with my single point of contact within the participating police force who in turn liaised with safeguarding leads to follow up the identified issue and ascertain what professional actions needed to be taken.

The lead police investigator for each case provided consent and approval for my access to each investigation file. The participating police force did not think that it was appropriate that young people involved in the cases be contacted. Some were deceased and others were recovering from the incident or were in custody. The participating police service wanted to use the learning to improve practice in the future and develop their responses to vulnerable young people. It was on those grounds that access was granted, with parameters for usage and data protection concerns managed. From a perspective of the Data Protection Act (DPA) I needed to access personal and sensitive materials in the investigation files in order to build case studies. The DPA generally prevents the onward sharing of this information for purposes other than which it was collected. However, because the materials were accessed to improve the response of the participating police force to peer-on-peer abuse and to enable it to fulfil its statutory duties to protect, in this instance the study and its objectives sat within Schedule 3 of the DPA – particularly, with regard to Schedule 3's reference to the administration of justice. As the review process surfaced additional safeguarding concerns for some young people involved in the cases, it had an immediate impact to the effect of Schedule 3 in addition to longer-term improvement of policing peer-on-peer abuse for the participating force.

Beyond the practicalities of ethical approval, the process of building the case files taught me a lot about the nature of peer-on-peer abuse, the challenges of researching the subject area and matters which the wider research community may want to consider in further developing this area of work. I conducted this review of nine cases as an individual, rather than as part of a wider research team. In the process I held a lot of traumatic information as a sole researcher, and over the three-year period displayed a physical reaction to the content of information files. While analysing the data I developed a skin irritation which doctors struggled to diagnose and treat. Once the study was completed the skin irritation went away. For me the emotional challenge of building peer-on-peer abuse case studies lay not in reviewing the details of the abusive incidents themselves but in the identification of a persistent mismatch between the contextual nature of the abuse and the individualised nature of the professional response. This repeated limitation in professional practice reduced the capacity of services to sufficiently safeguard the young people featured in the files and resulted in multiple missed opportunities to offer more effective outcomes for those involved.

In addition to this personal challenge, despite receiving ethical approval to access investigation files in keeping with the parameters of data protection, I felt continually aware of the sensitive nature of the materials I was reviewing. For me it was critical that the case studies I produced could be used to maximum effect to enhance professional practice and improve the safeguarding response to young people in England. It was only working through the process of building a contextual account that I have been able to appreciate the nature of the relationship between context and individual action in cases of peer-on-peer abuse and identify the significance of this for future research, policy and practice. Therefore, in producing this book and in sharing research messages in other papers, practitioner training and with the media, I have sought to take others through this same process. It is not enough to simply report the study findings. I have spent time building vignettes of the case studies, which are composite accounts rather than a reproduction of any one case, so that other people can go through the same contextual case-building process that I have done. The methodological approach of case review played a pivotal role in providing me with the perspective I now have, and so it was as important for me to develop narratives and tools through which others could build case studies as it was to communicate the thematic messages of this research. In doing this I feel that I have authentically engaged with the provisions of the DPA while working in the parameters of the ethical approval I was granted. Should my work have failed to engage in the process of improving the ability of statutory services to undertake their duties, then I would not have been satisfied that the work had fulfilled its duty, and potential, in keeping with the DPA.

Finally, in maintaining an ethical presentation of the case studies I have developed, it is important to acknowledge their limitations, and the limitations of the study in which they have been produced. Despite the relatively large number of young people featured in the review (n = 145), the nine case studies that I produced should not be viewed as representative of all peer-on-peer abuse incidents, nor are they intended to. As stated throughout this chapter, and as is illustrated throughout this book, the case review process is intended to illuminate, challenge and further the understanding of peer-on-peer abuse already established by an international research evidence base and acknowledged in media reports and policy documents. The case review findings are presented in the context of wider research into peer-on-peer abuse rather than in isolation, and the information gathered during case reviews have not been used to make generic comment on the nature of all cases of peer-on-peer abuse. All investigation files used for this study were selected from one police service area and may not reflect practices elsewhere in England or internationally. Furthermore, while multi-agency documents were featured in investigation files, it is likely that some information on wider safeguarding responses to each case were not included. Therefore, any reflection on implications of the case review for national and international policy and practice are contextualized with reference to wider studies into safeguarding responses to young people and the issue of peer-on-peer abuse, rather than drawing conclusions solely from professional practices in the files.

Setting the stage for a contextual account: vignettes and book structure

This chapter has illustrated the purpose of developing a contextual account of peer-on-peer abuse, the conceptual framework through which such an account can be built and the methodological approach I undertook to create a suite of case studies to further the contextual narrative I am trying to offer. Building on the research, policy and media evidence presented in the previous chapter, the remainder of this book devotes attention to the contexts associated with peer-on-peer abuse and the policy and practice implications of such an approach. The existing evidence base has already established that young people's home and family environments, their peer relationships, their school environments and the public spaces in which they socialise are all important for their social development and inform their experiences of peer-on-peer abuse. The purpose of this book is to use an international evidence base to provide a more detailed account of each context and to use the thematic evidence generated from the case study exercise to illustrate the dynamic relationship between context and individual behaviour/choice in the buildup to incidents of peer-on-peer abuse.

Working from social field to social field, the following four chapters of this book provide a cumulatively contextual picture of peer-on-peer abuse, before thematic implications for policy, practice and research are fully considered. In keeping with my intentions for delivering this book and the wider ethical considerations outlined in this chapter, each chapter on contexts features international research on that environment and its relationship to peer-on-peer abuse, thematic evidence that emerged from the case review process and a 'contextual vignette'. The contextual vignette is critically important to building the narrative this book sets out to achieve. It seeks to take the reader through the same process that I did when reviewing the nine cases in my original study. At the close of this chapter I introduce a peer-on-peer abuse vignette – a composite of the nine that I reviewed during the study. Each chapter of the following four chapters builds on the initial information provided by communicating the dynamics of the particular social field to which that chapter is dedicated as it relates to the vignette (as presented in Figure 3.2).

In using the vignette process in this way, alongside the thematic findings of the nine case reviews, I am seeking to contextualise the ways in which practitioners, the public, the media and academics understand the journeys young people take towards abusing or being abused by their peers, the choices involved on this pathway and the implications of this for professionals. Throughout the book I achieve this by using Bourdieu's social theory to refocus attention on the contexts in which peer-on-peer abuse occurs and the ways that these interplay with individual choices and behaviours, therefore asking questions of all of us regarding how we can prevent and intervene with this social problem.

The vignette I return to throughout this book involves the following incident:

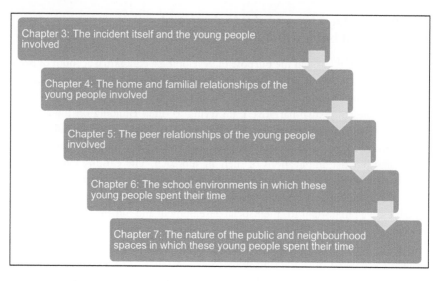

Chapter 3: The incident itself and the young people involved

Chapter 4: The home and familial relationships of the young people involved

Chapter 5: The peer relationships of the young people involved

Chapter 6: The school environments in which these young people spent their time

Chapter 7: The nature of the public and neighbourhood spaces in which these young people spent their time

FIGURE 3.2 The contextual vignette presentation in the book

The incident

- Lara was in a room when Melissa entered and stole something from her
- Lara asked why Melissa was always picking on her and asked for her property back
- Melissa said that if Lara does something for her first she would give her back her property
- Melissa told Lara to wait and left the room
- A few minutes later Melissa returned to the room with James
- Melissa said that Lara could have her property back if she had sex with James
- Lara told Melissa that she no longer wanted her property back and to forget it
- However, Melissa threatened to beat Lara up unless she had sex with James
- James raped Lara under the instruction of Melissa, while Melissa filmed it on her phone
- Later that day other boys began to approach Lara for sex

The three primary individuals involved in this case are Lara, Melissa and James. In keeping with the evidence base introduced in Chapter 2, these three young people have a number of individual characteristics, and display behaviours, associated with young people who have been abused by, or who abuse, their peers.

Individual characteristics of those involved

James	Melissa	Lara
• 14 years old	• 14 years old	• 14 years old
• Black British ethnicity	• Black British ethnicity	• Mixed Black Caribbean and White British ethnicity
• No recorded disability	• Recorded learning disability – although extent not specified	
• Living at home with biological family		• No recorded learning disability
• Frequently missing from home	• Historic child protection plan for neglect – nothing at present	• Living at home with biological family
• Erratic and low attendance at school	• Excellent attendance at school	• Historic child in need plan – nothing at present
• Arrests for robbery, drugs possession and violence on his record; no convictions	• One arrest and conviction for robbery	• Some record of truancy
		• One arrest and caution for criminal damage

The individual characteristics and life stories of James, Melissa and Lara are diverse. As suggested by the research evidence into peer-on-peer abuse, some were going missing from home or school (James and Lara) whereas Melissa was not. Melissa had a history of abuse but Lara and James did not. James had poor attendance at school but Melissa's attendance was excellent. And while all three had been in contact with the police, James' offending was far more established than the behaviours displayed by Melissa and Lara. So what could it be about the homes, peer groups, schools and neighbourhood in which James, Melissa and Lara spent their time which turned these personal characteristics into vulnerabilities associated with peer-on-peer abuse? The next section of this book draws attention to those social fields and, in detailing the wider evidence base on each, sets this vignette in context and illuminates the importance of understanding the relationship between individual behaviours and contextual dynamics for providing an effective response to peer-on-peer abuse.

Note

1 Not every case file had identified the gender of those involved; other cases had groups of suspects that were both male and female, and some cases involved the same complainant, so the complainant and suspect figures won't necessarily total the number of cases.

SECTION II

The contexts associated with peer-on-peer abuse

4

'I BLAME THE PARENTS'

When it comes to identifying the social contexts associated with peer-on-peer abuse, the family is often at the forefront of both government and media debate. As David Cameron, the then prime minister, stated in 2015:

> For me, families are the best welfare system there is – so I have never been shy about supporting them in the work they do. Marriage is now recognised in the tax system. Shared parental leave is now available for parents in the first year of their child's birth . . . if we really want to extend opportunity in our country, we need to intervene more directly to help the most vulnerable families in our country. Our troubled families programme, under Louise Casey, has changed lives. By radically changing the way we deliver services to the hardest-to-reach families in our country, we have tackled worklessness, addiction, truancy and anti-social behaviour. And I can announce today that almost all of the 117,000 families which the programme started working with have now been turned around – in terms of either school attendance or getting a job or both.
>
> *(Prime Minister's Office, 2015)*

Such rhetoric implies that a range of social issues stem from the nature of families and therefore by intervening with families governments can prevent social harm – a position that has been maintained across the political spectrum. In 2008 the then Labour Prime Minister, Gordon Brown, stated that 'the first responsibility when a child is in trouble or at risk of getting into trouble rests with the parents – "We must hold parents responsible"' (The Telegraph, 2008). Four years later, David Lammy, MP, one of the 2015 Labour candidates for the mayor of London, attributed young people's involvement in knife crime to a lack of a relationship with their fathers:

> Most knife-wielding young killers in London have absent fathers, Tottenham MP David Lammy said today. He issued the grim warning in the wake of

the fatal stabbing of 14-year-old Kevin Ssali as he stepped off a bus in Lee, south-east London, last month . . . Mr Lammy . . . said many single mothers on estates were 'yearning' for help to try to keep their children out of trouble's way. 'I have sat with too many parents, usually mothers, who have lost their children to knife crime . . . . Usually the child that has committed the offence comes from a background where the father has been absent'.

(Evening Standard, 2012)

These political positions are supported by a media and public discourse that routinely emphasises the roles of parents, or their absence, in determining young people's involvement in crime and violence. In early 2017 the UK media reported that the head of London's murder investigation team in the police had claimed that 'it's up to parents to tell their children to stop carrying knives' (Evening Standard, 2017). A YouGov survey in 2013 found that 41 per cent of parents and 44 per cent of professionals believe parents are partly to blame for grooming and child sexual exploitation (Channel 4, 2013). While five years earlier, Daily Mail columnist Amada Platell claimed that 'Britain's endemic culture of single-parent homes and fractured communities is the principal reason why violent crime is spiralling' (Mail Online, 2008). These sentiments were echoed by Sir Alan Steer in his review of behaviour in UK schools, when he said that:

You wonder what has gone wrong in these children's lives. Of course, the kids have a responsibility, but there are questions about what's going on at home. Parents have a huge responsibility. Government doesn't bring up children; parents do.

(The Guardian, 2008)

Seven years on and similar attitudes prevailed when a judge who presided over a sexual exploitation case in 2015 summed up by stating that 'the combination of inadequate parenting leading to rebellious children lacking supervision provided an opportunity' for young people to be abused (Mail Online, 2015).

If these accounts are accurate, then approaches to prevent peer-on-peer abuse should focus on the nature of family environments and the relationships that form within them. Are there particular family environments that protect young people from peer-on-peer abuse while there are others that increase the risk? The current parameters of the child protection system in England and Wales have created processes that are set to investigate peer-on-peer abuse through this lens (Firmin, 2017): It is designed to assess and intervene with young people's families in a bid to keep them safe (Parton, 2014). Should we do what Gordon Brown, Sir Alan Steer and others have suggested and question what is going on in a young person's home in order to understand why they experience, or engage in, violence at school, on the street or amongst their friends?

Returning to the case of James, Melissa and Lara introduced in Chapter 3, and exploring their experiences of family life with reference to international literature and findings from the cases I reviewed, this chapter does as the political discourse suggests. By exploring the evidenced relationship between family dynamics and incidents of peer-on-peer abuse, it investigates both the extent to which 'family matters' to the phenomenon in question and the extent to which the 'I blame the parents' narrative is over-simplistic. In doing so this chapter begins to illustrate why it is critical to understand young people's contextual experiences beyond their families in order to truly appreciate both the importance of family dynamics and their experiences of peer-on-peer abuse.

To begin with, let's revisit the case of James, Melissa and Lara – and consider whether their family environments suggest that the responsibility for what happened between them lay with their parents.

Returning to the case study: the family and home environments of James, Melissa and Lara

As detailed in Chapter 3, Lara was raped by James, and Melissa initiated the incident. In the buildup to this event, James' behaviour had been getting progressively challenging for his parents, his teachers and other professionals. He would go missing from home and wouldn't come back when his parents tried to call him; he was rarely in school, had robbed other young people of their phones and had carried weapons before. Both Melissa and Lara had also been arrested in recent months, but their offending record was far less prolific than James'. Lara had started to truant as well, whereas Melissa had an excellent attendance record at school. But to what extent did their home environments and family relationships contribute to the incident they were involved in or the behaviours they displayed in the escalation towards it? In keeping with the policy and public discourse outlined previously, the first question we need to ask is: what were their parents doing in the lead-up to the incident?

James	Melissa	Lara
• James lives with his mum, dad and older sibling	• Melissa lives with her mum and two younger siblings	• Lara lives with her mum and younger sibling
• James' older brother, who doesn't live with him, is associated with a street gang	• She was exposed to domestic abuse from early childhood. She witnessed her father physically and emotionally abuse her mother and his later partners	• She was exposed to domestic abuse in early childhood when her father abused her mother
• There is no record of any familial child protection issues in James' home environment (neglect, physical, sexual or emotional abuse)	• Melissa's father has a criminal record and has spent time in custody	• Her parents later separated when she was 8 years old
		• Lara has been unable to establish a relationship with her father since

- James' mother has raised concerns with his school about a change in his behaviour over the past year, stating that he repeatedly goes missing and does not answer his phone when she tries to call him

- Melissa's mother has attempted suicide and has persisting mental health concerns
- Melissa was on a child protection plan for neglect in early childhood but this was no longer in place at the time of the incident

He has had children with another partner since and doesn't want contact with Lara

- When Lara's behaviour begins to change, her mother contacts her school and comes in to see them to ascertain what she can do to support her daughter

James', Melissa's and Lara's families had a complex association with the incident in question. While James' mother had been raising concerns about a change in her son's behaviour, there doesn't seem to be anything about his home environment that related to his assault on Lara. His older brother had been involved in offending as part of a street gang, but he didn't live with James. We might wonder what influence James' older brother had on him. We could also ask how it could be that no concerns were raised about their family environment given that James and his brother were involved in crime. All of these issues are explored in this chapter and throughout this book – but at this stage it seems that James was relatively safe, protected and cared for when he was at home with his parents.

Melissa's family was quite different from James'. She had been exposed to domestic abuse at home, her father had a criminal record and her mother had experienced mental health issues when Melissa instigated the rape of Lara. These factors contributed to the fact that she had been on a child protection plan for neglect when she was younger. But at the time of the incident, professionals weren't as concerned about Melissa's home environment as they had been. She was no longer on a child protection plan, and her father wasn't living in the family home. But to what extent did her past experiences or her current family situation influence the decisions she made on the day that Lara was raped? Were they the reason she had started to commit offences despite her regular attendance at school? If Melissa had experienced a different family life, would she have still been involved in the incident in question?

Lara, like Melissa, had also been exposed to domestic abuse when she was younger. While her father no longer posed a risk in that regard (he was no longer living with, or abusing, Lara's mother), his reluctance to have a relationship with Lara negatively affected her well-being. But to what extent was any of this related to what happened to Lara on the day that she was raped? Did being exposed to domestic abuse or being rejected by her father make her vulnerable to what James and Melissa did? If Lara had been raised in a different family setting, would she still have been assaulted? Was the judge who presided over the 2015 sexual exploitation trial referenced earlier in this chapter right? Was it Lara's background that made her vulnerable to being abused?

If we were to apply the UK policy discourse and child protection frameworks outlined at the start of this chapter to the lives of Lara, Melissa and James, then we would look to 1) Lara's family to protect her from what happened and 2) James' and Melissa's parents to prevent them from abusing Lara. We would argue that Lara was raped by James and Melissa, in part, because: James and Melissa were exposed to criminality at home; Lara and Melissa had both witnessed domestic abuse; Melissa's mother had mental health issues that prevented her from adequately parenting her daughter; and James' parents (because of their own limitations and deficiencies) had clearly lost control of him. But does international research and case review evidence support this argument?

The extent to which 'family matters'

From the moment they are born, the nature of a child's home environment is central to their physical and mental development. It is within their family unit, both immediate and extended, that they first form and learn about relationships. Through this process children form attachments, learning how to trust, rely on and care for others and develop a sense of self and identity (Cassidy & Shaver, 2008; Warr, 2002). By building relationships with parents, carers and wider family members, and observing the relationships they have with one another, children learn social norms and values (Cassidy & Shaver, 2008). To this extent the type of family environment in which children are raised will inform the nature of the relationships that they form with their peers.

If, however, positive and protective family environments do much to equip children in their encounters with others, then what is the consequence for children who live in abusive, harmful or unprotective households? International research suggests that abusive home environments can negatively affect the ability of young people to identify and form healthy and safe relationships (Catch 22, 2013; Gadd, et al., 2013; Hackett, 2014; Nieuwbeerta & van der Laan, 2006; Vizard, 2006) – and in this way they have been associated with young people's experiences of peer-on-peer abuse. A total of 160 households featured in the nine peer-on-peer abuse cases I reviewed. Of the 145 young people who were associated with these homes, at least 33 per cent (n = 48) were exposed to, or experienced, harm in their families such as Melissa and Lara did.

Experiences of physical, sexual and emotional abuse in their families and exposure to domestic abuse between their parents and carers have been associated with abuse in young people's relationships. A broad range of other issues, from parental substance misuse, mental ill health and criminality within families, have also been found in the backgrounds of some young people who have been abused by, or who abuse, their peers. Such experiences have been associated with psychological dysfunction, trauma, detachment and a lack of empathy in young people (Aisenberg & Herrenkohl, 2008; Allenye, et al., 2014; Cassidy & Shaver, 2008; Gadd, et al., 2013; Vizard, 2006). These experiences within homes have also been found to undermine the ability of families to protect young people from other factors beyond the home, which may be negatively influencing their lives and relationships (Losel & Bender, 2006; Tremblay, et al., 2004). Beyond issues that may emerge within their biological families, children who are living in the care of the state are also thought to be at increased vulnerability to peer-on-peer abuse (Beckett, 2013; HM Government, 2016; Shuker, 2013a).

Each of these matters requires detailed exploration before a clear account can be provided of the relationship amongst families, individual young people and their experiences of peer-on-peer abuse. International research bolstered by the cases I reviewed provides a detailed evidence base with which to interrogate the persistent practice of intervening with families in order to prevent abuse between young people.

Exposure to domestic abuse and harmful gender norms

A number of young people who have abused, or who have been abused by, their peers have, like Lara and Melissa, been exposed to domestic abuse in their homes (Boswell, 2006; Catch 22, 2013; Gadd, et al., 2013, Hackett, Phillips, et al., 2013). Compared with young people living in non-abusive households, young people who have witnessed abuse between their parents have been found to have 'increased adolescent aggressive behaviour' (Herrera & Stuewig, 2011) – but the reasons for this, and the wider association between living with domestic abuse and being involved in peer-on-peer abuse, are complex.

Domestic abuse was the most consistently identified source of harm within the families that featured in the cases I reviewed – recorded in at least one household in eight of the nine. In at least half of the 48 households where harmful behaviours were documented in case files, young people were exposed to domestic abuse, for example:

> Sean's and Michael's mother . . . got into an argument with the father and has also been hit . . . . During an argument between his parents, [Sean's] father grabbed his mother, causing her to hit her head. She then hit the dad over the head with an iron.
>
> *(Case 7, murder, home of two suspects – Sean and Michael)*

Some scholars argue that, when young people witness physical conflict in their families, they learn harmful or 'aggressive' behaviours that they repeat in their encounters with peers (Losel & Bender, 2006) – a process sometimes referred to as 'social learning theory'. All examples of domestic abuse in the files I analysed featured the abuse of women by men. For the young people involved, this introduced, or for some reinforced, harmful ideas about gender and relationships which some went on to repeat (in both their actions and words) during interactions with peers. However, it is important to note that exposure to domestic abuse was not the only route through which young people in the cases accessed harmful gendered ideas. As subsequent chapters in this book demonstrate, they were also introduced to these social norms in their peer relationships, schools and neighbourhoods in which these relationships formed, and their interactions online. Furthermore, in four of the nine cases reviewed, there was evidence that young people who weren't living with domestic abuse were still exposed to harmful gender norms by their parents and carers. For example, in one case a young woman, Rita, was murdered by her ex-partner. Rita had left him after he stalked her online and threatened to harm her if she was seen talking to any other young men. Three of Rita's female friends were living in families who held similar stereotypical views about the roles of women in relationships and in society. In the year that Rita was murdered her friend Leila had been:

> hit by her mother after she was seen hanging around with boys and [when] officers attended to speak to Leila about a possible forced marriage with her cousin, she disclosed that her father had hit her.
>
> *(Case 8, friend of complainant)*

When Rita told her friends, including Leila, that her boyfriend was threatening her, they normalised his behaviour – they didn't think it was out of the ordinary that he would be jealous and thought that she should respect her boyfriend's wishes and not speak to other young men. Leila was not witnessing domestic abuse between her parents. But her experiences at home still reinforced the gendered norms that underpinned the behaviour of Rita's boyfriend.

In three cases, parents of young people suspected of abusing their peers, or witnessing the abuse of others, also drew upon gendered stereotypes to blame the young person who had been abused for what had happened to them. For example, after Melissa was charged with the rape of Lara, alongside James, Melissa's mother wrote the following statement on her social media account:

> I don't think they realised that the tart's [sic] version of events didn't go as planned in court. Her whole story was proved to be bullshit and her credibility was fucked.
>
> *(Case 3, social media entry, parent of a suspect)*

Parental responses that blame victims of peer-on-peer sexual abuse are not uncommon (Hackett, et al., 2014) and often serve to deflect responsibility and enable denial within families affected. However, these reactions, like acts of domestic abuse and other representations of gender stereotypes within families, reproduce harmful social norms which often underpinned the incidents that were under investigation in the cases reviewed. There was evidence within both murder and rape reviews that young people had drawn upon harmful gender norms when abusing their peers, and that these views often reflected the ideas and behaviours that some had encountered within their families. While also reflective of national and global ideas about gender and other social norms (UN Broadband Commission, 2015), problematic attitudes about gender and relationships within young people's families reinforced abusive social rules rather than supported young people to challenge them.

Beyond social learning theories, other studies suggest that, when young people are exposed to violence in their families, they learn how to suppress their emotions as a means of coping. This process affects a young person's ability to experience empathy and can also increase the likelihood that they will be abused by others (Herrera & Stuewig, 2011). Evidence of this pattern was difficult to establish using a case review methodology. However, different types of coping strategies, beyond emotionally 'shutting down', were reflected in case file material.

In some cases it was evident that for some young people, particularly those who were being victimised by peers, abuse between their parents impacted their ability to seek safety, security and advice at home. They appeared unable to share their fears with a parent, and within files this was always their mother, who was already trying to manage their own experiences of violence.

Other young people in the cases reviewed would attempt to cope by running away from home when a domestic abuse incident broke out. This was particularly true for young people who led their peers to abuse others (n = 20), 40 per cent of whom were going missing from home as a result of domestic abuse. When young people ran away from home in these cases, they ran to the street and their peers. When spending time on the streets, they were exposed to violence, exploitation, risks of gang association and others forms of offending. This exposure created situations in which young people relied upon adults and peers on the streets to keep them safe while they were there – relationships which often resulted in a young person's involvement in peer abuse and other forms of offending behaviour.

Therefore, while case file evidence, like wider research, suggested an association between young people's exposure to domestic abuse and their experiences of peer-on-peer abuse, this relationship appears to be a complex one with multiple explanations. There does not appear to be a simple intergenerational cycle of abuse – where young people who witness abuse go on to abuse others. This notion has been largely disputed in wider research (Widom, 1989; Women's Aid, 2007), and the case review evidence base would support this position. Rather, it seems that the interaction between domestic abuse in families, young people's responses to these behaviours and their interactions with other social contexts can create climates and situations that are fertile for peer-on-peer abuse. Practitioner responses in the cases that were reviewed often struggled to acknowledge the complexity of this relationship. For example, a potential association between young men's exposure to domestic abuse at home and their vulnerability to committing violent offences against peers was rarely addressed: all suspects, bar one, who were living with domestic abuse were bailed back to their home addresses without intervention while they waited for their trials to commence.

Without other sufficient protective factors, to be explored throughout this book, it appears that exposure to domestic abuse at home: creates a harmful impression of gender and relationship norms; normalises violence as a form of care; and limits the capacity of the home to be an environment which protects young people against peer-on-peer abuse. However, while exposure to domestic abuse was the most consistent form of abuse experienced by young people in the cases I reviewed, international research has also argued that the physical, emotional and sexual abuse of young people from their parents/carers increases their vulnerability to peer-on-peer abuse (Gadd, et al., 2013; Herrera & Stuewig, 2011; Losel & Bender, 2006; Vizard, et al., 2007).

Intra-familial abuse

Experiences of physical chastisement, neglect and other forms of abuse are considered to both serve as models for aggressive behaviour (in keeping with the idea of social learning theory introduced previously). Children who have been physically abused by parents, carers or other family members have been found to react in aggressive and violent ways to scenarios that do not necessarily warrant such a response (Teisl & Cicchetti, 2008). Abuse by parents and carers can affect young people's ability to form healthy, and non-abusive, attachments with others, including with their peers (Losel & Bender, 2006). When young people, particularly girls, are physically abused in their families, they are more likely to bully their peers (Barter, et al., 2009; Herrera & Stuewig, 2011).

Being sexually abused by family members is also thought to increase the likelihood that young people will bully their peers as well as be victimised by them (Herrera & Stuewig, 2011). Feelings of shame and self-blame can manifest as low self-esteem. This can in turn be exploited by peers or masked by those who have been abused through their own expressions of violence when they harm others. This pattern was evident for a young woman, Sara, who featured in a case I reviewed. Sara was sexually exploited by a group of her peers over a number of months. She had experienced chronic levels of abuse within her family in earlier childhood:

> Sara was exposed to violent and disturbing images at a young age and as such her emotional development is distorted. Sara watched her mother's boyfriend stab himself . . . aged 4/5 years. Sara's mother disclosed that she believed Sara was sexually abused at age 2.
>
> *(Case five, complainant)*

Professionals who worked with Sara largely agreed that these early experiences contributed to Sara's feelings of worthlessness and her perception that she should be sexually available to anyone at any given time.

While not always as extreme or extensive as the experiences of Sara, of the 46 young people who were recorded as being abused by their families in the cases I reviewed, 35 per cent had been neglected by parents/carers, just over a quarter (26%) had been physically abused, 11 per cent were known to have been emotionally abused, and documented evidence suggested that three had been sexually abused. These experiences appeared to create varying states of emotional detachment or a lack of empathy amongst young people who abused their peers and/or were abused by them (Aisenberg & Herrenkohl, 2008; Allenye, et al., 2014; Cassidy & Shaver, 2008; Gadd, et al., 2013). In addition, the impact of these experiences reduced the capacity of some families to protect young people from challenges they faced in their peers groups, schools and the public spaces in which they spent their time. When a child was being abused by their families, it was difficult for them to identify how these same people may also protect them from other forms of violence. In addition, like exposure to domestic abuse, experiences of physical, sexual and emotional abuse within families drove young people from their homes and onto the streets – sites in which they encountered and engaged in acts of peer-on-peer abuse.

As well as abuse from parents or carers, sibling relationships, and sometimes sibling abuse, have being associated with young peoples' experiences of peer-on-peer abuse. The behaviours of their siblings have been linked to the involvement of young people in acts of serious interpersonal violence (Hagell & Jeyarajah-Dent, 2006) and gang association (Catch 22, 2013; Firmin, 2011; Khan, et al., 2013).[1] One study in England found that both young men and young women who were gang-associated were four times more likely than other young people within the youth justice system to have a sibling already involved in gang-related offending (Khan, et al., 2013).

Young men who grow up in the shadow of siblings who are involved in violent and criminal offending have been found to look up to, aspire towards, or feel pressured into involvement in serious youth violence (Bourgois, 1995; Catch 22, 2013; Decker & Van Winkle, 1996; Moore, 1991). In the cases I reviewed, just over one in 10 young people were growing up in a gang-associated family (n = 17), and in more than 70 per cent of these examples familial gang association was the result of sibling, rather than parental, involvement in criminality. These associations drew influences and norms of the streets into what were often otherwise safe family environments. Examples of real and perceived threats of violence to family members from rivals, the storing of weapons and/or drugs in the family home, and the home being used by other young people as a base from which to assault peers, or just 'hang out', were all recorded in case files. As was the case with James, many parents struggled to fight against the influence of 'the street' on the behaviours of their children, and when one sibling was drawn away from familial values the battle to prevent the same outcome for younger siblings appeared even more pressured.

In the US and the UK, sibling gang association has been evidenced as impacting the safety and well-being of young women as well as young men (Aisenberg & Herrenkohl, 2008; Beckett, et al., 2013; Catch 22, 2013; Firmin, 2011; Khan, et al., 2013):

> As 20-year-old Jennifer noted: 'My brother is an elder member of a gang so that had a lot to do with it. We repped our area and cuz of my brother, I was immediately associated and I got involved'.
>
> *(Catch 22, 2013:41)*

While far from a determined outcome, having an older sibling involved in peer-on-peer abuse can constrain the choices of young people, who feel that they will be targeted by rivals of their older sibling or need to follow in their siblings' footsteps if they are murdered or sent to prison (Catch 22, 2013; Firmin, 2011). In an attempt to usurp such trajectories, some young people actively seek out alternative routes to establishing identities independent of their siblings, a tactic that can result in risk increasing as well as, in other cases, diminishing. I will always remember young women I met in 2009 and 2010 (while researching the impact of gang violence on women and girls) who discussed how they entered into intimate relationships with gang members who rivalled their families in a bid to fight against the gang association of older brothers:

> Yea, sisters find themselves in problems, but some then go looking for it, like Sacha, she went out with Micah knowing who he was just to piss her brother off. But then Bianca really didn't know who her boyfriend was [and that he was a rival of her brother] and when her brother found out believe she got banged up for real.
>
> *(Firmin, 2011:35)*

On such occasions, fighting against the influence of siblings escalated the risk that these young women would be abused by their peers. They became vulnerable to assaults from family members who thought their sibling's behaviour placed them at risk. They were also vulnerable to attacks from their partners, who believed they had been duped into relationships to gather information or set them up to be attacked in the future.

Research into sibling abuse more generally, and its influence over whether young people are abused by, or abuse, their peers requires far more investigation (Naylor, et al., 2011). Beyond gang association, just over three in 10 of the young people who were harmed at home in the cases I reviewed were physically and/or emotionally abused by a sibling before their involvement in peer-on-peer abuse. Such experiences, like exposure to domestic abuse, made home an unsafe space and pushed young people into the streets in search of care, relationships and protection:

> At the first missing episode Shane stated that he was being bullied by his mother and sisters and this explained why he had gone missing.
>
> *(Case 4, suspect, sibling abuse)*

In this excerpt, Shane was repeatedly going missing – and while this behaviour placed him at risk with the peers he was spending time with, he believed that it protected him from the abuse he was experiencing at home.

Wider familial factors

Beyond experiences of familial and domestic abuse, some young people are made vulnerable to peer-on-peer abuse because of a number of wider familial factors, including poor mental health and/or substance misuse amongst parents and carers.

Research has indicated that, in keeping with other factors highlighted thus far, parental alcohol misuse can push a young person out of home and onto the streets, or into their peer group, as they try to cope with the issue by staying away from home (Adamson & Templeton, 2012). Parental substance misuse and mental health problems within families have also been associated with young people who demonstrate aggressive and anti-social behaviours through to those who commit serious acts of violence against peers (Losel & Bender, 2006; Tremblay, et al., 2004).

The intersection between these factors and young people's experiences of peer-on-peer abuse was far less explicit in the cases I reviewed and require further exploration in international research. Available evidence suggested that 7 per cent of the 145 young people featured across the nine cases I reviewed were living with parents who were struggling with their mental health. For those parents, mental ill health undermined their ability to safeguard the young people in their care. Concerns were raised about one young man whose mother was not deemed well enough to act as an appropriate adult when he was charged with murder; and another mother, who having had attempted suicide previously, struggled to accept and support her son after he had raped a peer.

The challenge with such correlations is that parental ill health is often associated with wider structural, social and historical factors that are affecting parents' wellbeing and their ability to care for their chilren. Without considering these wider issues, parental substance misuse can be discussed in ways that serve to blame parents, often mothers, who are seeking to manage multiple experiences of deprivaton and violence rather than address the causes of those issues. As Featherstone, et al. (2016:9) have argued:

> Despite compelling evidence that mental health difficulties, violence and addiction issues are much more common in societies with high levels of inequality, such as the UK, we find little evidence that this is an issue that is considered in terms of its impact on policy and practice developments in child protection. This is all the more startling given the concern that has emerged around the impact of what has become known as the 'toxic trio' (parental mental health, substance misuse and domestic abuse) on children. The experiences of those trying to parent in a profoundly unequal society are subject to practices that misrecognise symptom for cause, rendering the possibilities of meaningful change less likely.

Care placements

In addition to increasing the risk that young people will be affected by peer-on-peer abuse, all of the familial dynamics explored thus far in this chapter can also result in young people being placed into the care of the state. Living in care, and away from their families, is a life experience routinely associated with young people who have been abused by, and/or abused, their peers (as noted in Chapter 2) (Beckett, 2011; Coy, 2009; Wood, et al., 2011).

Placing a child into the care of a local authority can aggravate individual or familial vulnerabilities associated with peer-on-peer abuse. Young people may be abused by peers within the residential children's homes in which they are placed (Barter, 2006; Kendrick, 2011). Evidence has also emerged of young people being drawn into exploitative peer networks by others who are already being abused by their peers and live in the accommodation into which they have been placed (OCC, 2012; Firmin, et al., 2016). In these circumstances, experiences of care can be directly related to peer-on-peer abuse, albeit this was not a pattern that emerged in any of the cases I reviewed.

In other situations, when young people are being exposed to, or experiencing, abuse at home, being taken into care can act as a means of protection. If a young person is in a safe and stable placement, being in care won't necessarily create further risks of abuse (Beckett, 2013; Shuker, 2013b). Instead, a care placement can end a young person's exposure to domestic or familial abuse and begin a process of their recovering from the impact these experiences have had on them. Being in care can also give young people an opportunity to engage in healthy and trusting relationships – with carers, professionals and other young people – and in doing so provide an alternative social environment to the ones in which they are being abused by their peers. For two young people in the cases I reviewed, one who led his peer group to rape a female peer, and one young woman who was involved in murder alongside her male peers, placements in care protected against previous experiences of abuse within their families. While these placements were insufficient to prevent their involvement in acts of peer-on-peer abuse, there was also no evidence in the files to suggest that the care placements they were in had increased the likelihood that they would abuse a peer. In this sense, being in care wasn't an associated factor – but the reason for them being in care (physical abuse by their parents) was likely to be.

Some young people are in care as a result of peer-on-peer abuse rather than prior to their experiences of the phenomenon. When young people are groomed into sexual exploitation or gang affiliation (Catch 22, 2013; Thomas, 2015), parents have reported losing their children to the street, or to exploiters, whose influence fractures the parent-child relationship and diminishes a parents' ability to keep their child safe. Such a trajectory was clear for two of the nine complainants who featured in my case reviews, who were both placed into foster care following abuse from their peers:

> Mother stated that 'there were things going on in Sophie's world that she did not have access to'. . . . She described that Sophie was 'being controlled by others who were more powerful' than her mother . . . . Sophie was taken to a police station by her mother, who stated that she couldn't cope with her behaviour and was later taken into care.
>
> *(Case 4, complainant's parent)*

Such illustrations, like research into parental mental ill health and substance misuse, point to the limitations of considering evidence of vulnerabilities within home environments in the absence of the wider social and structural contexts with which they intersect. Therefore, while being in care has been associated with young people's experiences of peer-on-peer abuse, the direction of this association is multi-faceted. Familial experiences which caused a care placement may be the actual reason for the association between being in care and young people's experiences of peer-on-peer abuse, whereas in other cases young people's experiences of care can directly expose them to, or aggravate vulnerabilities associated with, peer-on-peer abuse. Like evidence on domestic abuse, child abuse and other familial vulnerabilities noted thus far, evidenced associations between being in care and young people's experiences of peer-on-peer abuse suggest that families do matter in determining the vulnerability to the phenomenon in question.

Families matter – to an extent

The fact that James' brother was gang-associated, Melissa and Lara had been exposed to domestic abuse, Lara was unable to establish a protective relationship with her father and Melissa was neglected in a family where criminality and poor mental health were also issues, were all arguably matters that could have been associated with the incident of peer-on-peer abuse in which they were involved. Whether it is their histories of victimisation, the prevalence of their 'missing from home' episodes or their 'care' status, the individual biographies of young people affected by peer-on-peer abuse introduced in Chapter 2 suggest that, for some, the nature of their home environments are associated with their abusive experiences and behaviours. In some ways the relationship between individual and familial risk factors is obvious: if a young person is physically abused by their family and runs to the street for refuge – forming relationships in which they abuse their peers – then their individual behaviours, familial dynamics and experiences of peer-on-peer abuse appear interwoven. However, there is nothing determined about the association between domestic abuse, child abuse, mental health or substance misuse amongst parents and young people's experiences of peer-on-peer abuse. Instead 'most individual family characteristics explain only a small amount of variance in child problem behaviour' (Losel & Bender, 2006:50), and many children who encounter abuse at home do not go on to abuse, or be abused by, their peers. Even in the case study provided here it is not possible to consider the young person's behaviour and their experiences of familial abuse in isolation to the wider social contexts and dynamics of the street with which they were engaged during their escalation to peer-on-peer abuse.

Government policy and local practices have largely responded to the evidenced association between familial characteristics and peer-on-peer abuse – but not to the wider contextual factors that appear to influence this dynamic. The government's Troubled Families programme – launched in 2010 – was designed to intervene with families in order to prevent a range of social issues, including peer-on-peer abuse. It identified families who were in receipt of most intervention from social care, health and criminal justice agencies – largely to address issues such as their mental health, substance misuse, crime and violence. By putting in place a coordinated response to these families, it was envisioned that family members would successfully gain employment or re-enter education, and these outcomes would in turn reduce the prevalence of wider social issues such as peer-on-peer abuse.

Beyond national programmes, local engagement of families in the response to peer-on-peer abuse has largely focused on intervening with parents to intervene with their children – and in doing so follow the train of thought introduced by policymakers at the start of this chapter. Generally delivered through the provision of 'parenting programmes', these interventions attempt to increase the capacity of families to reduce the likelihood that young people will be involved in a range of anti-social behaviours – including those who abuse, or are abused by, their peers (Aldridge, et al., 2011; Catch 22, 2013; D'Arcy, et al., 2015). In keeping with the ethos of the Troubled Families programme, parenting programmes are designed to change the dynamics of families rather than change external factors that may be impacting the nature of family environments.

In addition to the state of families, in recent years the plight of children in care, and their experiences of abuse and exploitation, has also received increased attention from the government and the media. In 2013 an investigation was launched into the sexual exploitation of children living in care in Northern Ireland. In 2012 the then Education Secretary, Michael Gove, requested an Inquiry from the Children's Commissioner in England into the exploitation of children in residential care, which led to calls for 'urgent reforms' (OCC, 2012) to reduce the numbers of young people who went missing from, or were at increased risk of abuse while in, the care system. Three years later an Inquiry was launched to explore why so many young people who are in the care of the local authority end up in the criminal justice system (BBC, 2015e).

Where familial characteristics have been associated with peer-on-peer abuse, some authors have noted the violent, economically deprived or socially excluded spaces that such families are seeking to navigate (Aisenberg & Herrenkohl, 2008; Catch 22, 2013; Losel & Bender, 2006). Case review evidence, particularly of families such as James' who struggled to address the influences of external factors on their child's behaviour, are overlooked by approaches espoused by Troubled Families and parenting programmes. The most extreme expression of this in the cases I reviewed was young people who were taken into care as a result of their experiences of peer-on-peer abuse – not as a result of abuse they experienced in their families but because their families couldn't protect them from abuse by their peers. These contextual accounts of vulnerable families offer a point of diversion from the political narrative, introduced at the outset of this chapter, that locates risk of, and protection from, peer-on-peer abuse within families and individual choice. It is the untold story of parents/carers who lose their children to factors external to the familial environment which is often absent from accounts of the association between familial characteristics and peer-on-peer abuse – an association to which this book now turns.

The extent to which context matters to families

Young people are not parented by families or carers in a vacuum. As the evidence outlined thus far in this chapter suggests, the difficulties that emerge in families interact with factors in communities and wider society. On some occasions this interplay can exacerbate the impact of familial abuse. If a child runs away from an abusive household and into a violent peer group or neighbourhood setting, then the association of that home environment to the child's experiences of peer-on-peer abuse is amplified. If a child's family members hold harmful beliefs about gender and relationships and their peers demonstrate the same attitudes, each context reinforces rather than challenges the problematic ideals of the other. In both examples it is the interaction between family and other contexts that intensifies the association between difficulties in a child's family and their experiences of peer-on-peer abuse.

But what if there are no challenges within a child's family environment? What if we have done as Sir Alan Steer, Gordon Brown and David Cameron suggest and, when a child experiences peer-on-peer abuse, we look to their parents and find nothing of concern? Many young people in the cases I reviewed lived with safe and protective families, and yet they still experienced peer-on-peer abuse. And even when there were factors of concern present within their family networks, such as in the case of James or Lara, it wasn't completely clear that these matters had any direct association to their experiences of peer-on-peer abuse.

Rather than exist as independent islands, families form a part of streets, neighbourhoods and wider communities. The relationship that families have with these contexts informs both their individual approach, and capacity, to parenting. A critical challenge of the political narrative outlined at the opening of this chapter, and the Troubled Families and parenting programmes that have emerged from it, is that it offers a de-contextualised account of parenting power in two ways. Firstly, it espouses that what parents do or don't do is what matters most in relation to how children behave when they are in school, on the streets or socialising with their friends. The nature of these social settings, according to the 'I blame the parents' narrative, bears little relation to why a child may behave violently within them. Secondly, it presents any vulnerability that parents present to their children as if it also emerged in a social abyss (Featherstone, et al., 2016). Troubles within families are a family's own – they are created within that unit and can be addressed by changing the behaviour of that unit. However, it is a struggle to conceptualise families in this way, particularly when applying the contextual lens that this books adopts. Families interplay with a range of social contexts, and studies into peer-on-peer abuse and the role of families have demonstrated the ways in which factors beyond parental control can affect parents' ability to keep young people safe (Catch 22, 2013; Thomas, 2015).

Such experiences were captured in a BBC television documentary into young people convicted of murder under the law of Joint Enterprise[2] in 2014. In the documentary one mother talked about the influence of her son's peers on his behaviour and her ability to control them; she asked:

'Do you know what it's like to lose your son?'

(Guilty by Association, 2014)

When the documentary featuring this story was aired on television, I was in the middle of analysing the data from my case reviews and was struck by the similarity of this mother's account and those of the parents and carers featured in the investigation files I was reviewing:

The mother of Shane (Jacob's friend) had called the police to report her son missing, stating that she was struggling to manage his behaviour and that he was returning home with unexplained amounts of money and would pack a bag and stay with friends.

(Case 1, suspects' parents)

Shane's mother was losing control of her son and didn't understand why. Shane had gradually stopped listening to his mother and instead was under the influence of his friend Jacob. Jacob was Shane's friend – they went to school together and Jacob kept Shane safe at school when he had previously been bullied there. His reliance on Jacob had little to do with the nature of Shane's family, but this didn't stop this peer relationship from affecting Shane's home environment. As Jacob's influence increased, Shane began committing offences alongside his friend, hanging out with him at night and not answering the phone when his mum called. Shane's mother reached out to services for support, but it was difficult to identify a factor within her family that was contributing to this battle between her influence and that of Jacob on Shane's behaviour.

The struggle that parents face when confronting the influence of their children's peers plays out online as well as offline. In 2014, 14-year old Breck Bednar was murdered by someone he had met online – 18-year-old Lewis Daynes. Multiple interviews given by Breck's mother, Lorin LaFave, following his murder documented her attempts to disrupt the influence that Lewis Daynes, and the online world, had on her son (Murder Games: The Life and Death of Breck Bednar, 2016). She tried to restrict his access to the internet and counselled her son about her concerns. But these attempts did little to disrupt the relationship between Lewis Daynes and Breck – they remained in contact and, when Breck visited Lewis Daynes' home, he was murdered.

The fact that their contact was online extended the reach that Lewis Daynes had. It was difficult for Breck's mother to find any space in which she held primary influence over Breck. But as the cases I reviewed illustrate, even when young people are influenced by peers in person – at school or in their local community – it is still a struggle for parents to disrupt these relationships. Evidence of these difficulties has emerged in peer-on-peer abuse literature over recent years. Studies in the UK have documented the parental tug of war between the norms of the home and those that form outside of their front door:

> . . . it was freedom and the independence brought by being out 'on road', the social camaraderie, excitement and, importantly, the prospect of making money that overrode the influence of the family. Against these factors, parental controls and advice were limited (at best) and largely ineffective for young people, primarily young men who wanted to grow up and impress their friends or felt they had no foreseeable way of earning a living by legitimate means.
>
> *(Catch 22, 2013:55)*

From sexual exploitation through to studies into gang-related violence, parents have communicated the significance of extra-familial contexts in shaping the behaviours and decisions of their children. For some young people it is the pull of the street (as a result of grooming, coercion or fear), rather than the push of risky experiences at home, that leads to their association with peer-on-peer abuse (Berelowitz, et al., 2012; Catch 22, 2013; Thomas, 2015).

In these studies it is not an individual's approach to parenting but the environment in which they are expected to parent that appears central to an assessment of their capacity to keep their children safe. As critics of our child protection system have argued:

> Child abuse can therefore be manifested at the institutional or societal levels, as well as within families and with individuals. The activities of certain institutions, such as schools and the church, the processes of racial discrimination, social class exploitation, gender violence and the role of government and global corporations are all potentially implicated.
>
> *(Parton, 2014:188)*

Contrary to the Troubled Families agenda, you can't educate or sanction parents to a state in which they can control the influence of a wider range of social factors on their children. In the cases I reviewed I was struck by the number of parents who had proactively sought help in dealing with the fact that they were rapidly losing the ability to influence the decisions being made by their children. Parents of a quarter of the 76 suspects featured in the cases reviewed sought help from the police, schools and other services when they began to lose control of their children. These parents reported that their children were becoming violent at home, going missing, stealing from the house and refusing to adhere to boundaries. For the most part they received no support in response to their calls for help and when they were offered an intervention it was in the form of 'parenting programmes'. In short, they were offered support in order to improve how they responded to their children's behaviour rather than to disrupt the influence that other matters were having on their children. Research into a range of issues, including adolescent-to-parent violence

(APV) and gang association (Aldridge, et al., 2011; Condry, 2016), have consistently pointed to the limitations of the parenting programme agenda for many families affected by extra-familial risk. Such responses fail to acknowledge that while parents may not always have the capacity to keep their children safe from gang association, for example, this is not necessarily due to a deficit within their families that can be fixed with family-focused interventions.

The limitation of family-focused intervention is further illustrated by the fact that foster carers and those who manage residential children's homes also struggle to safeguard young people from extra-familial risk (Beckett, 2013; Shuker, 2013a). If a young person's vulnerability to peer-on-peer abuse is being exacerbated by family issues – such as domestic violence or physical abuse – then a placement in care may increase the protective nature of their home environment. However, this will not necessarily increase the extent to which the young people who live within them are protected from peer-on-peer abuse. As noted earlier in this chapter, in two cases I reviewed young people were taken into care because of child abuse in their families. This decision rightly safeguarded those children from physical abuse inflicted by their parents, but it was insufficient to safeguard them from negative influences that existed beyond the family homes they had left and set them on a trajectory towards peer abuse.

When a child has been placed into care because factors beyond their home have undermined the ability of their parents to keep them safe, the situation becomes even more complex. In these situations, care can arguably increase a child's vulnerability to peer-on-peer abuse. The decision to remove children from their families in these cases appears to be the result of community, rather than familial, risks (Shuker, 2013a). These children are often placed at a distance from the neighbourhoods in which they have lived (to be explored further in Chapter 7) to get them away from extra-familial risks. But these moves also separate children from safe families and therefore disrupt protective as well as abusive relationships. If children have safe relationships with their parents that have been undermined by matters beyond their family dynamic, then severing the relationship between a child and their family can undermine the relational safety a child enjoys (Shuker, 2013a). In such cases a care placement is not necessarily providing anything that the child is lacking in their familial environment. Instead it is intended to place the child into a home that exists within a safer community context, albeit also away from a safe family.

The limitations of using parenting programmes, parental intervention and care placements as responses to peer-on-peer abuse demonstrate the insufficiency of the 'I blame the parent' narrative. While international research and case review evidence has documented factors within families that have been associated with young people's experiences of peer-on-peer abuse, on their own they are insufficient to account for why some young people are abused by, or abuse, their peers. Some children who encounter abuse at home do not go on to experience abuse within their peer relationships. Furthermore, despite the efforts of their parents to protect them, some children who live in safe households are directly affected by peer-on-peer abuse when socialising with peers in school or in their local communities (both online and offline). For both of these reasons, asking questions about a child's upbringing or family environment will not sufficiently direct us towards the drivers of peer-on-peer abuse.

Conclusion: the contexts of parenting

In keeping with national policy discourse, the evidence documented in this chapter implies that:

- For some young people, home is not a safe or nurturing context in which they can be supported to choose, or exhibit, non-abusive attitudes or behaviours in their peer relationships
- Young people who encounter harm at home may develop a dependence on a family environment that is neither protective nor resilience-building should they encounter peer-on-peer abuse

However, unlike government policies which suggest that parental responsibility is the primary source of safeguarding young people from peer-on-peer abuse, the experiences of families documented in research, documentaries and the cases I reviewed indicate that living in a safe home is insufficient to guard against peer-on-peer abuse.

As was the case with the individual life histories of young people who have abused, or been abused by, their peers (Chapter 2), the lack of consistent narrative about the nature of families impacted by peer-on-peer abuse indicates that there is little about them which can be routinely associated with the phenomenon. While it may be easier to blame families, the evidence suggests that matters outside of young people's homes may be more closely associated with peer-on-peer abuse than the parents of those affected. The interactions of these homes with peer groups, school and neighbourhood settings, and the interaction of young people with these social spaces both online and offline, appear central. It was a challenge, and sometimes impossible, to consider the family factors outlined in this chapter without also considering how they related to young people's peer relationships, the violence they may be exposed to in their local community or the bullying they may have experienced at school.

Therefore, while victimisation and vulnerability in young people's families can be, and often is, associated with their experiences of peer-on-peer abuse, an absence of these factors is not necessarily enough to prevent it. For some young people, it is the nature of what is happening beyond the boundaries of their home that draws them into abusive situations. Crucially these extra-familial experiences can either exacerbate pre-existing limitations in parental capacity to keep young people safe (e.g. as a result of domestic abuse), or create limitations, undermining what, without these external factors, would be a safe and protective setting. The following three chapters explore the social rules of the peer group, school and neighbourhood contexts which may have undermined or exacerbated the family dynamics outlined thus far. Starting with peer groups, they provide a social stage upon which to explore the familial and individual characteristics that have been the focus of assessment and intervention to date – and significantly question the purpose and sufficiency of such an approach when seeking to disrupt abuse which is largely located beyond the home.

Notes

1 I have also received anecdotal accounts of young people being drawn into sexually exploitative networks by older siblings who are already being abused, although research into this is required.
2 Joint Enterprise is a legal tool used to charge individuals with an offence, that is, murder, if they were part of a group who took part in that offence in some way. According to the CPS,

> Joint enterprise can apply where two or more persons are involved in an offence or offences. The parties to a joint enterprise may be principals (P) or secondary parties (accessories/accomplices) (D). A principal is one who carries out the substantive offence (i.e. performs the conduct element of the offence with the required fault element). A secondary party is one who assists or encourages (sometimes referred to as "aids, abets, counsels or procures") (P) to commit the substantive offence, without being a principal offender. However, a secondary party can be prosecuted and punished as if he were a principal offender: Accessories and Abettors Act 1861. Secondary liability principles can be applied to most offences. The principles remain the same, whichever offence they are applied to. The principles are commonly used in offences of violence, theft, fraud and public order. A joint enterprise may or may not be pre-planned. Sometimes a jointly committed crime occurs spontaneously. The applicable law is the same in either case.
>
> *(Crown Prosecution Service, 2012)*

5

I GET BY WITH A LITTLE HELP FROM MY FRIENDS

By exploring the association between families and young people's involvement in peer-on-peer abuse in the last chapter, our attention was drawn towards factors outside of the home that undermine the ability of parents and carers to protect their children from the phenomenon in question. Although rarely the focal point of government policy, peer groups consistently emerge within peer-on-peer abuse literature as one of these influential extra-familial contexts. Young people have physically, sexually and emotionally abused others alongside their peers, and some are more likely to abuse peers when accompanied by friends rather than when on their own. Some young people are motivated to abuse peers, including partners, to gain peer approval or comply to peer group norms (Catch 22, 2013; Corr, et al., 2012; Franklin, 2004; Holland, et al., 1998). The nature of young people's peer groups, particularly if they are engaged in violent or aggressive behaviour, can be a stronger predictor that they will abuse peers or partners than violence within their families. In sum, the nature of young people's peer groups is of critical importance in informing their trajectory towards being abused by, or abusing, their peers, and goes some way to explaining the limitations on familial influence outlined in the previous chapter.

To an extent the significant weight of peer group influence is not that surprising. Most parents of teenagers, and those of us who can recall out teenage years, will recognise it as a time when what your friends say, think or believe often far outweighs anything else. A broad range of literature has explored, and evidenced, this sway towards peer group influence during adolescence (Frosh, et al., 2002; Gardner & Steinberg, 2005; Messerschmidt, 2012b). While this is far from a global pattern (Warr, 2002), in the UK, US and a number of other Western countries young people are encouraged to have many friends, and it is through friendship that status is often achieved. It then makes sense that if young people are seeking status, then they will adhere to the norms of their peers, even if these are counter to the norms of their families, in order to navigate 'being a teenager'. After all – what help are the safe social norms of your parents when you are trying to establish yourself as an individual amongst your peers – whether that is at school or in your local neighbourhood, online or in person?

The social rules of families are likely to bear little influence on the social rules of peer interaction in schools and other social settings. Peer groups provide young people with particular things that families can't – such as social status and belonging – when they are not at home. In his study on groups, Warr (2002) identified specific factors that hold and bond together 'youth' groups, including:

- Fear of exclusion from the group
- Desire to be accepted by, and to gain status within, the group
- Need for group loyalty and to abide by the moral codes set by the group

It is for these reasons that the social and moral code of young people's peer groups is said to often prevail over those set by wider societal norms within which they may be located (Cialdini & Trost, 1998; Franklin, 2013). Such is the significance of peer influence that a study which compared the impact of groups on individuals of different age ranges found that:

> Although the sample as a whole took more risks and made more risky decisions in groups than when alone, this effect was more pronounced during middle and late adolescence than during adulthood. Thus, relative to adults, adolescents are more susceptible to the influence of their peers in risky situations.
>
> *(Gardner & Steinberg, 2005:632)*

For most parents or carers this means that their young person must have a particular pair of shoes to wear to school because that is what all of their friends are wearing, regardless of whether their parent or carer thinks the shoes are nice. Or having been raised on music from their parents' generation, young people will begin to make their own music selections, strongly influenced by those of their peers, and often to the peril of their parents' eardrums. In many Western social contexts where social status is set by peer relationships (Warr, 2002), this tussle between peer and parental dominance is somewhat expected for the period of adolescent development.

However, in cases of peer-on-peer abuse, the influence of peer social norms becomes far more critical in three ways. Firstly, peer groups can act as an environment in which abusive behaviours occur – so a peer group can abuse together, with individuals taking part in behaviours that were they alone they would be unlikely to engage in. Secondly, the way that young people react to the individual experiences of their peers can normalise abuse. Therefore, even if a young person's peers aren't the ones who are abusing them, if they do not show concern for what their friend is experiencing, peers can reinforce rather than challenge norms which underpin abusive behaviour. Finally, young people are also known to disclose to peers, often before they tell an adult about their fears or worries. As such, if peers react in a way that recognises abusive behaviours and are equipped to seek help, they have the potential to intervene and disrupt abusive incidents from escalating.

To explore these critical points of association between peer group contexts and incidents of peer-on-peer abuse, this chapter returns to the case of Lara, James and Melissa before thematically considering their peer relationships with reference to:

1   The nature of peer group co-offending
2   The influence of peer group dynamics on young people's intimate relationships
3   Peer group dynamics – the roles of leaders and followers
4   Peer normalisation and the role of negative bystanders
5   Peer attempts at disruption and the potential for positive bystander intervention

Taken together, these aspects of peer influence on the phenomenon of peer-on-peer abuse illuminate what, to date, peer-on-peer abuse literature has recognised but insufficiently explored. They also question the relevance of policy and practice landscapes that do little to recognise or address the influence of peer relationships on young people's safety and well-being – or the impact these relationships can have on the capacity of parents to safeguard their children.

Returning to the case study: the peer group contexts of James, Melissa and Lara

As the previous chapter outlined, James' parents had been struggling to control his behaviour and he was often missing from home – but who was he with? In contrast, Melissa and Lara both had experiences of familial abuse and had started to commit offences (albeit to differing degrees). But were their peer relationships interacting with the social norms they had been exposed to at home in the escalation towards the incident in question?

James	Melissa	Lara
• James has a large peer network with whom he spends most of his time • Most of those involved in James' peer network are involved in criminal activity and violence, with many having convictions for robbery and drugs possession	• Melissa is described as a bully by other young people. She is acquainted with a number of young people but few would describe her as a friend • One of Melissa's friends is a few years older than she is and is being sexually exploited. This friend is repeatedly missing from home where she is at risk from physical abuse	• Lara is in a relatively safe peer group made up of both young women and young men • None of Lara's friends have a history of offending or violent behaviour • Lara tells her friends that James has been harassing her for sex

- James witnessed the attempted murder of one of his friends in the weeks before the incident in question
- A number of people in James' peer network are older than he is – they are in their late teens and early twenties

- This same friend tried to protect Melissa by threatening Lara to retract her allegation after the rape
- A number of Melissa's peers describe being afraid of her and of her father's reputation

- Her friends advise her to ignore James. They say that some boys are just like that and if Lara ignores James he will get bored and move onto someone else
- After she is raped by James, Lara meets up with her friends and doesn't tell them what happened to her

Compared with his home, James' peer group was a violent and dangerous environment. Not only did his peers engage in violent behaviour and offending on a regular basis, but they were also victimised. Because he spent most of him time in this social context, James was with his peers when he was missing from home. It is unlikely that James had much power in his peer group – he was considerably younger than some of the people with whom he was spending his time. For James' parents this dynamic was a considerable concern. What influence did they have over this peer context and how capable were they, on their own, of drawing James away from it?

Compared with James, Lara was safe within her peer group. She was not abused, exposed to violence or any other form of criminality in this setting. However, the social norms of Lara's peer group were not completely distinct from those of James. While they didn't behave in violent or abusive ways, Lara's peers acknowledged that some people did and normalised such encounters. As a result, when Lara tries to seek support from them in the weeks leading up to the rape, her friends fail to offer a positive intervention. Rather than acting concerned, speaking to a teacher or another trusted adult or confirming that James' behaviour was wrong, they displayed a certain level of acceptance. Not only did this reaction result in a missed opportunity for the abuse to be disrupted but it also prevented Lara from talking to her friends after she was raped. This is particularly problematic for someone like Lara who relies on her friends for advice and support, having been rejected by her father, and who has already been exposed to harmful gendered norms when she witnessed domestic abuse at home. But if they don't engage in abusive behaviours, why are Lara's friends accepting, to a certain extent, of abusive social norms?

Melissa's situation was very different from that of James and Lara. She was socially isolated and lacked a sense of belonging to a peer group – safe or unsafe. One of the few friends that Melissa did have was being sexually exploited. Exposure to the abuse of a female peer served to reinforce the patterns of abuse that Melissa has witnessed at home – when her father abused her mother and his later partners.

In addition, because Melissa was largely isolated, she had an increased reliance on the friends that she did have, especially when these friends stood up for her. However, in doing so, Melissa's friend reinforced a harmful idea that the victim was responsible for what happened to them rather than the perpetrator. Finally the reputation and norms of Melissa's family influenced her ability to form safe friendships. Her father had a reputation in his local community as being violent, and this affected how other young people perceived Melissa. In the absence of positive friendships, Melissa bullied her peers, increasing the social isolation that she experienced.

Three very different experiences of peer relationships – all of which informed the incident in question and which reflected the associations between peer groups and peer-on-peer abuse that were documented in wider research and the nine cases I reviewed. Twenty-one peer groups could be identified within the case files, and these were associated with 140 of the 145 young people featured. Exploring these relationships, as in the case study of Melissa, James and Lara, served to illuminate and extend what research has documented about the role of peer groups and peer relationships in incidents of peer-on-peer abuse. In doing so, this chapter begins to evidence why some parents are unable to safeguard young people from peer-on-peer abuse and the ways in which it is critical to foreground social context in any discussion which seeks to identify opportunities to intervene and prevent the phenomenon in question.

Peer group offending and peer group involvement in peer-on-peer abuse

While some young people will abuse peers on their own, research has evidenced that much peer-on-peer abuse is instigated by, or associated with, peer groups (Cialdini & Trost, 1998; Cowie, 2011; Warr, 2002; Zimring, 1998). Policies to respond to serious youth violence in England and Wales have been focused on group offending for more than a decade (Home Office, 2011). Such a position is recognition that young people appear to commit more serious acts of interpersonal violence more frequently when they are part of a group compared with when they are on their own. Research has begun to disaggregate sub-groups of young people who sexually harm much younger children as opposed to those who abuse peers – those in the latter group appear to have a profile closer to young people involved in group-based anti-social behaviour and engage in sexual and non-sexual harmful acts on a continuum of peer-based offending (Beckett & Gerhold, 2003). Through their exploration of the idea that 'numbers matter' (i.e. Lambine, 2013), researchers of multiple-perpetrator rape (MPR) have found that much of what occurs within MPR cases is about the group dynamic and not necessarily about the person who is being abused (Franklin, 2013). These studies indicate that the victim is a 'dramatic prop' (Franklin, 2013:59) for the social activity of the group (Lambine, 2013) and is objectified for the means of group social bonding (Bijleveld & Hendriks, 2003). As a result, it has been argued that it is this social nature of the MPR that explains the heightened levels of physical violence and humiliation experienced by the person being abused, with those involved trying to 'outdo' one another (Franklin, 2004;

Woodhams, 2013). Beyond peer sexual abuse, studies have identified that peer group offending can be the result of young people, particularly males, grouping together as a means of protection in violent neighbourhoods or schools (Warr, 2002). Such findings add weight to arguments that the social conditions within which peer relationships develop will inform the extent to which these groups engage in 'delinquent' or abusive behaviours (Weerman, et al., 2013).

Of the nine cases I reviewed, seven involved young people who committed offences while in a group (Table 5.1). The involvement of these groups exemplified

TABLE 5.1 Peer involvement in the nine incidents

Case	Example of peer influence
1	• Suspects assisted one another in sexually harming the complainant (e.g. holding the head of the victim while another suspect orally rapes her)
	• Suspects directed one another about how they should harm the victim
	• Harmful gender stereotypes were stated out loud during the assault
2	• One suspect had no recorded offences in his history and yet committed a serious sexual offence when initiated by two of his peers
	• Two suspects told a third when to join in the assault and when to stop
	• Two suspects held the complainant down while a third assaulted her
3	• One suspect told another suspect how to sexually assault the complainant
	• A suspect moved the head of the complainant while another orally raped her
	• Two witnesses laughed during the abusive incident
4	• Suspects approached the complainant after the initial abusive incident, stating that she now had to engage in sexual activity with them as well
	• Multiple members of the peer group groped and assaulted the complainant
5	• Suspects had sexually harmed and assaulted young women together
	• Suspects reassured one another and blamed the complainant
6	• Peers of the complainant normalised sexual harassment when she disclosed to them
	• Peer of the suspect followed him to the complainant's to demand sex following the initial rape
7	• Peers were recruited into the incident via social media conversations
	• One suspect used gender stereotypes held by the group to create an impression that (male) suspects needed to protect their status/reputation through the use of violence
8	• The peer group did not challenge those who spat at and punched the complainant
	• Young men in the peer group approached the complainant stating that she had to have sex with them as she was perceived to have done so with others
9	• One suspect told peers that if she didn't take part she would be assaulted
	• Two suspects had physically assaulted partners during the escalation period

the different elements of group involvement in offending documented in wider literature. From encouraging and directing what each group member should do, through to planning to seriously harm other young people, young people's peers informed their involvement in abusive behaviours:

As Table 5.1 illustrates, even in the two cases I reviewed where young men acted alone to murder (case 8) or rape (case 6) a young woman, peers of both complainants and suspects acted in ways that contributed to the social conditions in which escalation towards an abusive incident could occur. As was the case with Lara's peers, in these instances the acceptance of harmful gender norms and emotional or physical abuse amongst peers created a context that was conducive with the abusive incident itself and on some occasions provided an audience for abusive behaviours.

Audience provision and the ensuing violence and degradation that follows, as discussed in studies of multiple-perpetrator rape (Franklin, 2004; Woodhams, 2013), was certainly demonstrated by young people in rape files featured in the cases I reviewed:

> The boys moved Micha to three different public spaces . . . to orally rape her . . . at times it was a frantic assault, with statements such as 'It's my turn' and descriptions of the boys jeering while Micha was being assaulted.
>
> *(Case 1)*

> One of the boys stated that if she didn't do what he was asking his girlfriend would beat up Rema. The two boys anally raped Rema, and she was told to 'hack the pain'.
>
> *(Case 4)*

Such accounts illustrate the ways in which peer group expectations and norms inform peer-on-peer abuse incidents. In addition to facilitating acts of peer sexual abuse and group-based youth violence, peer group performance has also been found to factor in the nature of young people's intimate relationships (Connolly, et al., 2000; Corr, et al., 2012; Holland, et al., 1998) – a matter of note in the cases I reviewed and an issue to which this chapter now turns.

Impact of peers on young people's intimate relationships

Unlike adult partnerships, young people's relationships are often played out in public and in the context of a peer group. Sometimes referred to as the 'networked' nature of young people's relationships (Connolly, et al., 2000), the norms of peer groups interact with, inform and are informed by the intimate relationships that form within, or alongside, them (Corr, et al., 2012; Holland, et al., 1998). In theory, the close social proximity of young people's peer groups and intimate relationships creates opportunities for reinforcing positive and healthy relationships – if young people form intimate relationships within the gaze of their supportive peer group, then one would assume that the positive norms of that peer group would inform the nature of the intimate relationship and vice versa. Research into peer-on-peer abuse has implied that such a reciprocal relationship does indeed exist; however, for young people who abuse their partners and peers symmetry simply serves to reinforce harmful attitudes. Being part of a violent peer group has been found to increase the risk that boys will instigate violence in their intimate relationships (Barter, et al., 2009; Chung, 2005; Connolly, et al., 2000). Like Connolly, et al. (2000) in Australia, Barter, et al. (2009:188) identified that for boys in the UK 'peer violence was found to be the strongest predictor of [them] both experiencing and instigating partner violence'. In these instances, broader harm within peer groups set the stage (Connolly, et al., 2000) for relationship-based abuse to develop.

This stage-setting interplay between peer groups and intimate relationships was certainly evident in the cases I reviewed. While only one case involved an investigation into a teenage relationship abuse murder, eight of the nine files contained examples of teenage relationship abuse experienced by both suspects and complainants before the incident of peer-on-peer abuse that was under investigation:

> In an (online) conversation with Josh, Selena (his girlfriend) states that another man likes her. Josh replies by saying 'don't make me come there and beat the colour out of hes [sic] skin.'
>
> *(Case 1, Josh, who was a suspect in a rape case)*

> During an argument with his ex-partner, Mitchell punched her in the head and threw a lighter in her face.
>
> *(Case 9, Mitchell who was a suspect in a murder case)*

In one sense, these instances were distinct from the abusive incidents under investigation. The young woman being abused by Josh in Case 1 was not involved in the rape that he participated in weeks later, and when Mitchell murdered a male peer in Case 9 the partner that had been abusing was not present. However, the explicit and public presence of relationship abuse within peer groups contributed to peers sustaining harmful social rules about gender, relationships, consent and power in the escalation towards a serious incident. These are the types of social rules that Powell (2010) identified when she used Bourdieu to explore the norms underpinning attitudes towards consent amongst young people in Australia. In such contexts, both young people's relationships and their peer groups reinforced rather than challenged the norms underpinning abusive incidents. In the cases I reviewed, this left young people with limited access to social spaces that operate to non-abusive and safe rules.

Assessing the weight of peer group influence over young people's intimate relationships suggests a need to recognise not just peer group norms, but also peer group dynamics, when exploring the nature of peer-on-peer abuse. What is it about the roles that young people occupy within their peer groups which means that the social rules of this context can dominate how they interact with their partners and peers? Illustrating the reach of peer group influence into individual decision-making, and the way that individuals engage with the social rules at play in this context, is critical to fully understanding the association between groups and the nature of peer-on-peer abuse.

Peer group dynamics

Young people's peer groups are not homogenous. They are a collection of individuals who all have their own sense of power and identity which in turn is informed by, and informs, the nature of the group. To understand the relationship between groups and individuals involved in peer-on-peer abuse it is important to understand the dynamics of the groups themselves. An exploration of group dynamics, however, is relatively limited in peer-on-peer abuse literature which, generally speaking, either locates abuse in 1:1 relationships (sometimes associated with peer groups) or fails to specify where group activity was a feature of note in the data explored. In investigating group roles, and leadership, in group offending, MPR theorists have begun to illustrate group dynamic in cases of peer-on-peer abuse (Bijleveld, et al., 2007; Porter, 2013; Porter & Alison, 2001). Their work has further contributed to how we understand the notions of 'peer group performance' and 'group bonding' during abusive incidents. With followers seeking to demonstrate group loyalty and impress leaders, and leaders achieving or sustaining power within the group as the result of an assault (Bijleveld & Hendriks, 2003), young people's status, and sense of belonging, within peer groups can be solidified or undermined during abusive incidents.

The cases I reviewed afford an opportunity to consider how these aspects of peer group dynamics unfold during an instance of peer-on-peer abuse. Utilising the leadership model developed by Horvath & Woodhams (2013), it was possible to establish the group roles played by 123 young people across the nine cases. 'Suspects' or 'witnesses' to the abusive incident played the roles of leaders, followers, positive bystanders (who discouraged harmful behaviour) and negative bystanders (who encouraged harmful behaviour).

Only 16 per cent (n = 20) of young people featured in the files initially assumed a leadership role during an abusive incident. Evidence suggests that, in keeping with literature on group dynamics during sexual assaults, these young people primarily led through their own participation in abusive behaviours, acting first for others to follow:

> Rema didn't feel like she had a choice (as Marshall) 'kept harassing her via texts and phone calls'. When she said she didn't want to have sex with Marshall, again he said – 'just come'. (Rema was) anally raped and then Marshall invited friends – 'he did ask her if she wanted to and she shrugged her shoulders and didn't say yes or no because she felt that since he had forced her once

he would do it again'. Four boys then anally raped her. (Rema was) threatened with physical violence by two others boys who were present.

(Case 5, rape, suspect young man)

The foregoing extract demonstrates how, through his actions, Marshall set the parameters of consent, and behavioural expectations, for the remainder of his peer group to follow. In doing so, the followers and complainant in the case adhered to the rules that Marshall set in motion. Followers repeated Marshall's behaviour, and Rema, the young woman they were abusing, despite not consenting and therefore being raped, saw no point in resistance. Rema's adherence to the social norms that were set out by Marshall and embodied by his peers illustrates the dynamics within Marshall's peer group and the power that he had within it. Recognising peer group dynamics in this instance is integral to understanding Rema's response and vulnerability, and punctuates a need to explore the potentially variable extents of culpability amongst followers.

To establish the power and influence of individuals within peer groups during abusive incidents it is important to consider the other contexts with which they may interact. As was the limitation of the accounts of familial vulnerabilities outlined in the previous chapter, seeking to conceptualise the influence of peer groups, and individuals within the group, in the absence of the wider contexts in which these peer groups form, is arguably insufficient. While some of this broader contextualisation is developed in the following two chapters, it is important to highlight two key points here.

Firstly, young people's social networks can provide them with the social capital that they need to safely navigate violent school or neighbourhood contexts. It is in a young person's interaction with these other social spaces that young people identify a motive for associating with violent peer groups – who provide them with a means of survival. Is this what happened to James?

Secondly, studies into group dynamics have suggested that young people who lead abusive incidents may come from more troubled and abusive familial backgrounds than those who follow them (Franklin, 2013; Lambine, 2013; Pitts, 2008). Young people who have been emotionally impacted, or otherwise, from abusive/neglectful experiences at home may demonstrate abusive and harmful behaviours towards peers when they are on their own as well as when they are with their peers – such as Melissa did. However, young people who are in safe familial settings, and have not been negatively impacted in this way, only experience a need to engage in abusive behaviours when in the company of their peers such as James.

These assumptions were somewhat reinforced in the cases I reviewed. The 20 young people who led the abusive incidents were more exposed to abuse within their homes than those who followed them. Of the young people in my cases for whom data were available (n = 68), those who led abusive incidents were more likely to have been exposed to domestic abuse and child protection issues at home than their peers. It is perhaps these entrenched histories of abuse which also explain why, in five of the six rape cases, there is evidence that those who led the abusive incident (all young men) sexually offended alone as well as alongside peers.

The ways in which peer group dynamics interact, through individuals, with other social contexts is considered in later chapters and require further investigation. However, at this stage they indicate a relationship amongst 1) harmful rules in the homes in which domestic abuse is a feature, for example; 2) a leader who embodies these rules and replays them in peer groups by leading abusive acts (and achieving power/status in the process); and 3) the broader harmful contexts in which peer groups form that provide a motive for young people to gain social capital through association with an abusive peer network.

Evidence of peer group dynamics in the cases I reviewed illustrates and extends the information on group influence that currently features in peer-on-peer abuse literature (Barter, et al., 2009; Catch 22, 2013; Losel & Bender, 2006). Potentially, it is not just an association with a violent or aggressive peer group that creates a risk of an individual's involvement in peer-on-peer abuse but their role within this social setting, their potential desire for belonging and/or status within it, and their motivation for this desire all require consideration. In the cases I reviewed some young people appeared to engage in a race for a place within their peer group by attempting to lead others, and thereby exemplify their own leadership credentials, once the primary leader in their group has set an abusive train in motion. Evidence of young people changing roles during abusive periods supports the idea, espoused earlier in this chapter, that engage-ment in group-based abuse can be motivated by social bonding (Lambine, 2013), which in turn is both a cause and consequence of a pursuit of unequal gender relations and harmful ideals of masculinity (Franklin, 2004). While followers and bystanders in the cases did not seem to commit serious offences alone, in ways that those who led did, they dynamically assumed leadership roles when in the company of their peer group:

> Mervin [who had been following Wayne] directs Lorna to 'walk up the stairs or I'll beat you up' and told her 'pull them down before I kick you in the head'.
>
> *(Case 1)*

This type of behaviour was particularly pertinent in cases that involved a sequence of rapes (rather than one-off incidents) (n = 3) where young men led during some rapes and on other occasions followed their peers. For example, in one case a peer group had a leader who, through his behaviour and language, directed the group during initial offences. Over time, followers embodied their 'feel for' the rules in this peer group, realising power and status as achieved through their peer relations and through their abuse of young women. Some of these followers went on to lead assaults without the direction of their primary leader. Such detailed accounts of peer group dynamics and roles require far more investigation within peer-on-peer abuse literature, and are arguably critical to informing the development of dynamic assessments of, and interventions with, young people suspected of abusing their peers. They also highlight a need to understand the potentially differing drivers of those who follow or stand by and encourage young people who abuse their peers – a matter to which this chapter now turns.

Followers, 'peer recruitment' and negative bystanders

In addition to young people who assume a leadership role when abusing peers, there are others who follow their lead (and who never become leaders) or stand by and support the abusive behaviour that is taking place but who don't get directly involved (negative bystanders). The process of becoming a bystander or follower can occur in a number of ways. Some young people may intentionally 'recruit' others into exploitative peer networks as a means of deflecting attention away from them and thereby avoiding abuse themselves (Beckett, et al., 2013; Berelowitz, et al., 2013; Firmin, 2011). In other circumstances young people have unintentionally introduced peers to exploitative experiences when they have been accompanied by their friends to the parties or parks where they are all abused together. Instances of accompaniment can also result in young people either witnessing the abuse of their peers or seeing their peers abusing others (Allen, 2011; Beckett, et al., 2013; Firmin, 2011). In addition to witnessing abusive incidents, young people often hear about the abuse of their peers (Barter, et al., 2009; Cossar, et al., 2013) or know that their peers are abusing peers/partners (Chung, 2005; Holland, et al., 1998) before professionals or other adults become aware.

The fact that some young people will be aware of, or become involved in, acts of peer-on-peer abuse have prompted some scholars and policymakers to promote theories of 'equal culpability' (Allen, 2011; Porter, 2013). They argue that the role of negative bystanders and followers encourages the behaviour of leaders, and as a result are central to the commissioning of abusive behaviours. However, others have argued the opposite, stating that the presence of a group can coerce followers/bystanders to engage in or encourage abusive behaviours, whereas leaders may abuse peers even in the absence of an audience (Lambine, 2013). Furthermore, studies into bystander intervention more broadly have highlighted the significance of the wider contexts in which individuals act to disrupt abuse (Powell, 2011). If young people are standing-by in a peer group, or a broader social setting such as a school, that promotes the harmful social rules which underpin abuse, then they are at risk of harm themselves should they intervene. Whereas if young people are in social contexts that promote safe and pro-social rules, then they are better equipped themselves to recognise, intervene and disrupt abuse.

The complex web that drives young people to follow or stand by during abusive incidents was evident in the cases I reviewed. Young people were drawn into abusive behaviours and witnessed the abuse of their peers when spending time with them at school or in parks, etc. On these occasions young people, who were once bystanders, or those being abused, were groomed explicitly or implicitly into direct involvement in the abuse of others. A total of 6 per cent of the 145 young people featured in the files moved from being bystanders to becoming directly engaged in the abusive behaviour at the point of the incident under investigation:

> Sadie and Porscha (who had initially tried to defend Sam as positive bystanders) were seen egging on Serena and when Marcus came in they were laughing (becoming negative bystanders).
>
> *(Case 3)*

In this example, Sadie and Porscha were drawn into an abusive incident as a means of self-protection. They initially tried to defend their friend Sam; however, they were in a school environment where they had felt unprotected and unsafe before. As the situation escalated they switched from trying to support Sam to aligning themselves with Marcus and Serena as a means of keeping safe. They didn't agree with what was happening and they were clearly able to recognise that the situation was wrong – but in that particular context this peer group was unable to keep their friend safe. When bystander engagement manifests in this way it exemplifies the use of so-called 'symbolic violence' (Bourdieu, 1992): young people conform to harmful social rules as a result of powerlessness and a need for self-protection at times of crisis – even if this is ultimately to their detriment.

In addition to highlighting the relationship between peer groups and the social environments in which they form, evidence on bystander and follower behaviour in the cases I reviewed provided further insights into the interaction between peer group and family norms introduced in the previous chapter. For some young people, following the lead of others into abusive experiences was correlated with a process of distancing from and dismissal of their parents/carers. On such occasions, followers, such as James, transmitted harmful peer norms into safe household environments, disrupting previously secure familial attachments in the process.

If young people's social status, and via this their safety or sense of belonging in extra-familial settings, is established by their peer relationships, then they may rely upon those peers and distance themselves from their families. James' family relationships were unable to fulfil the purpose being realised by his peers. Likewise, Lara's family was unable to protect her from what James and Melissa did. While the harmful norms in the homes of leaders sometimes appeared to cross into young people's peer groups, safe familial norms did not appear to have the same impact. Instead, harmful norms outside of young people's families infiltrated the safe home dynamic, particularly when parents attempted to prevent young people from seeing the peers who they felt gave them a sense of status, safety and protection. As subsequent chapters demonstrate, such examples of cross-context social norm pollination are not only reserved for interactions between peer groups and households: through the behaviours and attitudes of followers, as well as leaders, the nature of schools and neighbourhoods can also be shaped by, as well as shape, young people's peer groups.

The process of peer recruitment and bystander involvement in peer-on-peer abuse requires far more attention as does the impact of peer social norms on family relationships in cases of peer-on-peer abuse. But despite the limitations in the evidence base, what is known about bystander involvement, and the exemplification of this in the cases I reviewed, demonstrates the extensive reach of abusive social rules through peer relationships. In addition to informing the behaviours of followers and bystanders, the spread of harmful social norms can result in the normalisation of abusive behaviours across peer networks.

Processes of peer normalisation

Beyond their direct engagement in abusive behaviours, young people's peer groups can display adherence to harmful social norms through their beliefs and attitudes. Research has illustrated a range of ways in which shared values within peer groups can create contexts which are conducive with abuse even if the group itself doesn't directly engage in abusive behaviour (Barter, et al., 2009; Chung, 2005; Henggeler, et al., 2009). In a study into relationship abuse, Corr, et al. (2012) identified examples of value systems within peer groups that required individual members to control their partners. They argued that:

> For some young men . . . control could be a collective endeavour, facilitated via social media, to insult; those men deemed unable to keep their girlfriends on lockdown.
>
> *(Corr, et al., 2012: 8–9)*

In the foregoing example the peer group promoted the idea that young men had to control their female partners and used social media to ridicule those who appeared unable to do this. Through this process they normalised incidents where young men abused their girlfriends, even though they were not directly involved in any abusive incidents themselves.

Even when abusive behaviours aren't encouraged, if a peer group accepts that others will display harmful behaviour it can lead them to normalise (or accept) abuse. Such processes of peer influence have been evidenced across literature into serious youth- and gang-related violence in the UK (Catch 22, 2013; Centre for Social Justice, 2009; Pitts, 2008; Ralphs, et al., 2009; Spindler & Bouchard, 2011). This evidence base documents processes through which the collective social experience of peer groups normalise violent encounters, manipulation and harmful gender norms. As was the case with families (Chapter 4), evidence regarding peer group cultures indicates that broader social and structural norms influence this process of peer normalisation. A study into the role of families in facilitating gang membership stated that:

> Most of the young people and family members interviewed saw factors outside the family as having a greater influence on their gang association. Issues widely seen as more significant included growing up in a 'hostile' environment where gang membership, criminality and violence [were] normalised;

> negative experiences of school; the pull of peer subculture . . . and the search
> for identity, independence and respect.
>
> *(Catch 22, 2013:4)*

Evidence documented in the cases I reviewed brought to life the process and impact of peer group normalisation. Examples were found in five of the six rape cases and all three murder cases, where the peers of young people who were abused by, as well as those who abused, their peers failed to challenge the harmful social rules that informed that behaviour. In six instances (four rapes and two murders), young people who were being bullied or harassed during the escalation towards their rape or murder did what the literature suggests and spoke to their friends (Cossar, et al., 2013). However, the reaction of their peers normalised, rather than problematised, their concerns – as was the case for Lara. In a similar case, when a young woman told her friends that she was being sexually harassed in school, they told her to ignore it and it would stop. This reaction was informed by a belief that sexual harassment was a relatively normal, albeit annoying, behavioural characteristic of some of the young men they knew. A different reaction may have prompted earlier help-seeking behaviour. Following their advice to ignore rather than challenge harassment, when this young woman was later raped she did not tell her peers, or anyone else, what had happened to her for an additional 23 months. In another case a young man was being threatened over the phone and on social media by a peer who went on to murder him. This young man told his friends that he was being threatened and on one occasion even texted someone to say he thought he was going to 'be killed'. None of the friends he spoke to appeared alarmed enough to seek help or suggest that he do so. Online bullying of this nature had been normalised to the point that it was accepted; even threats to kill did not yield a response that challenged that dynamic. By normalising what was happening, young people shut down routes to safety and in doing so contributed to the abusive incidents that followed.

In addition to highlighting the negative process of peer normalisation, research has also started to evidence the ways in which young people have sought to disrupt, rather than reinforce, harmful attitudes and behaviours. Albeit less evident in the cases I reviewed than processes of normalisation, I was struck by the attempts that young people made to disrupt abuse as it escalated. Evidence of positive bystander engagement demonstrates the potential for peer groups to be a source of prevention for peer-on-peer abuse. Positive peer group intervention could prove to be a critical component of a contextual account of, and response to, peer-on-peer abuse.

Positive bystanders and attempts at disruption

Research into peer disclosure (i.e. Cossar, et al., 2013) has clearly evidenced the ways in which young people have attempted to intervene with, or at least positively counsel, their friends who are at risk of being abused and/or abusing others.

Likewise, bullying literature (i.e. Cowie, 2011) has provided examples of young people who have challenged bullying behaviours amongst their peers and risked their own social status and sense of inclusion as a result.

The risk of being ostracised when challenging harmful behaviours has also been linked to wider social contexts and structures (Frosh, et al., 2002) – when young people go against the social norms of their group they may also be acting against social-cultural expectations of gender, for example, that the group itself has embodied. Nonetheless, young people can, and do, disrupt harmful behaviours. Local projects in the UK and other countries have supported young people to act as positive bystanders, challenging bullying and abusive behaviours in the peer groups and schools (Anti-Bullying Alliance, 2005; EDC, 2013). These programmes identify the different ways in which young people have intervened to keep their friends safe, including offering advice, refusing to support bullying behaviours, seeking help from others and sometimes, physically intervening. In a bid to encourage this, researchers have advocated the need to develop contexts that are conducive to bystander intervention whether in workplaces, neighbourhoods or in schools (Cowie, 2011; Powell, 2011), claiming that the most effective means of engaging bystanders to positively intervene with abuse is to create the social conditions that faciltate such an intervention.

Accessing evidence held in the cases I reviewed provides one route to understanding the dynamics of bystander intervention within peer groups affected by peer-on-peer abuse. In the nine cases, bystanders intervened in the escalation towards abusive incidents in three different ways. Firstly, and most frequently, young people provided counsel. This method, most readily cited in the wider evidence base (i.e. Cossar, et al., 2013), involved young people verbally advising their friends either to seek help from an adult or professional (if they were being abused) or to reconsider their involvement in an escalating abusive scenario:

> 'I told her to get out but she was scared. I told her to go to her year head, but she was scared her parents would find out. They were not good boys.'
>
> *(Case 8, statement of a peer)*

Secondly, albeit less commonly, young people demonstrated to their peers that there were alternative ways that they could behave – that a different choice/life was possible. This approach went beyond providing verbal advice as it involved young people acting in ways that were counter to the abusive norms being adopted by their peers. Whenever they did this young people demonstrated that, despite the dominant harmful rules at play, alternative courses of action were possible. This approach was particularly evident when trying to intervene with young people's intimate relationships. Of the 49 young people whose intimate relationships were documented within the case files, 33 per cent appeared to be in safe intimate relationships. In one case a young person drew upon her experience of being in a safe relationship to demonstrate an alternative course of action to a friend whose own abusive relationship was leading her into offending behaviours.

Finally, and least prevalent in the cases reviewed, were attempts by young people to physically intervene as an abusive act was taking place. Three of the nine cases reviewed featured young people, all of whom were friends of suspects, who physically intervened during abusive incidents:

> (Yusuf) arrived (having heard that a girl was having sex with some boys he knew) and when he realised that she was not consenting he challenged the behaviour of the group and helped her to escape.
>
> *(Case 1)*

> Maleek saw (Kim) and grabbed her by the head and pulled her up. At this point a bus pulled up and Kim ran onto the bus and saw some of her friends. The boys followed Kim onto the bus, and Maleek started slapping her. Kim's friend (Shaye) tried to stop them, but Josh punched Shaye in the head to make her stop. Another of the girls, who was a cousin of Maleek, told him to stop.
>
> *(Case 4)*

Arguably, physical interveners were seeking the same goal (i.e. 'safety') as negative bystanders but differed in their preferred method to achieving this. However, instances of physical intervention in the cases I reviewed largely compromised the status of young people within their peer groups whereas being a negative bystander maintained or improved a young person's status within the peer group through their engagement in abusive behaviours.

Ultimately, whether they sought to intervene through advice, involvement in alternative relationships or direct physical intervention, young people in the cases I reviewed intervened without seeking the assistance of adults. Although they were willing to challenge their peers, it appears that these young people were not willing to abandon them or risk isolation from their peer groups as a result of 'snitching'. The big question is why, and it is a question that requires further investigation. Not understanding this sufficiently seems like such a missed opportunity for us all. Is it because young people lack the confidence that adults will know what to do? Is it that they think adults will make the situation worse? Or is that they feel like nothing can be done by adults to improve the situation they are in? Ultimately, if some young people are recognising risk and seeking to prevent it from escalating, we need to identify ways in which they can see adults, including professionals, as safe partners in that endeavour.

Conclusion – peers: present within and yet missing from the debate

Research into peer-on-peer abuse routinely identifies that young people who are associated with 'aggressive', 'violent' or 'offending' peer groups are at increased risk of being abused by, or abusing, their peers (Barter, et al., 2009; Chung, 2005;

Corr, et al., 2012; Cowie, 2011; Franklin, 2004; Losel & Bender, 2006; Warr, 2002). By using case review evidence to detail the involvement of peers in abusive incidents, peer group dynamics, the development of intimate relationships in peer groups and normalising peer group processes, this chapter has explored why this association between peer groups and peer-on-peer abuse has been identified by international research. Evidence of bystander intervention has furthered this understanding, raised questions about why young people engage differently with harmful peer norms and highlighted the significance of peer group influence on young people's sense of safety.

Given the weight of peer influence on young people's social decisions it is hardly surprising that such factors not only influence abusive incidents themselves but also the capacity of parents to prevent young people from being involved. The fact that a detailed account of peer influence is largely absent from policies intended to prevent or intervene with peer-on-peer abuse is therefore a concern. While UK policy to address serious youth- and gang-related violence has acknowledged the group nature of offending, wider policy programmes to reduce violence and safeguard children remain squarely focused on intervening with children and their families. Statutory child protection procedures are built around the idea that it is the role of the state to prevent families from abusing their children or to intervene when families are unable to protect their children from abuse (HM Government, 2015). The interventions offered are in keeping with the parenting and Troubled Families programmes discussed in the previous chapter: assess and address deficits within families rather than external factors that may be undermining safe families. There is no reference to peer group influence within child protection or safeguarding assessments (Firmin, 2017) and therefore nothing to direct practitioners towards extra-familial dynamics that may be associated with peer-on-peer abuse.

These omissions in policy and practice are not completely unrelated to the peer-on-peer abuse research agenda. Beyond the examples from Holland, et al. (1998), Connolly, et al. (2000), Chung (2005), and Barter, et al. (2009), there is little within teenage relationship abuse literature that assesses the nature of the interplay between peer groups and instances of peer-on-peer abuse. Likewise, despite indications that addressing young people's association with 'deviant peers' is central to systemic responses to harmful sexual behaviours (Henggeler, et al., 2009; Letourneau & Borduin, 2008), literature in this field is yet to fully explore potential differences between young people who harm their peers within groups as opposed to those who harm alone (Hackett, 2014; Latchford, et al., 2016). Research has identified an association between peer groups and peer-on-peer abuse, but has often failed to fully reflect upon the implications of this for government policies, interventions or assessments. Interventions are still largely designed to change the behaviours of individual young people rather than the rules at play within the peer groups in which they demonstrate abusive behaviours (an approach that runs counter to the theoretical lens offered by this book). Given that literature implies that younger people are more likely to sexually offend in groups than alone (Finkelhor, et al., 2009; Gardner & Steinberg, 2005; Porter & Alison, 2006; Warr, 2002), this is an omission that warrants attention. Evidence on peer group dynamics in cases I reviewed, and particularly the experiences of bystanders and followers, indicate that some young people who abuse their peers, even in the most extreme ways, can move directly across from the normative to abusive and violent end of Hackett's spectrum (Chapter 2) as a result of peer group norms – a finding that if true may have significant implications for approaches to assessment, intervention and sentencing (and is explored in Section III of this book).

All of this requires further study before conclusions about peer influence, and what this means for intervention, can be drawn. However, at this stage in the book, three matters are clear:

1) A contextual account of peer-on-peer abuse must foreground the influence of peer dynamics on the phenomenon
2) The nature and reach of young people's peer groups can undermine the influence that their families can have in preventing incidents of peer-on-peer abuse
3) The nature of abusive peer groups, and the social norms that they hold, are informed by the social contexts in which these friendships develop

It is to that latter point that this book now turns. What are the social environments in which abusive peer groups form? What role do these settings play in shaping contexts conducive to peer-on-peer abuse? What potential do these contexts have for facilitating and enabling the attempts at positive bystander intervention identified in this chapter? And finally, what contribution could these contexts make in bolstering the influence of safe and protective families? Could the contexts in which peer groups form reproduce the norms of safe households and in this way enable parental influence to infiltrate peer contexts that appear impenetrable thus far? To begin exploring these questions the next chapter looks at the educational environments in which peer groups form and assesses the extent to which they are associated with the nature and prevalence of peer-on-peer abuse.

6

EDUCATION, EDUCATION, EDUCATION

Young people spend much of their waking day in school, and even more time socialising with their school friends in person and online in the evenings, weekends and during school holidays. Schools are routinely identified as 'sites of social development' for young people. It is within their school environment that many young people learn and practice skills for forming same-age relationships, independently of familial supervision. This relative independence from the family is important. As a young person's family doesn't directly shape the nature of their school environment/s, when young people are at school they are dependent upon others who manage and influence the social norms of this space to ensure they are safe when they are there. Teachers, other school staff and students create and practice the social norms of the school environment – in addition to the statutory frameworks, provided by policymakers, to which schools operate. All of these players – staff, students and policymakers – determine the rules at play within schools and in turn the nature of an environment in which young people form some of the peer relationships explored in the previous chapter. In this sense the school is potentially of greater influence in shaping the norms within young people's friendships groups than their families. As a consequence, during adolescence, young people are developing with a dependence on those who inform the nature of their school environments as well as with a dependence on their family to safeguard them from peer-on-peer abuse. The significance of this relationship, and the extent to which it has been recognised in policy, practice and research, is the focus of this chapter.

An association between the nature of school environments and young people's experiences of peer-on-peer abuse is well established in international literature. Relationships between students, between staff and students, and within staff teams can create cultures that are conducive with or challenge peer-on-peer abuse (Centre for Social Justice, 2016; Cowie, 2011; Ringrose, et al., 2011). The attitudes of both individual young people, and the peer groups which form within the social and cultural structures of a school, are informed by these relationships. Researchers concerned with youth violence have noted evidence of young people carrying weapons to school as a means of protection against risks they face within educational settings. Young people who have sexually harmed peers have been found to experience academic and behavioural difficulties at school – difficulties which cannot be reduced to the individual characteristics of the children affected, but instead are the result of the relationship between the school environment, the child and other social and environmental factors explored in this book.

In keeping with this evidence base, and despite the dominant policy discourse on the role played by families in safeguarding young people from violence and abuse (explored in Chapter 4), the role of schools in safeguarding young people is recognised in UK government policy, guidance and inspection frameworks. National statutory guidance 'Keeping Children Safe in Education' (2016) is revised annually. It states that:

> All school and college staff have a responsibility to provide a safe environment in which children can learn.
>
> (DfE, 2016:5)

However, until 2016 the issue of peer-on-peer abuse within schools was largely noticeable by its absence within this statutory document. Following a national consultation in 2016, as concerns regarding peer-on-peer abuse and sexual violence in schools intensified (Women and Equalities Committee, 2016a), greater attention has been paid to the issue in the most recent version. Statutory guidance now states that:

> Staff should recognise that children are capable of abusing their peers. Governing bodies and proprietors should ensure their child protection policy includes procedures to minimise the risk of peer on peer abuse and sets out how allegations of peer on peer abuse will be investigated and dealt with. The policy should reflect the different forms peer on peer abuse can take, make clear that abuse is abuse and should never be tolerated or passed off as "banter" or "part of growing up". It should be clear as to how victims of peer on peer abuse will be supported.
>
> (DfE, 2016:19)

This increase in recognition is testament to the escalating pressure on governments to have a response in place for peer-on-peer abuse. However, questions have been raised regarding the sufficiency of the amendments made thus far (Women and Equalities Committee, 2016a). The revised guidance contained three paragraphs advising schools on their response to peer-on-peer abuse compared with 10 pages dedicated to responding to the abuse of students by staff. Research into the scale of peer-on-peer abuse in schools suggests that the prevalence of this issue far outstrips the numbers of allegations made against staff annually (BBC, 2015d; Ringrose, et al., 2011), and yet statutory guidance has not reflected this weighting.

Inconsistent recognition of the association between schools and young people's experiences of peer-on-peer abuse can be found in a number of other policy documents and initiatives. Successive governments have published guidance for schools on a range of extra-familial safeguarding issues, including gang association (DCSF, 2010), radicalisation (DfE, 2015) and sexual exploitation (DfE, 2017). All of these documents note the safeguarding role played by schools, and their ability to be a protective factor against risks that young people face within their peer groups, communities or online:

> Protecting children from the risk of radicalisation should be seen as part of schools' and childcare providers' wider safeguarding duties, and is similar in nature to protecting children from other harms (e.g. drugs, gangs, neglect, sexual exploitation), whether these come from within their family or are the product of outside influences.
>
> Schools and childcare providers can also build pupils' resilience to radicalisation.
>
> *(DfE, 2015:5)*

They also note that schools can be environments in which abusive behaviours and attitudes thrive, and as a result young people can be recruited or groomed into harmful networks via peer associations in school:

> Where schools or other educational establishments, such as colleges, have concerns about the safety or welfare of a child in relation to gangs, they should inform the senior member of staff with designated responsibility for child protection and ensure that the police or local authority's children's social care services are contacted. Schools can be well placed to pick up signs of gang activity and identify those at risk of harm from gangs, including siblings of gang members and children and young people at risk of sexual exploitation and abuse by gang members.
>
> *(DCSF, 2009:39)*

The collective message across these many policy documents, therefore, is schools can both protect young people from peer-on-peer abuse, and other extra-familial risks, in addition to creating risks associated with the phenomenon. Either way, schools appear central to safeguarding young people from peer-on-peer abuse.

Despite these acknowledgements, when responding to a national inquiry into sexual harassment and sexual violence in UK schools, in 2016 the government initially refused to make sex and relationships a statutory component of the national curriculum (Women and Equalities Committee, 2016b), even though multiple studies, inspections, inquiries and campaigning groups had argued that this provision is the cornerstone of a school's safeguarding role. In early 2017 the government announced that 'relationships and sex' education would be made statutory via the Children and Social Care Bill. This is a significant development and offers the chance of progress on this agenda; however, the details of the curriculum are yet to be confirmed. At present, in the absence of consistent access to education on relationships, respect and consent, a number of schools are ill equipped to meet the needs of students who are dependent upon them for part of their social development.

Therefore, despite ad hoc recognition of the roles played by schools in safeguarding young people from a range of issues in some policy documents, central pillars of government policy, that is, particularly their statutory guidance on keeping children safe in education, do not provide a consistent framework through which schools can safeguard young people from peer-on-peer abuse. Compared with the national Troubled Families programme and the legislative child protection frameworks dedicated to building the capacity of families to keep young people safe from violence and abuse (documented in Chapter 4), work with schools appears significantly lacking.

The remainder of this chapter explores how significant a policy gap this is – and the extent to which school environments should feature more centrally within research, policy and practice concerned with peer-on-peer abuse specifically, and the welfare of adolescents more generally. Returning to the case study of James, Melissa and Lara, and then exploring international research and policy frameworks associated with education and peer-on-peer abuse through the lens of the 30 schools featured in the nine cases I reviewed, this chapter evidences:

1   The extent to which schools are identified as locations in which peer-on-peer abuse occurs
2   The impact of inappropriate responses to abusive incidents from professionals and students in creating/sustaining problematic school cultures
3   Approaches that have been taken to develop 'whole-school approaches' which seek to create safe and supportive social cultures within educational settings

Cumulatively, a consideration of these three factors demonstrates a need to recognise the nature of school cultures, and not just young people's attainment and behaviour within educational settings, when assessing the likelihood of peer-on-peer abuse occurring. Highlighting the significance of school environments in this context draws attention to the limitations of the national and international policy landscape and begins to raise questions regarding the suitability of child protection frameworks (which are primarily focused on family interventions) for safeguarding young people from peer-on-peer abuse.

Returning to the case study: the school environments of James, Melissa and Lara

Chapter 5 illustrated the association between the peer relationships of James, Melissa and Lara and their experience of peer-on-peer abuse. Lara's peers were unable to recognise harmful sexual behaviours when Lara approached them for support. A number of James' peers were involved in violent offending, including robbery, whereas Melissa was relatively socially isolated, struggled to form peer relationships and, of the friends she had made, one was being sexually exploited. But to what extent were these peer relationships informed by the cultural and social norms of the schools that they attended? Does understanding their experiences within school provide some explanation for the attitudes and behaviours of their peers?

James	Melissa	Lara

- James, Melissa and Lara attend the same school and are in the same form class
- Their school has recently been rated as 'good' by inspectors across all categories and is aware of the impact of gang-related violence on their student body
- Students report bullying by Melissa in the years before the incident, but individual staff members struggle to recognise Melissa as a 'bully' and instead refer to her as 'headstrong'. They are aware of Melissa's vulnerabilities at home and want school to be her 'safe place'
- A number of young men, including James, have been individually reprimanded for physical violence and sexual harassment in school over two years. Incidents include punching a girl and pinning her to the floor, threatening rape and grabbing girls in the corridors between lessons. The school has responded with detentions and reprimands but has not referred James to children's social care. They offered James' mum a parenting programme when she reported her concerns about his change in behaviour
- Other professionals working with James regarding his offending behaviour are keen to have James in school as often as possible. When James is in school, teachers try to stagger the time he leaves to avoid him coming into contact with rivals on his way home
- It is on school property that Lara is raped. Once Lara discloses the rape to a member of school staff (on the same day as the incident), the police are notified immediately
- After the rape Lara is approached by other students for sex, and she leaves the school a week later

The first thing to note about the information presented here is that James, Melissa and Lara share the same school environment. Therefore, while they have different peer groups, and their families do not have contact with one another, they encounter one another at school and in this setting are exposed to a shared set of social norms. It is also important to note that school, in this case, provided the context for the rape itself and in this sense is directly associated with the incident. The social and cultural norms established by students and staff in the escalation towards this rape are to a certain extent more significant than the rape itself for understanding the association between the nature of this school environment and the incident in question.

When Lara told a member of staff about the rape, the school contacted external agencies and an investigation was launched. At this stage the severity of the incident was recognised and steps were put in place to offer a response. Yet, in the months and years preceding the rape, staff and students were less consistent in their recognition of harmful and abusive behaviours. James was one of a number of young men who had been displaying harmful sexual behaviour at this school. While school staff recognised that this behaviour breached school rules and initiated sanctions when the behaviour was identified, these reprimands only seemed to 1) respond on a case-by-case basis rather than address the cumulative effect of sexual harassment on a school culture and 2) treat physical assaults and threats to rape using the same sanctions as they would for shouting in class or forgetting homework. The seriousness of the behaviour, the way in which it was escalating and the impact it may have been having on the wider student body were not reflected in the response that was put in place – and external agencies were not engaged. Likewise, Melissa's behaviour towards other students lacked recognition that was sufficient enough to address its impact on the student body. Therefore, although at the point of the rape the school responded efficiently, other students did not share the concerns of staff, and some approached Lara for sex in the days and weeks following the assault.

It is therefore somewhat unsurprising that Lara's friends responded in the way that they did when she told them of her concerns. James' behaviour was in keeping with that of other young men in the school and was being responded to by staff as something some boys did sometimes like any other form of 'bad behaviour'. The limited response to the behaviour of Melissa could have further limited the faith that the student body had in the ability of staff to keep them safe while simultaneously creating another avenue through which harmful behaviour could be normalised within that setting.

In addition, the social isolation that Melissa and James experienced in school increased their dependency on the friends they did have – even though these peers were being sexually exploited and were involved in, and being subjected to, street-based violence, respectively. Melissa's experiences of abuse within her family and the influence of James' peers no doubt informed the behaviours they displayed in school. While Melissa was relatively powerless at home, as was James with his peers, both were able to acquire a sense of power in school – albeit via the abuse of others. The interplay between the social norms of the peer groups explored in Chapter 5, and the home environments documented in Chapter 4, with the young people who attended this school was an important factor in the development of the social norms displayed by staff and students. Yet, as noted by others (Cowie, 2011; Losel & Bender, 2006), the school was not a docile context that was only 'done to' by these external environments. Each young person engaged with the school environment in different ways, culminating in the creation of a social setting that was conducive to the rape occurring.

So to what extent are the patterns and behaviours displayed in this case illustration replicated in policy, research and the nine cases I subjected to review? The remainder of this chapter explores this question with reference to the four thematic areas noted previously, and in doing so demonstrates the centrality of school environments to our understanding of peer-on-peer abuse.

School as a site of peer-on-peer abuse

While we may intuitively think that children, upon entering their school gates, are safely protected, media reports, parliamentary inquiries and extensive international research have evidenced that for some school is an unsafe place to be (BBC, 2015d; Centre for Social Justice, 2016; Frosh, et al., 2002; Messerschmidt, 1994; Peguero, 2009; Ringrose, et al., 2011; Women and Equalities Committee, 2016a). Young people have experienced physical, sexual and emotional peer abuse when attending school and within the relationships that they form at school. Sexual harassment in school corridors, weapon carrying, threats and bullying behaviours that have resulted in young people avoiding school altogether, or committing suicide in extreme cases, have all been documented across this international evidence base. Cumulatively these works have clearly illustrated the scale and nature of incidents in which young people, in the UK and globally, are exposed to abusive and violent behaviours in their schools – experiences that were also documented in eight out of the nine cases I reviewed.

In five cases all, or part, of the abusive incident that was then investigated by the police occurred within the school environment:

- In two cases young women were raped on school property
- In one case young people were recruited in school to take part in a murder that occurred later that day
- In two cases young women were groomed into abusive peer groups through associations in school

In four cases (three of which also featured in the five cases just mentioned), young people were threatened at school following the incidents under investigation:

- In one case, young people who gave evidence following the murder of their friend were physically assaulted by other students at school in attempt to get them to withdraw their statements
- Likewise, in three other cases young women who had been raped were threatened or attacked in school for telling the police what happened to them

In all of these cases, and a further two, young people experienced violent and abusive behaviours in school which, while not directly associated with the incidents under investigation, informed their expectations of peer relationships and safety. For example, in five cases young people had been physically assaulted by peers in school in the years before their involvement in rape offences. In keeping with the wider literature on bullying and school-based violence (O'Brien, 2011; Muelle, et al., 2015; Thomson & Gunter, 2008; Trotter, 2006), for some of these young people it was the school environment, and not home, where they first encountered abuse.

Young people have reported experiencing physical and emotional abuse within school across a spectrum of severity. For some, a real or perceived threat of physical assault has motivated them to harm others or carry weapons as a means of self-protection (Frosh, et al., 2002; Squires & Goldsmith, 2011). When the crime survey in England and Wales first collected information on the experiences of young people aged 10–15 years old, those who reported experiences of violent crime were more likely to be harmed by someone who was at their school than those who reported experiences of theft (Office of National Statistics, 2013). Some studies have found that as a result of physical abuse in schools some young people have avoided school altogether – resulting in periods of truancy or extended non-attendance (Centre for Social Justice).

Of the 145 young people featured in the cases I reviewed, at least 69 per cent of them were exposed to physical violence in school. In five cases, this violence occurred during the escalation towards the abusive incident. A total of 92 per cent of young people in the cases reviewed experienced, used, or were exposed to emotional abuse and bullying behaviours in school. Far from being a concern reserved for young people featured in the cases I reviewed, or in the UK more widely, across the world an estimated 246 million girls and boys experience school-related violence every year (UN Women, 2015). In 2015 the UN published a briefing paper which outlined the various ways in which young people experience violence, particularly what they referred to as 'gender-based violence', within schools across the world (UNGEI, 2015).

The UN's specific reference to gender-based violence is an important one. As the profile of peer-on-peer abuse suggests (Chapter 2), young people's experiences of abuse in their relationships is often informed by gendered power dynamics – and it appears that these play out in their interactions at school. Young men's experiences of physical violence and pressures to carry weapons, outlined previously and identified in the cases I reviewed, promote harmful notions of masculinity which underpin abusive incidents. For example, in seven cases I reviewed, suspects, who were predominantly young men, were threatened by older students within school during their first year. These experiences required them to adopt stereotypically masculine identities, based on status, strength and fear, in order to stay safe at school. Some of these young men reported that such experiences normalised the idea that school was an unsafe space and provided a motive to use violence (and sometimes carry weapons) as a means of self-protection (Squires & Goldsmith, 2011).

For young women, experiences of peer abuse in school are also highly gendered. Studies have routinely evidenced the extent to which young women disproportionately experience sexual violence and harassment in school. In 2010, in a survey of 16- to 17-year-old women, a third reported that, like Lara, they had experienced unwanted sexual touching in UK schools. In 2014 a national organisation, GirlGuiding, surveyed its members (aged 13–21) and found that three in five (59%) had experienced sexual harassment at school, college or work in the past year. A freedom of information request to police forces in England in 2015 found that more than 5,500 allegations had been made of sexual offences in schools in the previous three years. This included 4,000 complaints of physical sexual assaults and more than 600 rapes. While these figures included allegations against staff and the ages of some instigators were absent in reports, at least a fifth of all allegations made reference to peer-on-peer incidents of sexual abuse.

Such survey data captures the scale of young women's experiences of sexual harassment at school that they have reported in wider research into partner exploitation and abuse and the sharing of youth-generated images (sometimes referred to as sexting):

> There is some boys in the school that like keep asking me to have sex with them and I am just like 'no', like on a daily basis . . . like they will walk around school and try dragging me into corners and feel me up and everything and it's just irritating because they don't understand.
>
> *(Barter, et al., 2009:110)*

> Like I could be with my girls and then we would just be standing anywhere in the school and then the boys will come as they are together, they just come and then touch us up, and yeah we will be like, 'Get off, get off' and they will be like 'Shut up' and stuff like this.
>
> *(Ringrose, et al., 2011:33)*

Five rape cases and one murder case I reviewed featured accounts similar to these, impacting 47 per cent of young people in my study before, during and following the incidents under investigation. Four young people who were raped by peers had been exposed to sexual harassment at school in the months beforehand. On these occasions, their experiences at school normalised abusive social rules related to consent, respect and relationships – rules that were then played out during their own experiences of abuse:

> Sam and Jeff used to touch Rema regularly during the day as they were all attending the same school . . . . The boys would also grab the girls in the corridors and simulate the 'daggering' dance move on them.
>
> *(Sexual harassment of students in the school of Rema, Case 4 – who was later raped by Jeff and his friends)*

In addition to those who were abused, young people who were investigated as suspects in five of the six rape cases had been sexually harassing other young people at school before the rapes in question:

> [Reuben was] on record as having told a girl 'I will rape you', forced the head of another girl towards his groin area, and another allegation of indecent exposure.
>
> *(Reuben's school record, Case 3, he later raped a peer)*

While the experiences and behaviours of Reuben, Jeff and Rema – and others documented in wider research – are shocking, they are not necessarily sufficient to create problematic school cultures that normalise abuse amongst students. The response to these behaviours and experiences are equally, if not more, important. If young people experience physical, sexual or emotional abuse in schools and these behaviours are challenged by the staff and other students, then the behaviour is presented as exceptional and unacceptable – rather than normal and expected. For example, as documented previously in this chapter, young people have carried weapons into school when they feel unsafe there (Cowie, et al., 2008; Squires & Goldsmith, 2011). Why would they feel unsafe – would exposure to physical violence at school be enough? Or is it that they feel that professionals in, and outside, of school can't keep them safe when violence occurs and they are there?

Schools manage a range of risks every day, with hundreds, if not thousands, of young people in their care with a variety of experiences and needs. It is likely that some vulnerability will play out as abusive and concerning behaviours for some young people. It is also likely that some of these behaviours will be informed by matters beyond the school's control, such as fear of violence in the local neighbourhood (to be explored in Chapter 7) or experiences of abuse at home (Cowie, 2011; Frosh, et al., 2002; Losel & Bender, 2006). School staff can't prevent what children are exposed to at home or in the street. When young people have their mobile phones stolen on their way to school, when they view pornographic materials on their phones with school friends on the bus, or they are exposed to domestic abuse at home in the evenings, these experiences occur in social fields beyond the control and reach of the norms of the school environment. And yet all of these experiences can inform how a young person then behaves at school, and the ways in which teaching professionals respond to these behaviours when they emerge is the responsibility of the school. Their responses will serve to normalise or challenge problematic behaviours, and so it is to this relationship – between professional responses and abusive behaviours – that this chapter now turns. In doing so, the chapter further explores the ways in which the social field of the school is associated with peer-on-peer abuse.

Problematic responses from staff and students

There are a range of ways in which the behaviours, attitudes and decisions of school staff and students can inform the nature of an association between a school culture and young people's experiences of peer-on-peer abuse. Three distinct, and yet related, ways in which incidents are responded to, identified and/or prevented are documented in research and were evident (to varying extents) in the cases that I reviewed:

1   School staff and/or students may deny or minimise young people's experiences of peer-on-peer abuse, or may display attitudes, values or behaviours which reinforce harmful gendered norms which in turn create cultural contexts that are conducive with peer-on-peer abuse
2   School staff may respond to incidents in ways that fail to address their serious-ness or impact
3   School staff may respond to the symptoms of peer-on-peer abuse rather than address the abuse itself – and through this process can further harm or isolate young people who have been victimised

Each of these are considered here, before this chapter explores the ways in which whole-school approaches to safeguarding young people can create sites of safety, rather than abuse, for the young people who attend them.

The increasing concern about sexual harassment in UK schools over recent years has provided multiple accounts of school responses which have failed to recognise abusive behaviour as problematic. In both a BBC Five Live investigation (BBC, 2015d) and a GirlGuiding survey (2014), referenced previously in this chapter, young people described how their complaints of sexual harassment or assault were responded to by school staff as 'as just a bit of banter – "boys mucking around"' (GirlGuiding UK, 2014). Such reactions are thought to have come from senior leadership within schools as well as teaching staff:

> My abusers were the most popular boys in the school; they played on all the sports teams. The principal at the time tried to put it down to 'rugby locker-room banter' and didn't seem surprised at all (a boy, 15, who was assaulted in a classroom by three of his friends)
>
> *(BBC, 2015d)*

Accounts such as these are alarming and illustrate the most severe expressions of problematic professional responses to peer-on-peer abuse that contribute to abu-sive school environments. Some studies into bullying cultures within schools have also raised concerns about the inability of school staff to consistently identify and respond to abusive or harmful behaviours (Barnes, et al., 2012; Chambers, et al., 2010), particularly when they draw upon gendered stereotypes or rely on explicit encounters of physical aggression to identify an incident as harmful.

In the cases that I reviewed, practices such as these were rarely recorded in case file material. In two examples, staff appeared reluctant to identify behaviour as 'bullying' or 'harmful', as was the case with Melissa, because of an awareness of the wider vulnerabilities that the young people in question were experiencing. In being unable to identify ways in which to sanction problematic behaviour while also safeguarding the welfare of a vulnerable young person, staff in these examples created permissible contexts for abusive behaviours.

Even where professionals don't actively endorse bullying in schools, they can do so, by proxy, via an acceptance of the harmful gendered norms which often underpin abusive behaviours between young people (Benton, 2014; Chambers, et al., 2010; Messerschmidt, 2012a; Powell, 2010). School environments have been identified as sites which often reconstruct, rather than challenge, problematic expectations of gender roles and identities (Benton, 2014; Chambers, et al., 2010; Bourdieu, 2001; Frosh, et al., 2002, Messerschmidt, 2012a; Ringrose & Renold, 2011) as a result of both staff and student behaviours: from stereotypical masculine norms being encouraged in school sports clubs (Light, 2007) through to gender-stereotyped subject allocation which results in few young women studying science (Institute of Physics, 2015). These patterns, although not directly related to peer-on-peer abuse, are in keeping with the norms that underpin abusive behaviours (Barter, et al., 2009; Corr, et al., 2012; Powell, 2010; Ringrose, et al., 2011). The contribution that this can make to creating school cultures that are conducive with young people's experiences of peer-on-peer abuse warrants some attention. Expectations for boys to be in control, to dominate, to not show emotion, etc., are all relevant to their experiences and instigation of physical, sexual and emotional abuse. Likewise, 'victim-blaming' attitudes have been directly associated with attitudes towards women and girls which suggest that if they are abused they must be at fault in some way or hold partial responsibility for encouraging the behaviour of those who have harmed them.

At least 75 per cent of the young people featured in the cases I reviewed were attending schools where stereotypical gender ideals were reinforced by the behaviour and attitudes of staff and/or students. This was most explicitly demonstrated by the response of students and staff to abusive incidents themselves. In keeping with examples from wider research (GirlGuiding, 2014; Ringrose, et al., 2011), in three of the cases I reviewed students drew upon gendered norms of victim-blaming when blaming young women who had been raped:

> After a few minutes he stopped and left Lisa there. She put her clothes back on and went to join her friends. Later that day boys in the school started shouting 'sket' at her.
>
> *(Case 6, Lisa, a young woman raped at school)*

These were the same attitudes that were identified within peer groups (Chapter 5) and, to a lesser extent, families (Chapter 4) associated with peer-on-peer abuse. Problematic student attitudes were compounded by professional practices engaged in victim blaming. Cases contained examples of staff who, instead of focusing on the behaviours of those who were being abusive, suggested that young women change their behaviour in order to avoid sexual assaults:

> School stated that [Rema, aged 12] was 'getting into lots of arguments at school, people calling her names and spreading rumours'. 'Some of the boys

were boasting that they had sex with her'. Emails state that she had a behaviour mentor in school due to 'her attitude, behaviour, and acting out in school'.

(Case 5 – Rema a young woman sexually exploited by a group of peers some of whom she met at school)

Evidence of such problematic, and gendered, responses from staff and students in the cases reviewed indicates that some of the abusive behaviours documented in previous chapters were in keeping with the social rules at play in the schools they attended. Rather than act as a social field which challenged the rules at play in the peer groups explored in the previous chapter, a number of schools that have been the subject of research, inquiries and cases I reviewed have adopted social norms which facilitate peer-on-peer abuse.

In addition to practices which failed to address abusive social norms and behaviours are those which seek to do so but fail to make an impact. Research into bullying, peer victimisation and violence in schools has evaluated and critiqued a number of interventions designed to disrupt harmful peer behaviours (Cowie & Hutson, 2005; Cross, et al., 2011; Glover, et al., 2010). Government guidance on addressing bullying (DfE, 2014) recommends that schools record, and monitor the effectiveness of, interventions put in place to address bullying, but the responses they recommend are largely focused on the use of sanctions and behaviour management rather than adopting whole-school approaches to safety and violence prevention. The characteristics of a whole-school approach are explored later in this chapter, but they are noted here as a contrast to responses which sanction harmful behaviours in an individualised lens, rather than address the cumulative impact or cultural foundations of school-based victimisation. An inability to sufficiently address school-based violence can in turn create contexts that are conducive with, or facilitate, peer-on-peer abuse (Barnes, et al., 2012; Chambers, et al., 2010; Cowie, 2011) and in this sense can be as problematic as staff responses which normalise or fail to acknowledge abusive incidents.

In the cases I reviewed, the challenge of using traditional school-based sanctions to respond to abusive behaviours, including sexual harassment, was clearly evident. For the most part, teachers in the 30 schools featured in the cases I reviewed used school sanctions (such as referral to the head teacher, detentions, withdrawal of privileges or being placed on report) in response to problematic behaviour:

> Following sexual harassment of female students, he was taken out of class and **spoken to** about his behaviour . . . . Staff member who witnessed this left the school due to stress the year after.
>
> *(Case 3, bold type added by author)*

There appeared to be three limitations with this approach which in turn contributed to a process of creating harmful social norms within schools. Firstly, the use of school sanctions in response to harmful sexual behaviour runs counter to research which advocates the use of systemic and therapeutic interventions for young people who sexually harm others (Hackett, 2014; Letourneau & Borduin, 2008). They implied that behaviours such as these were, like talking in class or running down a corridor, forms of 'acting out' which were to be expected and did not warrant further concern or investigation. Secondly, the use of sanctions to address individual incidents independently of each other left the cumulative impact of these behaviours largely unaddressed (Cowie, 2011; Cross, et al., 2011; Harber & Sakade, 2009). Finally, sanctioning the behaviour did not necessarily address what was driving it. The relationship between problems outside of school – such as abuse at home or violence on the streets – and young people's behaviours within school was not disrupted through a sanction-based, incident-management approach to peer-on-peer abuse. Taken together, these three limitations in the use of sanctioning to address peer-on-peer abuse constructed the phenomenon as a 'behaviour' issue (and therefore in keeping with national policy) and not a 'social' one (being presented by this book and others who have researched school-based bullying and violence) (Barter & Berridge, 2011; Cowie, 2011; Harber & Sakade, 2009).

Denial, problematic gendered attitudes and the use of insufficient sanctioning in the cases I reviewed all contributed to victim-blaming behaviours amongst students following the incidents that were under investigation. In keeping with wider research, relationships between school staff and students can create cultures that challenge or reinforce bullying behaviours more generally (Chambers, et al., 2010; Cowie, 2011; Harber & Sakade, 2009; Barnes, et al., 2012; Root, 2005). In their study of 'sexting', Ringrose, et al. (2011) documented physical touching in corridors, verbal abuse from peers and the pressure to engage in sexual activity, all intensified through social media networks, as part of two school cultures in which abusive behaviours were normalised amongst students, as well as staff.

For example, in one case where a student was raped on school property, the head teacher refused to allow the police to interview other students during school time, stating that this would 'aggravate circumstances'. This decision reduced the ability of the police and school staff to offer reassurance and identify if other students had similar experiences to that of the complainant. The complainant in this case was later physically assaulted by other students for giving statements to the police. In all such instances, professionals failed to respond as problems escalated, and in doing so incubated rather than challenged the norms and undermined the confidence of parents:

> Attempts to get statements from five young people in the school – all said they were too afraid to take part . . . . All were supported by their parents not to provide information as they were 'afraid of local gangs and **problems that would arise at school**'.
>
> *(Author, bold type added by author)*

Even when young people didn't actively assault or blame those who had been abused, in seven cases problematic school cultures still influenced attitudes of students to the point that they normalised or accepted abusive behaviours in ways similar to that of Lara's friends. While they were not abusive themselves, and were not directly involved in the abuse of Lara, they normalised her experiences of sexual harassment – and in Chapter 5 it wasn't clear why this was. Details presented earlier in this chapter suggests that the inability of staff in Lara's school to respond to bullying by Melissa and problematic sexual behaviour displayed by James amongst other young men informed how Lara's peers responded to her attempt at seeking support. They were attending a school in which staff appeared unable to protect them from sexual harassment or wider bullying behaviours. Despite the expectations laid out in national statutory guidance (DfE, 2016), for this peer group there was an increasing expectation that abusive behaviours occurred at their school – this was just what happened – it was not a safe place to be.

Beyond examples where staff identify, but fail to sufficiently address abusive behaviours, cases I reviewed evidenced examples where professionals responded to the symptoms of peer-on-peer abuse in schools rather than the abuse itself. Government guidance on bullying makes reference to the importance of identifying the causes of poor behaviour and the potential victimisation of someone who is also harming others (DfE, 2014). Research into bullying has provided extensive evidence of the overlap between victim and perpetrator identities in schools, and the importance of recognising this complexity in practice (Cowie, 2011; Glover, et al., 2010; O'Brien, 2011). However, serious case reviews, inquiries and research into peer-on-peer abuse have all provided examples of where young people who have been abused by peers are sanctioned by professionals in schools and a range of other agencies – who only see the impact that abuse has on a child's behaviour and not the abuse itself (Beckett, 2013; Berelowitz, et al., 2012; Coffey, 2014; Jay, 2014; Pearce, 2013).

When responses such as these were identified in the cases I reviewed, young people who were being victimised by peers, or who were vulnerable and on a pathway to abusing others, were sanctioned rather than supported. For example, in three cases (two rapes and one murder) school staff were aware that young men were going missing and 'sofa surfing' but did not explore the drivers of this behaviour – these young men later abused others alongside the peers they had been going missing with. In other instances, young women who were abused both in and outside of school became physically abusive towards staff and other students. In all examples of this in the cases I reviewed, schools used punitive sanctions to manage this behaviour, including issuing detentions and exclusions:

> **School moves Susan to another part of the school to avoid contact with the boy**. . . . Susan is having 'problems' with another girl in her class – **school changes Susan's timetable so that she is not in class with this girl**. In the following month, Susan is reported to be 'abusive swearing, walked out of lessons without permission'. In the New Year, staff log that Susan has been threatened by someone from a different school . . . . Truancy recorded in the following week and school **assigns a mentor to Susan** – the following week Susan is recorded as making 'rude and offensive comments during

mentoring time, threatening a member of staff' – **school gives a fixed-term 3-day exclusion.**

(Case 4, bold type added by author)

None of the interventions outlined in this example sought to identify what was causing Susan's escalating behaviour (in reality it was that she was being routinely raped by a group of boys, some of whom were in school with her).

Therefore, while the abusive behaviours within schools documented at the outset of this chapter are concerning, their nature and prevalence within schools are contributed to by the way in which those who use school spaces (staff and students) respond to those behaviours. Bullying cultures, inter-student emotional abuse and problematic gendered hierarchies in some school environments all inform the nature of young people's peer relationships and the abuse they experience within them. Drawing upon the examples identified in my primary study as illustrations of an international evidence base, it is clear that staff and student responses to incidents, wider gendered norms and bullying behaviours in general can serve to create school cultures that facilitate, rather than challenge, peer-on-peer abuse. As Cowie (2011) has argued, to understand bullying behaviours, and particularly young people who bully others, they must be viewed:

> in the wider social context in which children and adolescents are growing up, where there are strong peer pressures for both boys and girls to behave within the strictly regulated dominant behaviour patterns required by the culture.
>
> *(Cowie, 2011:41)*

It is in the interplay between the problematic peer norms explored in the previous chapter, and the harmful school norms explored in this chapter, that Lara's peers, (and the bystanders referred to in Chapter 6) were unable to support and safeguard their friend. If staff and students within a school are able to respond to the behaviours/attitudes outlined thus far in ways that offer challenge and safety, then they can provide young people the opportunity to act differently, and counter to the abusive peer cultures to which they may have been exposed (Chapter 6). Policymakers, charities and academics have referred to this as taking a 'whole-school approach' to both gender equality and safeguarding – a practice that is variable around the country, was largely wanting in the cases I reviewed, and to which this chapter now turns.

Towards whole-school approaches: advancing the policy landscape

While it is clear that abusive behaviours within school, and the response of staff and students to this, go some way to creating contexts that are either conducive with, or challenge, peer-on-peer abuse, it is critical to consider the role/s that policymakers play in addressing these challenges. As outlined at the opening of this chapter, government guidelines play a role in setting the agenda, expectations and capabilities of schools, and in communicating their role in the safeguarding agenda. In their recognition of the global scale of peer-on-peer abuse in schools the UN has argued that inclusive and equitable quality education will not be possible:

> Unless gender is recognized as a driving factor in school violence, strong monitoring frameworks are adopted and genuine commitment is made to eliminate gender-based violence in schools.
>
> *(UNGEI, 2015:16)*

As a result, many of the advances made in challenging abuse within schools has been enabled through the evaluations of school-based interventions and the incorporation of these findings into government policies and practices. Much of this work has centred on international calls for 'whole-school approaches' (AVA, 2016; Cowie & Hutson, 2005; Cowie, 2011; Cowie, et al., 2008; EVAW, 2010a; The Bristol Ideal, 2012) to addressing abuse and violence in schools – and the response of local and national governments to such recommendations. A whole-school approach is defined as one that:

> addresses the needs of pupils, staff and the wider community across the curriculum and the entire learning environment within a school. It aims to develop an ethos and environment in a school that supports learning and promotes the health, well-being and safety of all.
>
> *(The Bristol Ideal, 2012:1)*

This approach is built upon the idea that there is a relationship, illustrated throughout this chapter, between the culture of a school and the experiences that young people have within it. Taking a whole-school approach to respond to peer-on-peer abuse would include: the training and support of staff to ensure a consistent and effective response to the impact of abusive incidents; the creation of policies, procedures and structures to address, and prevent, the issue of concern; and support for young people – those who are abused by, or who abuse, their peers, as well as those who witness abusive incidents – where required. In essence, the entire learning environment is developed to prevent and combat peer-on-peer abuse.

Policymakers in a range of countries have picked up on, and promoted, this method over recent years. In Australia, for example, state policymakers in Melbourne have committed to prioritising support for school environments to adopt this holistic approach (Our Watch, 2016). In early 2015 I had the privilege of visiting practitioners and campaigners in Melbourne who have promoted whole-school approaches. They highlighted the role that governments play in ensuring whole-school approaches are consistently practiced across states and countries. Described as the provision of an 'authorising environment', academics and practitioners argued that in the absence of encouragement from governments some schools would be unwilling, or feel unable to, adopt a whole-school approach. Some would believe that in being proactive they would give the impression that their school, as opposed to others, had particular issues related to peer-on-peer abuse. For others schools, if state priorities were concerned only with academic performance to the exclusion of issues related to relationships, consent, equalities, etc., this reduced their space, time and capacity to prioritise the development of a response to peer-on-peer abuse. Whereas, if creating a school environment equipped to address/prevent the issue of peer-on-peer abuse was a state priority, schools were authorised to invest in taking this approach.

In the US, whole-school approaches have been developed to address what has been termed 'dating violence' (abuse in young people's intimate relationships) and have been evaluated over a number of years. Such practices are important given the evidence that young people's experiences of partner abuse often overlap with wider experiences of bullying in school (Barter, et al., 2009; Firmin, 2011; Vivolo-Kantor, et al., 2016). These programmes are intended to create school environments in which young people can recognise and practice healthy relationships. In taking a whole-school approach these interventions are not solely concerned with 'teaching' young people about what a healthy relationship is. Rather they attempt to build physical and cultural school environments equipped to challenge abusive behaviours – from identifying hotspot locations or times of day when abuse occurs through to student-wide awareness-raising activities to promote bystander interventions (Barter, 2009b).

Violence-reduction programmes in Scotland have implemented learning from the US and Australia to develop bystander initiatives for secondary schools. The Mentors in Violence Prevention programme (Mentors in Violence Prevention, 2016) is designed to create student cultures in which peers feel safe and encouraged to intervene when peer-on-peer abuse is escalating. Peer-support programmes to address bullying have also been subject to evaluation in the UK and abroad (Cowie & Hutson, 2005; Rigby & Johnson, 2005). Similar to the dating violence interventions outlined previously, bystander interventions and peer-support programmes appear to be most effective when delivered to young people in contexts where the entire school environment has been equipped to support the approach – as in they are programmes that form part of a whole-school approach rather than an isolated intervention. It is not enough to teach young people how to recognise abuse in the hope that they will intervene – they have to be in an environment in which they feel safe to make an intervention. One study, for example, found that while peer-support programmes increased how safe some young people felt at school, they did not impact safety in particular parts of a school environment – such as the toilets, corridors and staircases (Cowie & Oztug, 2008). Bystander and peer-support programmes, therefore, appear most useful as part of a whole-school approach – and when used in this way could prove critical for maximising the attempts at positive bystander intervention identified in Chapter 5.

Unfortunately, in the cases I reviewed the lack of support for bystander intervention and peer support in a number of schools that were featured resulted in staff being unaware of the abuse that was escalating in the environments that they managed. In one college, young people were recruited throughout the school day to take part in a fight, and while a large proportion of the student body was aware of what was going to happen, nobody informed a teacher – later that day a young person was murdered. Likewise, in another case a young woman was threatened in school and physically assaulted over two weeks by fellow students in the buildup to her being raped. Her school was completely unaware of the physical and emotional abuse that she had experienced at school or the fact that she had moved houses to temporarily live with another relative in a bid to avoid victimisation on the walk home from school. In both cases in the absence of an intervention, the school environment became one in which abusive behaviours and ideals were normalised amongst the student body, were hidden from staff and escalated towards serious incidents of peer-on-peer abuse.

The lack of a whole-school approach not only affects the ability of students to create safe peer cultures but also results in inconsistency amongst the response of school staff. Whole-school approaches are as much about creating a minimum standard of practice amongst professionals within schools as it is about shaping the behaviour of young people – in fact, it is the relationship between the two, as illustrated throughout this chapter, which creates safe school environments. Levels of inconsistency amongst school staff was evident in the cases I reviewed. The problematic responses of some staff outlined previously were not representative of all professionals featured in all cases. While some professionals struggled to look beyond problematic behaviours of young people who had been abused, others demonstrated the professional curiosity that has been called for to identify the causes. In one case, investigating why a student had begun to have violent outbursts in some classes put a teacher at direct odds with one of her colleagues, who stated that:

> Shauna's mother is coming into the school tomorrow and I have not been invited to attend the meeting? Why should I not be there? This is made worse by the fact that Miss X vouched for her, saying that she hasn't ever done anything like this in her classes previously . . . . I do not think that (references to) character is really appropriate; it just undermines me. Shauna may have never sworn (at) or assaulted Miss X before, but I have never lied in my job; in this case I have nothing to gain in doing so except more paperwork.
>
> *(Case 6, report by Shauna's teacher, young woman who was raped)*

Some months after this incident, Shauna disclosed to Miss X that she had been raped on school property; had Miss X responded differently and not suggested that something must be causing Shauna's change in behaviour, then this disclosure may never have occurred. Such examples demonstrate effective individual practice in absence of the 'whole-school approach'. Ultimately, Shauna was afforded an opportunity to make a disclosure to the individual teacher that had noticed her. However, this response did not make Shauna's school safe. Once Shauna had told a teacher, an investigation was launched and other students attacked her to try to get her to withdraw her statement; in the end Shauna was moved to another school. The support of one teacher was not enough to negate the wider cultures held by her student body or by other staff members who failed to recognise Shauna's victimisation.

When professionals are unable to keep young people safe in school, they move them out (Firmin, et al., 2016) – an approach that was used in eight of the nine cases I reviewed. The use of relocation, often referred to as 'managed moves' between schools, implies that school cannot be made safe for those who are moved. It sends a message to the wider student body that sometimes the only way to keep them safe is to intervene with them – as individuals – as the school environment itself is not for changing. The individualistic narrative that surrounds the use of relocation suggests that when a young person is moved from a school the risk of peer-on-peer abuse leaves with them. In this sense the use of managed moves implies that the risk of abuse is located with an individual young person and not the wider cultural fabric of a school – a conceptualisation critiqued by many (Cowie, 2011; Losel & Bender, 2006) and at odds with the entire ethos of a whole-school approach.

In England the inability to consistently provide whole-school approaches to addressing peer-on-peer abuse persists. This persistence is not helped by the continued lack of an 'authorising environment' to adopt whole-school approaches such as the one advocated for in Australia. Despite the approach being recommended by multiple reviews and cross-parliamentary inquiries (Berelowitz, et al., 2013; Ofsted, 2012; Women and Equalities Committee, 2016a), the government has only recently agreed to put sex and relationships education on a statutory footing, and the Keeping Children Safe in Education guidance remains insufficient for marshalling wider responses to peer-on-peer abuse. It is critical to view the challenges of responding to harmful behaviours amongst students in light of this wider policy gap.

Whether exemplified through a failure to disrupt escalation towards an abusive incident, or the mismanagement of abusive incidents after the fact, extensive evidence exists of the implications of not taking a whole-school approach to respond to, and prevent, peer-on-peer abuse. While school professionals are in no way responsible for the abusive actions of individual young people, they share a responsibility similar to those held by parents/carers when young people are abused in a familial context. In both instances, parents who manage a home and teachers who manage a school have some influence on the cultural context in which those abusive acts take place. Yet the government has not offered anywhere near the clear legislative framework, guidance or resources provided to the families agenda as a way of authorising the involvement of schools to act in the way that is required.

Conclusion: schooling safe cultures

When the roles that school environments play in preventing or facilitating peer-on-peer abuse is under-identified, space is left for individualised accounts of the phenomenon to flourish. Far from being unique to the cases I reviewed, the extent to which peer-on-peer abuse is informed by school cultures is reflected in a broad evidence base concerned with bullying, school policy development and peer-on-peer abuse. However, much of this thinking is still absent from child protection policies, practices and research agendas which remain primarily focused on families. When I attended the conference of the International Society on the Prevention of Child Abuse and Neglect in 2016, intervention with families remained the primary, and to a large extent, sole, focus of research papers and panel discussions. Thankfully, keynote contributions from the World Health Organisation and Professor David Finkelhor called for greater attention to be paid to schools as a key location of violence and abuse prevention. However, it was clear from the evidence being presented from scholars around the world that international child protection experts had some way to go before schools are to receive the level of attention required to sufficiently evidence their role in safeguarding young people from violence and abuse.

By drawing together research into bullying and school safety, with criminological, gender-based and even geographical literature, and building upon it with case file and policy evidence, this chapter has evidenced the multiple ways in which practices in schools can create cultural contexts that are conducive with peer-on-peer abuse. When school environments feature abusive behaviours, harmful gender norms, normalising responses or the absence of a whole-school approach, social rules are created that reproduce and sustain, rather than challenge, peer-on-peer abuse. As outlined at the outset of this chapter, the relationship that young people have with school staff, their fellow students and education policymakers is therefore one of dependency. Young people depend on others who use and govern their school environment to ensure that it is one in which positive social norms are promoted and harmful behaviours are disrupted. It is an environment primed to influence the nature of their relationships and where some have their first experiences of abuse and violence – and yet they cannot rely on their parents to make them safe when they are there.

While much of what has been documented in this chapter relates to school environment themselves, some matters concern the extent to which schools can challenge abusive norms that emerge in contexts external to it but which affect the behaviour of students. As much as the abusive actions of individual young people can't be considered in absence of the wider contexts in which they occur, neither can the cultural context of a school. Some of the young people that schools are trying to safeguard experience harm elsewhere – the effects of which are brought into the school environment. The homes and peer groups documented in previous chapters have some impact on the norms that are introduced to schools via their students. To develop these ideas further the following chapter considers the impact of neighbourhood on all of the environments explored thus far, and its relation to peer-on-peer abuse. While the behaviours of Lara's friends are largely explained with reference to the school environment in which they spent their time, more information is required to fully appreciate the motivating social factors for Melissa and James. Once this social site has been explored, the following chapter will be drawn together with the three that preceded it. Taken together the chapters in this section are used to explore notions of location interplay, consent and dependency, and will collectively provide a contextual account of peer-on-peer abuse.

7

THERE'S NO PLACE LIKE HOME

Young people's peer relationships (Chapter 5) form within local neighbourhoods in addition to the schools explored in the previous chapter. Research into both peer-on-peer abuse and adolescent development identify streets and other public spaces as 'sites of socialisation' for young people in many Western social contexts. The nature of these public spaces informs the nature of young people's peer relationships and can provide a motivation for the activities with which they are engaged (Squires & Goldsmith, 2011; Warr, 2002; Wikström, et al., 2012). If these environments are ones in which sexual harassment is normalised or the threat of violence commands a defence from particularly young men who navigate them, then the nature of a neighbourhood will also be associated with the peer-on-peer abuse that occurs within it.

As well as being associated with abusive behaviours and peer group formation, neighbourhoods play host to families, schools and other social contexts which they are informed by and inform. As indicated in previous chapters, the nature of families and, for example, the extent to which they have to contend with the impacts of local crime and violence will inform the association of familial characteristics with peer-on-peer abuse, and the same can be said for schools. When young people are exposed to violence, victimisation or other harmful experiences in their communities, they can adopt the norms of those spaces and recreate them in other settings – such as when they are with their families or when they are in their classrooms. Young people's engagement in neighbourhood dynamic, therefore, can inform their peer and family relationships and the range of social contexts in which they spend their time.

The fact that young people encounter harm on the streets is not surprising in the sense that this is often where they spend their time. Parks and streets provide public areas where young people can form relationships and friendships without the adult supervision that they experience at home or in school. Given that young people form relationships in public spaces, it arguably follows that any abuse that may occur in those relationships is likely to also take place in those same environments. However, as was the case with schools explored in the previous chapter, if those who use and govern the public spaces in which young people socialise challenge the abusive norms and behaviours within them, then parks, streets, transport hubs and other localities could be social sites of safety. It is far from inevitable that because young people spend time in public spaces that these environments will be directly associated with any incidents of abuse that they experience. Their local park could be a place where young people are supported to form healthy relationships, for example, and their interactions on the bus journey to school could be ones through which safe and supportive friendships are formed.

National policymakers have provided some direction in recognising the fact that violence and abuse occur in public spaces. For the most part, these have been confined to the management of individuals who compromise the safety and well-being of others in public spaces. The introduction of anti-social behaviour orders (ASBOs) in the 1998 Crime and Disorder Act is one such example of this. According to the Crown Prosecution Service, ASBOs are 'civil orders to protect the public from behaviour that causes or is likely to cause harassment, alarm or distress' (Crown Prosecution Service, 2017). Conditions can be placed on these orders that prevent individuals from entering into areas where they have caused harm or distress previously and can therefore be used in response to individuals who pose threats associated with peer-on-peer abuse in public spaces. These orders can be used on young people as well as adults, and particular provisions were made so that 'parenting orders' could be placed on the carers of young people who have been made subject to an ASBO if it was thought that this could impact the behaviour of the young person in question. ASBOs are one of many policy initiatives such as dispersal orders, behaviour order contracts and gang-injunctions that have been provided to manage, and disrupt, the behaviour of individuals who are thought to compromise the safety of others in public spaces.

Much of the foregoing has been rooted in community safety, rather than child protection policy, and is largely concerned with managing individual rather than environmental risks. In recent years, some government departments and parliamentary inquiries have begun to recognise a relationship between the nature of public spaces, the professionals who manage those spaces and the young people who encounter harm when in those spaces. In 2014 the Transport Select Committee conducted an Inquiry into security on the railways and reported that 'child protection at railway stations is an emerging issue' (Transport Select Committee, 2014:20) upon hearing evidence about sexual exploitation, missing children and gang association and key transport hubs around the country. It made recommendations to transport providers and the British Transport Police that it should have targets, and monitor practice, in relation to the protection of children and young people who use railway services. Likewise, the government's policing department, the Home Office, revised its Ending Gang Violence and Exploitation strategy in 2016 to explicitly reference localities in which young people were at increased risk of exploitation and abuse (HM Government, 2016).

While this direction of travel is promising, and moves some way beyond the targeting of individuals in public spaces that was common to civil orders and injunctions, approaches to address the public space dynamics of peer-on-peer abuse remain in their infancy. The most evident consequence of this is the continued use of relocation to safeguard young people who are at risk in their local communities. While there are no accurate figures available, work in local areas across England and Wales (as well as inspection reports and government policies) acknowledge that in the absence of change in the environments in which they encounter harm, young people will be moved out of them (Berelowitz, et al., 2013; JTAI, 2016). However, in doing so we make the young person the problem and the individual who has to shoulder the responsibility of making the abuse stop – they are moved and therefore they are intervened with. Neighbourhoods, in comparison, remain as abusive as they always were and continue to be spaces in which other young people are exposed to harmful norms and behaviours.

It is the association between neighbourhoods and peer-on-peer abuse – and the limited policy recognition of this relationship to date – that is the focus of this chapter. The term 'neighbourhood' is used to reference not just the street, but public space localities such as shopping centres and transport hubs in which young people socialise. Once again, media accounts and policy documentation will be drawn together in this chapter and exemplified with reference to the neighbourhood spaces that featured in the nine cases I reviewed. Six of these cases investigated abusive incidents that occurred completely, or partially, in public spaces including parks, stairwells and bus stops. Beyond the incidents themselves, 86 per cent of the 145 young people featured in the cases reviewed, including 75 per cent of all suspects, experienced or were exposed to abusive behaviours and/or had their safety compromised in their local neighbourhood. These experiences often occurred in the escalation towards the offences that were under investigation or in the form of retaliation in the aftermath of the incident. In all occasions, exposure to abuse within young people's local neighbourhoods informed the nature of their relationships with peers, parents and professionals and was often associated with their experiences of peer-on-peer abuse. And yet policymakers appear to have insufficiently incorporated neighbourhood-based risks within a safeguarding agenda – regarding these issues as concern only for those working in community safety, crime and disorder.

The mismatch between the current policy landscape and the evidenced association between public spaces and young people's experiences of peer-on-peer abuse is explored in this chapter, with reference to the following key themes:

1   The physical and emotional victimisation of young men on the street and the gendered pressures this puts on them to protect themselves and those around them

2   The sexual harassment of girls and young women on the street

3   The normalisation of violence between young people in public spaces by pro-
     fessionals, adult members of the public and other young people
4   The use of relocation to physically remove young people from public spaces in
     which they encounter harm

Evidence of each of these factors has been documented in criminological and sociological research and is explored here with reference to that evidence base and illustrated
through examples taken from the nine cases that I reviewed. By focusing on these
themes, the particular dynamics of the interplay between the social norms in neighbourhoods and young people's experiences of peer-on-peer abuse can be brought to
the fore – and a case made for their more prominent consideration in safeguarding policies and practices beyond the use of relocation as means of keeping young people safe.

Before these four thematic areas are considered in detail, this chapter revisits, for
a final time, the case study of Lara, Melissa and James, and explores the extent to
which their neighbourhood-based interactions informed the abusive incident in
which they were all involved – and the schools, peer groups and families to which
this experience was associated.

Returning to the case study: the neighbourhood experiences of James, Melissa and Lara

In the previous chapter we learnt that James was at risk in his local neighbourhood –
his friend had been attacked and his school was playing a key role in keeping him
safe by trying to have him with them, and not out on the streets, as much as possible. James' peer group was also largely street-based, and so the nature of his local
neighbourhood was likely to have informed the dynamics of his peer relationships.
Information about Melissa and Lara provided thus far, however, has offered less of
an insight into their interactions in their local neighbourhood. In learning about
how all three engaged with, and used, public spaces before, during and following
the incident, what more are we able to decipher about the social drivers, risks and
protective factors associated with their experience of peer-on-peer abuse?

James	**Melissa**	**Lara**
• James spends most of his time out in his local neighbourhood – particularly the local park and surrounding streets. This is where James is when he is missing from home or not in school	• Melissa associates with a local gang outside of school and has recently started to commit robbery offences alongside them	• Lara spends little time out in the local neighbourhood apart from going to the local shopping centre and cinema with her friends

- When James was 10 his bike was stolen from him in his local park and he reported the incident to the police. This was the only time James reported being victimized, despite being physically attacked on other occasions after this

- James is violent to other young people in the park and has been accused of robbery as a result

- James has also witnessed some of his friends sexually assaulting girls that they bring to the park

- Melissa's peers outside of school are separate to James' although they are aware of one another

- One of Melissa's friends was being sexually exploited by a group of young men – there are suspicions that they are friends of James

- Melissa hangs around some disused garages near the estate on which she lives, and it is where she has been seen with local gang members

- Melissa is often missing from home and thought to be on the street, but unlike James this behaviour is not reported to the police

- Lara knows that Melissa and James are linked to different local gangs but she doesn't come into contact with either of them on the street – she is only with them when she is in school

- After the rape Lara is attacked on a street near her school by a girl who claims to be friends with Melissa. Lara begins to feel increasingly unsafe in her local area after this incident, and a few months later her whole family is relocated for her own safety

In keeping with some of the evidence presented in Chapter 5, James had an early experience of victimisation which stimulated his need for 'protective' peer relationships. James needed a peer group that would help him feel safe when on the streets – even though from a professional perspective associating with violent or aggressive peers is likely to be considered anything but protective. James was exposed to and engaged in violence on the streets – rather than in his home – and it was clearly a space in which social norms encouraged abusive, hyper-masculine behaviours. James had also witnessed sexual violence in his local park, an experience which both reinforced and will have been reinforced by his exposure to harmful sexual behaviours at school. While Melissa brought abusive norms at play in her family home into her school and peer relationships, for James engagement in the social rules of the street shaped his peer relationships, disrupted his education and were the primary source of the norms that underpinned his involvement in the rape of Lara.

Melissa's peers had experienced sexual exploitation on the streets, and she became gang-associated in this space. Melissa's difficulties at home exacerbated her vulnerability to risks on the street. Unlike James, Melissa was never reported missing by her family, and professionals were therefore unaware of the amount of time she was spending out in her local neighbourhood or who she was with when she was there. Melissa's experiences of the street reinforced the messages that she received at home and at school in relation to the victimisation of young women, and provided the foundations of a motive for her to associate with those who abused young women rather than become one of those who they abused.

In comparison, Lara had been safe in her local neighbourhood. She used local community resources and was not at risk when doing so. This changed after Lara was assaulted in school. Once she sought help from professionals, Lara was threatened with retaliation and was unsafe in her local community as a result. In this sense the harmful social norms that Lara was exposed to at school transferred onto the street once she sought support. This increased, rather than addressed, her vulnerability and resulted in her being moved not only out of school but also out of her local neighbourhood. By relocating Lara, professionals stripped her of all the positive friendships and peer relationships that she had – and as Chapter 6 demonstrated her friends were non-abusive and relatively safe. Rumours that Lara had lied about the rape were shared online by the peers in her school. These rumours travelled with Lara when she was relocated, and she was bullied in her new community and school. By moving Lara, professionals also implied that she was the problem that needed to be changed – as opposed to the harmful spaces in which she spent her time – potentially impacting her emotional well-being and creating feelings of self-blame. Meanwhile, James and Melissa remained unsafe in their local area, engaging with social rules that still required them to prove themselves in order to stay safe and avoid victimisation on the street. The school and community contexts of which these young people were a part remained abusive, and peer-on-peer abuse persisted, despite Lara's relocation.

All four themes identified in the introduction of this chapter – street-based victimisation of young men, sexual harassment of young women, practices which normalise harm in public spaces and the use of relocation – were all identified in this case study. But to what extent are they reflected in the cases I reviewed or the wider research and policy landscape concerned with peer-on-peer abuse? The remainder of this chapter demonstrates that, while there is clearly an evidence base for associating young people's experiences of peer-on-peer abuse with the nature of their neighbourhoods, insufficient recognition of this relationship at a policy level has contributed to a response that uses relocation as a means of addressing public-space risk, rather than intervention with public spaces directly. As was the case with schools explored in the previous chapter – the use of relocation communicates to young people that the only way to keep them safe is to move them out of contexts in which they encounter harm and that these environments cannot be changed: an approach which is rooted in individualised responses to peer-on-peer abuse and fails to ensure that other young people who use those same social spaces but have not been relocated feel, and are, safe.

Young men's victimisation on the street

James was first victimised at the age of 10 when his bike was stolen from him. This experience, and the inability of his parents or services to keep him safe in his local community, provided a motive for James to associate with a violent peer group which would in turn act as a source of protection. When young men like James are victimised on the streets, these experiences are gendered in a way similar to that recorded about schools in the previous chapter (Anderson, 1999; Beckett, et al., 2013; Young & Hallsworth, 2011; Pitts, 2008; Wikström, et al., 2012). The street, like the school, is a social space in which gendered norms are engaged with, embodied, reproduced or challenged. Young men are expected to protect themselves on the street and have to demonstrate their ability to do so in competition with one another.

Experiences of street-based victimisation serve to establish the status, and therefore masculinity, of some young men while simultaneously undermining the status of others. Young men experience robbery or abuse on the streets; those who are abusing them are often seeking status, and establishing their masculinity, via the control of male peers. Likewise, those who are abused appear vulnerable and their masculinity is undermined (Anderson, 1999). While victimisation, or a lack of power, is not a prerequisite for a young person's abuse of others, research into young people who abuse their peers suggests that it is a factor for many (Gadd, et al., 2013; Losel & Bender, 2006) and, importantly, is not confined to a history of intra-familial abuse. For the young people in the cases I reviewed, street-based experiences of abuse were far more common than experiences of abuse within their families.

Although young men's accounts of street-based victimisation have been documented in qualitative research over decades, the scale of these experiences has been notoriously difficult to establish – largely because of under-reporting. However, the decision to include 10- to 15-year-olds in the national crime survey from 2013 has shed some light on the scale and nature of the issue across England and Wales. According to the 2013 survey, 10- to 15-year-olds experienced 821,000 incidents of crime, 465,000 (57%) of which were violent incidents and 314,000 (38%) were incidents of theft. A total of 77 per cent of the reported violent incidents were perpetrated by males, the majority of whom were also aged 10 to 15. Mobile phones, clothing, cash and bicycles or bicycle parts together accounted for nearly two thirds (65%) of all items stolen from children. Around a fifth (21%) of violent incidents experienced by children resulted in them receiving medical attention. When these figures were compared with adult responses to the survey, statisticians found that 10- to 15-year-olds are more likely to be a victim of violent crime than adults.

If the social rules of the street are informed by a fear, and real experiences of, robbery and physical violence, then the social capital that comes with a violent peer group is essential for the safe navigation of this space. The nature of the street creates a motive for forming an abusive peer group, rather than only informing the cultural rules of peer groups that are already in existence within it. Like James, many young people who engage with the rules of the street align themselves with violent peers in order to survive (Anderson, 1999; Pitts, 2008; Warr, 2002). These experiences were well documented in the histories of suspects featured in the cases I reviewed, 95 per cent of whom had been physically abused on the streets of their local neighbourhood well before the rapes and murders in which they were later involved. The vast majority of these suspects (bar two) were young men, who were assaulted and threatened as they spent time alone in their local area, trying to make friends and socialise independently of their families. The street became the source of both their victimisation and their protection, a vicious cycle widely documented in studies on gang-associated young people (Anderson, 1999; Beckett, et al., 2013; Young & Hallsworth, 2011; Pitts, 2008).

The violence that young men encounter on the streets not only informs the nature of their peer groups, but it can also affect the nature of their familial relationships as it did with James. Researchers have documented the strain that street-based violence can have on parent-child relationships, the impact of which was explored in Chapter 5 (Aisenberg & Herrenkohl, 2008; Catch 22, 2013; Losel & Bender, 2006). For young people who have grown up in safe and supportive households, experiences of physical violence on the street can draw them into abusing others as a means of survival. Studies into young people who display anti-social behaviour have found that 'a negative (neighbourhood) environment seems to encourage anti-social behaviour, particularly in young persons with no massive familial and personal risks who develop more behaviour problems during adolescence than in childhood' (Losel & Bender, 2006:55). Likewise, another study showed that young people who had murdered peers were far more likely to have done so in the contexts of robberies and criminally active groups compared with those who murdered adults or family members. Such patterns were evident in the cases I reviewed. Suspects were far more likely to have encountered physical abuse on the streets than they had done at home, and for many it was the risk of the streets and not in their homes that informed the abusive norms they held and practiced. For example, in one case all three male suspects, who raped a young woman that they had met online, had previously experienced physical violence and threats from other young men in their local neighbourhood, whereas none were exposed to physical abuse at home:

> Ethan stood at a bus stop when he was approached by a group of 20 males. They showed him a picture of his (social media) page and stated that they knew he was from another area. One of the males took a knife from his back pocket and put it up his sleeve. Another male also had a knife. Ethan ran from the stop into a shop and was chased by the group who then waited for him outside.
>
> *(Case 2, experiences of Ethan before his involvement in a rape)*

These patterns emerged in murder, as well as rape, cases that I reviewed. For example, a young man who murdered his ex-girlfriend had been repeatedly victimised in his local neighbourhood in the preceding years but did not appear to have had any violent or abusive experiences at home:

> [Kush was] surrounded by a group of males and had his bag poked by a sharp implement. He was patted down and slapped around the head. [On another occasion he was] searched by a lone male and had his phone taken.
>
> *(Case 8, experience of Kush before his involvement in a murder)*

Such incidents bring to life figures about the scale of street-based victimisation (Office of National Statistics, 2013) and illustrate the emotionally abusive nature of the physical assaults experienced by some young men. Stereotypical expectations of masculinity, associated with status, strength and an ability to have power over others, afford a tone of humiliation to such incidents. It is not simply the physical pain that may result from being 'slapped in the head' that is important in such cases – rather it is the emotional scars that may result from such interactions and the extent to which these inform the way an individual behaves in the future. When you've been slapped in the head, or had your phone or bike stolen, how will you stop this from happening to you again? For the young men in the cases I reviewed, as appears to be the case for those featured in other studies (Anderson, 1999; Beckett, et al., 2013; Pitts, 2008; Warr, 2002), the safest way to navigate their local area, and not be victimised again, was to victimise others – partners, peers, younger children, adults and so on. In adopting abusive identities, these young men embodied the social rules of their local areas and reproduced them – maintaining the abusive nature of their neighbourhoods rather than challenging or changing them.

Accounts of this pathway into peer-on-peer abuse are most profoundly established in research into young people associated with street gangs or involved in weapon-enabled street crime. A number of researchers have already evidenced the ways in which streets are particularly unsafe for young people who navigate gang-affected neighbourhoods (Catch 22, 2013; Firmin, 2008; Pitts, 2008), and so it is somewhat unsurprising that experiences of street-based harm were particularly pronounced for suspects identified as gang-associated in the cases reviewed (Table 7.1).

For 85 per cent of the young people in the cases I reviewed, physical victimisation on the street was interwoven with a fear of crime in gang-affected neighbourhoods and/or the pressures of gang association. Fears of gang association appeared far less prevalent within the schools (Chapter 6) and families (Chapter 4) featured. For example, a number of schools featured abusive social norms and harmful sexual behaviours, but these were not necessarily associated with the presence of gang members within the school community – whereas crime was often a common feature of the neighbourhoods featured in the cases reviewed.

TABLE 7.1 Young people exposed to harm in neighbourhoods by gang association

		Gang-associated	Not gang-associated	Total
Exposed to harm in neighbourhood	**Frequency**	50	6	56
	% within young people exposed to harm in neighbourhoods	89.3	10.7	100.0
	% within gang-associated individuals	100.0	24.0	74.7
	% of total	66.7	8.0	74.7

The physical violence documented in this chapter thus far predominantly represents the experiences of young men on the streets. However, research and the cases that I reviewed have also indicated that young women are also victimised in public spaces – and in ways that are also relatively gendered. While street-based violence between young men is built upon, and reinforces, gendered stereotypes about power, masculinity and status, the abuse of young women provides a vehicle for young men to assert their authority in front of one another and reproduce harmful gendered power dynamics between young women and young men – in ways similar to that documented in Chapter 5.

In keeping with research into gender, crime and offending more broadly (Dobash, et al., 1995; Stanko, 1994), young women in the cases I reviewed appeared to become increasingly unsafe on the streets in the escalation towards, or in the aftermath of, the abusive incidents in question. Before this, young women seemed to be victimised at home by family members or by partners in their intimate relationships, rather than by same-age peers on the streets. A lack of safety in their intimate relationships or at home increased the reliance of some young women on street-based peer association – as was the case with Melissa. This is in keeping with wider research which has suggested that young women who are abusive are more likely to live in violent households compared with young men who are more likely to associate with violent peer groups (e.g. Barter, et al., 2009). But overall this dynamic was rare – young women only featured as suspects in three of the nine cases and in each case harmful experiences at home, and in one case in their relationships, pushed them into the streets and in turn forged reliance upon violent peer groups.

What was more common were accounts such as Lara's where the street became unsafe for young women after, or during, their experiences of peer-on-peer abuse. Before the incidents in question, young women, unlike a number of young men in the cases, did not have an extensive history of street-based victimisation. However, once they sought help for the abuse they had experienced at school or within their peer groups, they were attacked on the streets by other young people who had allegiances to those who had harmed them in the first place.

Where we see an exception to this rule in the literature and in the cases I reviewed was regarding young women's experiences of sexual harassment on the street. These appeared to occur on a scale in keeping with young men's experiences of robbery and street-based violence, and in doing so informed their expectations of peer interactions and consent.

Street-based sexual harassment

In 2015, at a time of multiple national investigations and public inquiries into child sexual abuse in England and Wales, an independent review was conducted of the nature and scale of child sexual exploitation cases in Rochdale (Coffey, 2014). Amongst a number of things, the review found that young women were being abused in local communities where the sexual harassment of girls, including those travelling to school in their uniforms, was normalised. Young women were used to being approached by adult men and their peers, having people comment on their bodies, proposition them sexually, follow them home and on occasion 'grope' (sexually assault) them. The picture painted by the review of young women running a sexual harassment gauntlet on the streets of Rochdale just to get to and from school echoed the evidence on sexual harassment in school corridors being evidenced by inquiries and research at the same time (and documented in the previous chapter). Repeated exposure to sexual harassment on the streets resulted in young women being socialised in public spaces where they were accustomed to being sexually objectified, and limited the extent to which they or other members of the public could recognise abusive behaviours (Coffey, 2014). Far from being unique to the young women of Rochdale, the Everyday Sexism Project, launched by Laura Bates in 2011, has documented in excess of 100,000 experiences of sexual harassment and abuse experienced by women and girls in public spaces in the UK (Bates, 2014) and has continued to chart these encounters on a global scale. Since the launch of the project, women in multiple countries have contributed to Bates' cataloguing of gendered harassment and abuse, demonstrating the culturally insidious nature of sexism in many Western countries and the extent to which young women will encounter abuse in public spaces.

In keeping with this evidence base, the cases I reviewed documented multiple incidents of young women being sexually harassed and threatened by young men in the streets in the escalation towards both their rape and murder:

> Tasha (complainant) did not like Sean (suspect) and told her friend (Lacey). (Three weeks prior to the offence) Lacey told Sean and he threatened Tasha over the phone and made threats to Tasha when he saw her on the street.
>
> *(Case 1, rape)*

> Monica (complainant) [was] at a bus stop with a friend when Michael and Drew (suspects) saw her. Both boys slapped her . . . . When she tried to leave, Michael punched her in the face and told her 'If you come around here then you have to do things for us'. Drew took her into someone's garden nearby where he digitally penetrated her, stating 'Do you want to come to (the local area) or not'.
>
> *(Case 4, rape)*

These experiences set the stage for the assaults that would later follow and put in place a practiced set of social norms in which young women could be sexually, emotionally and physically assaulted by young men in public spaces and in the view of their peers. Not only did this affect young women's expectations of safety in their local area but it also normalised the problematic social rules which young men were engaged with when they behaved in this way. A total of 84 per cent of the suspects featured in the cases I reviewed (predominantly young men) were exposed to some form of sexually abusive or harassing behaviours in their local neighbourhoods before their involvement in the rape or murder of a peer. Young men formed peer groups and intimate relationships in these same environments – peer group and relationships that were documented in Chapter 5.

Considering previously described peer groups in this light furthers our understanding of the relationship between harmful social norms, peer group formation and instances of peer-on-peer abuse. However, as was the case with abusive behaviours in schools, it is less the presence of sexual harassment or physical violence on the streets and more the response to these incidents from peers, professionals and members of the public that contributes to the process of normalisation. Chapter 6 illustrated how even if some young people demonstrate abusive behaviours or attitudes at school, when these behaviours are challenged by staff, students or others who used that space (via a whole-school approach), abusive norms can be undermined and positive ones asserted. However, where responses failed to recognise or disrupt abusive behaviours, they contributed to the process of normalisation – and it was through this that individual incidents of abuse cumulatively created cultural contexts conducive with peer-on-peer abuse. It is therefore essential to explore how policy and practice have attempted to respond to the association between neighbourhoods and peer-on-peer abuse, and the ways in which this played out in the cases I reviewed, in order to fully account for the role of public spaces in a contextual account of abuse between young people.

Normalisation of violence in public spaces: 'that's where girls get raped'

The street-based sexual harassment and physical abuse of young people documented thus far seems to occur within public spaces in which violence is part of the cultural fabric. In some neighbourhoods, violence, criminality and abuse appear to have become routine to the point of fatalism for some young people (Beckett, et al., 2013; Young & Hallsworth, 2011; Squires & Goldsmith, 2011). It is notable that for many young people, especially young men, most, if not all, of the violence that they experience occurs in public spaces – they are not encountering these risks within the safety of their own homes and sometimes not even in school. In keeping with this evidenced trend, it seems that young people are rarely murdered by peers when they are at home or at school. Instead, media reports generally document young people being murdered by their peers on the streets and in other public spaces:

> Teenager, 16, stabbed schoolboy on bus full of horrified passengers on the victim's 16th birthday
>
> *(Mail Online, 2013)*

> Boy, 16, stabbed to death at London playing field after attending friend's 16th birthday party
>
> *(Mirror, 2016)*

It is of note, therefore, that two of the three murder cases I reviewed occurred on the streets, in broad daylight and in front of other members of the public. The one case that did not follow this pattern involved the murder of a young woman (as opposed to a young man) by her ex-partner when she was at home – a qualitatively different experience in keeping with wider research into gendered experiences of relationship-based abuse (Stanko, 1994).

The public normalisation of peer-on-peer abuse is not reserved to murder or other acts of serious youth violence. Research into multiple-perpetrator rape has routinely identified the use of public spaces during group-based acts of sexual violence (Horvath & Woodhams, 2013). Studies into harmful sexual behaviour have also evidenced that young people who abuse their peers, as opposed to younger children, often do so in public spaces[1] instead of private dwellings (Hackett, 2014; Latchford, et al., 2016). In keeping with this emerging evidence base, statutory inquiries into sexual exploitation have identified parks, hotels, disused garages and high streets as places in which young people are groomed into sexual exploitation (Coffey, 2014; D'Arcy & Thomas, 2016; Jay, 2014).

With public space comes visibility. When I first began reviewing cases of peer-on-peer abuse, I couldn't help but wonder why, in keeping with the wider evidence base, the cases I were analysing had occurred in view of so many people. Surely if you wanted to harm someone it made more sense to do it in private where you were less likely to be caught by the authorities? However, considering the incidents under investigation in light of peer-on-peer abuse research, the public nature of the phenomenon appears interwoven with both its development and its function.

In terms of development, it is important that incidents of peer-on-peer abuse are not considered as vacuous, one-off events. Research has captured the cultural normalisation of violence that can occur within localities in which violence is anticipated as a result of recurrence (Beckett, et al., 2013; Pitts, 2008). As this book has demonstrated, there are escalatory events that occur before incidents of peer-on-peer abuse. For example, in one case I reviewed a young man who was murdered in the same transport hub that he and his peers had been fighting in the day before. In fact, violence between the two groups had been escalating within the same public space for some time, and while each incident was disrupted by the police and relevant transport service the cumulative impact that these incidents may have had on the transport hub was not addressed – in a fashion similar to the management of incidents as opposed to the cumulative impact of incidents in schools documented in the previous chapter.

Further interrogation of the evidence regarding the use of public spaces for incidents of peer-on-peer abuse also suggests that legacies of violence in some environments, as well as young people's direct engagement with them, can create an additional historical layer of normalisation that make such acts permissible – or even expected. Areas may become 'known' as ones in which violence just happens, regardless of whether those who know this information have actually encountered violence there themselves (Beckett, et al., 2013; Ralphs, et al., 2009). Through this process, 'legacy normalisation' provides a further scaffold to prop up the process of escalation and acceptance of abusive norms within public spaces which both create contexts that are conducive with peer-on-peer abuse. In three of the six rape cases I reviewed, legacy normalisation was evident – once in a park, once in a stairwell and on another occasion in a school toilet. On these occasions, witness statements documented examples of young people identifying that sexual violence was routine in some of the areas where they spent their time. One young man was recorded as saying to a young woman he and his peers were abusing on a stairwell:

> Do what we say or we'll take you to the cupboard (a caretaker's space in the local estate) where the paedophiles go.
>
> *(Case 1)*

What was even more interesting in this particular case was that the attitude expressed by this young man appeared to be shared by some local professionals and members of the public who were also aware of risks on that particular housing estate. Before their involvement in the rape that was the subject of the case review, a number of young men had been issued with behavioural contracts in response to their 'anti-social behaviour' on the estate. During the rape itself, three residents walked past and did not intervene; two of whom also refused to give evidence to the police once an investigation was launched because of a fear of reprisals. The response of professionals and the public in this case gave the impression that the young men involved were perceived as a nuisance in the local community, were the subject of police and community safety intervention and were to an extent feared by, and therefore able to control, adults with whom they shared this public space. They were not seen as vulnerable by professionals, even though interrogation of their backgrounds indicated that a number had been abused at home and all had been victimised in their local community. There hadn't been a child protection response to the group, and so at best their behaviours were seen as solely criminal and at worst beyond the control or influence of other residents. The cumulative result of professional and public responses to the young men involved in this case, twinned with the established legacy of sexual violence on the housing estate, created social conditions that enabled and normalised, rather than challenged and disrupted, abusive behaviours. As was the case with schools in the previous chapter, in a context like this the potential for safe bystander intervention would have been severely limited (Cowie, 2011; Powell, 2011).

In addition to being informed by harmful norms that operate in neighbourhood spaces, the public-space nature of peer-on-peer abuse is also functional. Research into multiple-perpetrator rape (Franklin, 2004; Woodhams, 2013) and violence between men (Polk, 1994) has demonstrated the ways in which public spaces provide an audience and a set of social rules which can motivate some abusive behaviour. Research into serious youth violence, and increasingly, sexual exploitation, has evidenced the street, and other neighbourhood localities, as environments in which harmful gendered norms are in operation (Pitts, 2008; Young & Hallsworth, 2011). By abusing peers in these public spaces young people are able to realise the expectations of the social rules at play within the locality, and to a wider audience in accordance with societal expectations of masculinity. Polk (1994), for example, considers public drinking houses and the surrounding streets as environments in which other men are watched by their peers as they fight to demonstrate/regain their status, within a cultural context in which harmful rules about masculinity are in operation. As explored in Chapter 5, peer groups provide an audience for young men to perform in accordance with gender-stereotyped norms, either when they abuse/control young women or when they establish their status in conflict with one another.

Therefore, while it may be counter-intuitive for young people to abuse one another in some of the most visible ways possible, the public-space nature of peer-on-peer abuse is in keeping with the development and function of the environments in which peer-on-peer abuse occurs. It is not simply that young people experience different forms of gendered-based violence on the streets that associates public spaces with the nature of peer-on-peer abuse. Instead, public spaces provide contexts that are conducive with, and enable, peer-on-peer abuse. As is the case with schools, families don't hold much influence over the nature of public spaces, whereas professionals, members of the public and others who use and manage these spaces do. While families make up the communities in which much of these incidents occur, so do local businesses and other public services. In recognising the public nature of peer-on-peer abuse, questions arise as to the role of public – as well as private – approaches to safeguarding young people.

Relocation, relocation, relocation

The interplays between neighbourhoods and individual young people (along with the families, peer groups and schools to which they are associated) have the potential to safeguard young people from, or facilitate the likelihood of, peer-on-peer abuse. In the face of physical violence and sexual harassment within public spaces that normalise abusive behaviours, it may appear, for some young people, that violence and abuse are inevitable parts of neighbourhoods in which they live (Beckett, et al., 2013; Pitts, 2008; Ralphs, et al., 2009; Squires & Goldsmith, 2011; Stanko, 1994). The inability of professionals to intervene in a way that disrupts the nature of that space, the harmful social norms that may have developed there along with historic accounts of abuse in that locality, and young people's routine exposure to robbery, sexual harassment and other forms of violent crime can create a sense of inevitability about peer-on-peer abuse in some public spaces. While arguably overly pessimistic, this outlook can be further reinforced by the use of relocation as a response to peer-on-peer abuse.

The use of relocation as a means of safeguarding young people is recognised in both policy (HM Government, 2016) and research (Farmer & Pollock, 2003; Shuker, 2013b). Young people are moved from abusive households into care and into different local areas if the abuse they encounter is more locality based. Through this process Shuker (2013a:129–130) notes that rather than disrupt those who are abusive, for sexually exploited young people 'a far more common approach is moving the young person to a new location where distance prevents them from seeing adults or peers who pose a risk'.

Relocation, therefore, is positioned as a means by which young people can be removed from the abusive public-space environments highlighted in this chapter. In this regard, decisions to relocate young people in the cases I reviewed were in response to young people themselves, as well as professionals, identifying that the risks they faced were inherently interwoven with their local neighbourhood:

> I know most of the boys arrested in connection with this offence and if it became public knowledge that I have assisted police and provided evidence against them I would be subjected to serious violence before or after the trial . . . . I am aware that some, especially Eli, uses violence against people on a regular basis . . . . I would fear for my safety, my family's safety and our property.
>
> *(Case 1, view of bystander who intervened)*

> A move must be facilitated so that the family can leave (the local area) and avoid all possible threats and recriminations.
>
> *(Case 4, view of professionals)*

However, using relocation as a safeguarding mechanism has been critiqued by those who argue that safety for young people is not necessarily physical (Shuker, 2013a). Shuker argues, moving a young person may achieve their physical safety (and even this is questionable for some) but at the same time it can undermine their relational safety (the safety they experience through secure relationships) or their psychological safety (their identity, sense of self and well-being) – as was the case with Lara. Shuker's concerns were realised for some young people who were relocated in the cases I reviewed. One young man, for example, who was relocated after he disrupted a sexual assault, had to move away from his family and all his friends after he was threatened with reprisals for intervening. He became increasingly socially isolated, fearful and angry in his new placement. Another young woman who was relocated after she was repeatedly raped by young men in her local area was threatened online by their peers and abused again in her new placement by other young people who were there.

Beyond the ramifications for those who are moved, the use of relocation has potential impacts for those who remain. When young people are relocated it leaves the impression that the neighbourhood cannot be made safe. What then are those to do who are left behind? As outlined earlier in this chapter, young people's use of violence on the streets can be in response to a fear for their personal safety – fears that can be further aggravated by the process of relocating their peers. For those who are left behind, continued involvement in violent behaviours may appear to be the safest option – a means of 'surviving' violent neighbourhoods that are beyond the control of professionals (Cepeda & Valdez, 2003; Young & Hallsworth, 2011; Pitts, 2008). The young people in the cases I reviewed who remained in their local neighbourhoods after the incidents, most of them suspects, continued to encounter violence and abuse. Evidence of male suspects being abused in their local neighbourhood and then embodying the rules of that neighbourhood to abuse others, while still being afraid themselves, indicates a resolution to a life in which violence is a central feature. Arguably, in the absence of a change in the social conditions of the neighbourhoods, the suspects in the reviewed cases acted in ways to ensure their status within harmfully gendered and abusive spaces, and therefore realise 'safety', through the continual harm of others in their local area, even if arguably this safety was never realised.

Safeguarding in public spaces: beyond community safety

To an extent the UK government has recognised the relationship between young people's experiences of peer-on-peer abuse and the nature of the neighbourhoods in which they live. Since 2011 the Home Office has been delivering against an Ending Gangs and Violence strategy – which in 2016 became the Ending Gangs and Exploitation strategy – to target neighbourhoods and specific public environments where exploitation occurs. Support was offered to areas that identified themselves as gang-affected, constructing the issue as one that affected whole neighbourhoods rather than just individuals. Likewise, in recent years police forces have begun training hoteliers, taxi firms and those who run businesses on high streets to look out for the signs of exploitation and report it when they have concerns (Figure 7.1) (D'Arcy & Thomas, 2016; JTAI, 2016).

However, there are two main challenges with these initiatives to date. The first is that they are largely driven by central and local departments that lead on community safety, crime and justice as opposed to child protection and safeguarding. As such they are constructed as approaches to managing crime and disorder rather than safeguarding vulnerable children. Scholars have argued that a persistently criminal justice, rather than welfare-focused, response to young men's experiences of street-based violence has pushed them to seek protection through their own engagement in violence and abuse (Squires & Goldsmith, 2011). When systems are unable to keep a young person safe within chronically violent neighbourhoods, abusive behaviours can become acts of survival (Pitts, 2008; Young & Hallsworth, 2011). While some may argue that it doesn't matter who leads as long as a response is put in place, the departmental ownership of these issues has practical implications. At a local level those who lead on this agenda are largely based in community safety and policing. Children's social care services are tasked with fixing families – as outlined in Chapter 4. The impact that these community issues have on families, such as James', are rarely accommodated for with such a siloed approach.

Secondly, while these interventions are constructed around neighbourhoods and public businesses, the interventions that they support remain largely individualised. The Ending Gang and Youth Violence work has largely resourced interventions for

FIGURE 7.1 Operation MakeSafe campaign poster, Waltham Forest
Metropolitan Police

individuals and families within areas identified as being affected by gang violence. Likewise, the training for taxi drivers and hoteliers is based on the idea that they can identify and refer concerns about the safety of young people in public spaces – rather than being about the role that they play in making public spaces safer.

While the national child protection mantra is that 'safeguarding is everyone's business', in reality this is about everyone being aware and able to refer concerns into safeguarding agencies (i.e. social care), rather than recognising the contribution that everyone makes to creating safe social spaces.

Australian academics have long promoted 'situational crime prevention' as a means of addressing child sexual abuse and other forms of violence (Smallbone, et al., 2012). In keeping with the ethos of this chapter they recognise situations which facilitate abuse and promote approaches that seek to disrupt these situations. In this model, professional practices and the response of community members to abusive behaviours becomes integral to creation of safe or unsafe spaces (Firmin, et al., 2016). In the same vein promoted via whole-school approaches, situational crime prevention highlights the need to respond to the cultural norms within a given situation or area, and not just respond to incidents, in order to change the shape of an area and prevent its future use as a site for perpetrating abuse (Barter, 2009b; Cowie & Hutson, 2005).

The UK appears to be some distance from recognising the safeguarding potential of professionals, young people and other members of the public who contribute to the norms, behaviours and structures within public spaces. Compared with the Troubled Families programme and traditional child protection agendas, there is little in place to provide a strategic framework in which public spaces, and those who manage them, can be strategically and operationally included within safeguarding processes. And yet in the absence of a comprehensive safeguarding offer that addresses risk in public spaces, young people are moved out of unsafe areas by children's social care, akin to managed moves across schools, in a bid to keep them safe.

Conclusion: public-space risk and community safeguarding

The association between the nature of young people's neighbourhoods and their experiences with peer-on-peer abuse could be construed as being primarily about their victimisation on the street and the impact that this has on their sense of safety. It is true that in the cases I reviewed, and the wider literary evidence base, young people's experiences of violence on the streets can create a reliance on abusive peers, disrupt familial relationships (which can't protect young people from street-based risk) and result in disengagement from education. However, evidence presented in this chapter implies that it is the nature and efficacy of responses to these experiences (by peers, professionals, parents, policymakers and members of the public) which is more significant. Let's return to the case study example. If, when James had his bike stolen, there had been a response which challenged that behaviour, disrupted it, prevented it from happening again and made James feel safe, he may not have relied on a group of violent peers to keep him safe in his local neighbourhood from that point forward. Likewise, if having reported the rape she experienced Lara had been supported by her peers, protected in the local community and made to feel safe, then she may not have been relocated. The inability to keep James safe following his first experience of victimisation, the persistent exposure that Melissa had to street-based sexual harassment, and the need to relocate Lara for her own safety all combined to communicate a message that the neighbourhood they lived in was unsafe and would remain unsafe, and that there was nothing that could be done to change that.

In this example, stereotypical societal norms about gender roles informed and impacted James' experience of street-based violence. His later engagement in violent crime on the streets provided him with an audience, and through these performances he could reclaim his masculinity that had been undermined during the first assault he experienced. Sexual harassment and harmful sexual behaviours were being associated with a local park where abuse was expected to occur. His experience of services, along with Melissa's and Lara's, was that incidents were responded to via policing and when this didn't work young people were relocated. This four-stage process of neighbourhood normalisation (illustrated in Figure 7.2) communicates the more complex relationship between the nature of local neighbourhoods and young people's experiences of peer-on-peer abuse.

It is through this process of multi-layering of normalisation that neighbourhood spaces become ones in which 'girls get raped' (as the young men in a case I reviewed described) and that is just it, rather than ones in which young people can form relationships and socialise safely. Through a combination of public space risk and a lack of community safeguarding, the nature of neighbourhoods becomes an important component of a contextual account of peer-on-peer abuse.

In drawing out the contextual nature of peer-on-peer abuse through in-depth consideration of the social sites most consistently associated with the phenomenon, Chapters 4 through 7 have situated the behaviours and individuals documented in Chapter 2 within a social framework. Policy and media accounts of peer-on-peer

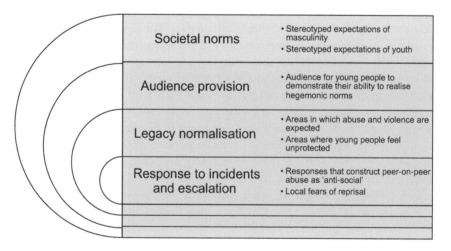

FIGURE 7.2 Neighbourhood normalisation process

abuse in England have generally failed to recognise the interplay between social, as well as familial, contexts which exist for the young people who experience the phenomenon. However, research into different manifestations of peer-on-peer abuse, when drawn together and exemplified using case-review illustrations, provides a cumulative and compelling evidence base that peer-on-peer abuse is contextual in nature and thus requires a contextual response. The following three chapters explore this conclusion with reference to location-based interplay, the notion of consent and adolescent dependency, in order to consider the implications of this account for how professionals, academics and the public engage with the issue of peer-on-peer abuse in the future.

Note

1 Whereas those who abuse younger children do so in private settings – such as homes.

SECTION III

The implications of a contextual account of peer-on-peer abuse

8

LOCATION, LOCATION, LOCATION

The four chapters in the previous section have detailed how and why in Western social-cultural contexts, such as UK, US and Australia, scholars have argued that public and social environments, including peer groups, schools and parks, are associated with both adolescent socialisation and the nature of peer-on-peer abuse. By examining each of these environments in turn this book has built upon this argument and demonstrated not just the significance of these environments but also the importance of the *interplay* between each of these contexts, and the roles of professionals, policymakers, parents, the public and other young people in creating or shaping the nature of these contexts.

Ultimately, it is the interplay between environments, and not just the environments themselves, which requires attention from parents, safeguarding professionals, the media, policymakers and the public more broadly. In the case of Lara, James and Melissa the nature of their families, peer relationships, school environment and their interactions in neighbourhood spaces all informed the incident with which they were all involved. The nature of each of these contexts informed one another and was informed by the professionals, adults and other young people who also used and governed those spaces. When the harmful norms in Melissa's home were reinforced, rather than challenged, by the norms held by her peers and the cultures that had developed in her school, her routes to identify and explore safe relationships were undermined. If Lara's school or her friends had challenged the norms of domestic abuse to which she had been exposed at home, they may have supported her to identify James' behaviour as harmful and seek support from professionals to challenge what James was doing. Furthermore, while abusive peer groups are, on their own, a concern, the extent to which they undermined the authority of James' parents and therefore their capacity to keep him safe from significant harm is also of note.

In considering the relationship between abusive behaviours, practitioner responses and policy engagement within homes, peer groups, schools and neighbourhoods in turn this book have identified that siloed accounts of, and responses to, each social context can only take us so far. While they rightly draw our attention to the fact that peer-on-peer abuse is informed by a range of individual, familial and social characteristics, neither research nor the policy landscape has provided an adequate account of the influence that each of these environments has on one another as abusive behaviours escalate. It is this account of interplay that warrants, and is given, further attention in the remainder of this chapter, through consideration of the:

- Social nature of vulnerability – the way that it is exacerbated, and sometimes constructed, in the interplay between social spaces
- Weight of peer group influence compared with other social fields
- Instances in which young people come together in, or share, abusive spaces
- The direction of contextual influence and interplay

Taken together, these four sections provide an account of the relationship between social field interplay and peer-on-peer abuse – a relationship that requires greater exploration and recognition in research, policy, practice and public discourse.

The social nature of vulnerability

In the absence of a contextual account of peer-on-peer abuse, vulnerability has been constructed through an individualistic lens, pathologising young people and families affected by the phenomenon. Despite an escalating critique of accounts that reduce the risk of peer-on-peer abuse individual characteristics (Henry, 2008; Letourneau & Borduin, 2008; Brodie, 2013; Losel & Bender, 2006), the behaviours and characteristics of individual young people continue to be assessed as predictors of peer-on-peer abuse. This approach to assessment would lead us to conclude that it was something about James' behaviour/personality in and of itself that made him vulnerable to committing a sexual offence. It was the fact that James was missing from home all the time that led him to rape Lara – right? Surely if someone had reduced the extent to which he was out then the rape would never have happened?

The problem with such accounts is that they fail to explore the contextual reasons that led to James being missing in the first place. There is no evidence to suggest that he just woke up one morning and decided to behave like this. James was out on the street with people who had groomed him into offending – a consequence of his need for protection in a local neighbourhood in which young men experienced violence and intimidation. James became vulnerable to peer-on-peer abuse by virtue of his interaction with harmful environments, and not just as a result of his own behaviour. If James hadn't sought protection from a local gang, he may have been victimised by them instead (i.e. Pitts, 2008). Likewise, choosing a different group of friends might have only protected James if violent peers weren't required to give him the social capital needed to navigate his local neighbourhood safely.

The limitations of an individualised account of vulnerability are even more explicit when one considers young people like Lara. While the fact that she had started to truant from school and had been known to children's services in her past may have garnered the concerns of some professionals, these characteristics did not cause the rape she later experienced. There was nothing about Lara's life story that suggested James and Melissa would rape her on that day – arguably Lara would never have been raped if she hadn't been in school with James and Melissa, or if her school had responded differently to James and Melissa's behaviours beforehand. Lara was vulnerable to rape because of the interplay between James, Melissa and their school, as well as the relationship between James' home, peer group and neighbourhood, and the way that this interplayed with the social norms of their school. In essence, Lara's vulnerability was constructed in her school environment and was located in the relationships amongst that environment, other students and the other social-cultural contexts in which they spent their time. All other things being equal, in another school Lara may not have been vulnerable to peer-on-peer abuse at all.

Far from being a finding unique to the experiences of Lara and James, a range of studies have implied, or evidenced, the social construction of vulnerability during adolescence (Barter, et al., 2009; Letourneau & Borduin, 2008; Messerschmidt, 2012b). The process of constructing vulnerability through contextual interplay was evidenced in all nine cases that I reviewed. For some young people, every single environment they were in reinforced and/or failed to challenge harmful norms that informed the abusive behaviours they displayed or were exposed to. Yet others were exposed to, and engaged with, competing social norms in the different environments in which they spent their time – the safe relationships that young people experienced at home, for example, often clashed with the sexual harassment they witnessed in school corridors (EVAW, 2010a; GirlGuiding UK, 2014; Peguero, 2009). Young people's peers in school may have been supportive and safe, but those they encountered on the street often painted a very different, and harmful, picture of friendship (Pitts, 2008; Young & Hallsworth, 2011). Figures 8.1 and 8.2 depict the ways in which these dynamics played out for lead suspects and complainants featured in two of the cases I reviewed. Environments in bold type involved harmful behaviours and norms; underlined type involved harmful norms but safe behaviours; and those in italic type were ones in which safe behaviours and social norms were dominant.

The young people featured in Figures 8.1 and 8.2 were exposed to a range of social scripts. Their vulnerability to being abused, or abusing others, was constructed through the interplay of these scripts and the engagement of young people in the process. Consider the complainant in Figure 8.2. The fact that she was bereaved of

	Case (6) complainant	Case (6) lead suspect
Individual young person	• *Female* • *Age 13* • *Black British* • *No vulnerabilities*	• **Male** • **Age 15** • **Black British** • **Previous victimisation** • **Sexually harasses peers for two years**
Home	• <u>Supportive</u> • <u>Separated parents</u> • <u>Disagreements with mother regarding contact with father</u> • <u>Mother raised concerns about complainant's well-being after assault before disclosure</u>	• **Neglect** • **Older sibling gang-involved** • **Lack of capacity to parent** • **Mother raised concerns about suspect's behaviour two years before rape**
Peer group	• <u>Supportive</u> • <u>Non-abusive</u> • <u>Harmful gender attitudes/beliefs</u>	• **Sexually and physically abusive** • **Gang-affiliated** • **Fights with other young men from different peer groups**
School	• **Gang-affected** • **Sexual harassment and abuse between students** • **Rivalries between students at nearby schools** • **Lack of capacity to safeguard students** • **Aware of escalation but only respond with school-based sanctions**	
Neighbourhood	• *Minimal interaction with, and not harmed in, local neighbourhood* • *Goes to the shops with friends*	• **Physically and emotionally abused in the local neighbourhood** • **Peer group developed there as a means of self-protection**

FIGURE 8.1 Social scripts for Case 6

a parent would usually be considered a characteristic rendering her vulnerable to abuse and exploitation (Berelowitz, et al., 2012). However, had this young woman engaged with different social settings, particularly with a non-abusive peer group and in a safe neighbourhood, then the fact that she was bereaved would probably have been a characteristic that bore little or no relation to a risk of peer-on-peer abuse. For it to be associated with peer-on-peer abuse, the experience and impact of bereavement needed to be exploited by someone (her ex-partner), within environments in which this was possible (her peer group and neighbourhood). Furthermore, the complainants in both Figures 8.1 and 8.2 were in relatively safe homes, but this was insufficient to safeguard them from peer-on-peer abuse. Vulnerability was not only constructed through an exposure to, and interplay, of abusive norms in a range of social settings. It was also informed by the weight of influence that unsafe extra-familial environments had on the behaviour of young people compared with safe familial spaces.

	Case (8) complainant	Case (8) lead suspect
Individual young person	• 15 years old • Female • Asian British • Bereaved of a parent	• 14 years old • Male • Asian British • Previous victimisation
Home	• Described as 'strict' • Parent tried to keep daughter at home and did not seek support when concerned about her • Older sibling had been missing	• *No details of concern collected regarding the family home*
Peer group	• **A small number of young men in the group were gang-associated** • **Three young women had been missing; one has been taken into care** • **Young men had experienced robbery and assaults** • **Individuals were physically violent towards, and in front of, each other** • **Peer group formed in the neighbourhood and a range of schools**	
School	• Not harmed in this environment • Peer group in school was supportive • School was unaware of the risk posed to the complainant in the peer group and neighbourhood and was unable to safeguard	• **Gang-affected** • **Described as having 'airport-style security' at the entrance** • **Physical abuse between students** • **Neither abusive incident nor peer group is located in the school**
Neighbourhood	• **Two local shopkeepers were aware of the risk faced by the complainant and urged her to speak to her family. They were aware but did not try to intervene** • **Approached by young men for sexual activity** • **Physically assaulted on the street and verbally abused**	• **Physically and emotionally abused by his peers and those slightly older** • **Threatened and had his phone stolen** • **Linked to gang-affiliated young men in the local area**

FIGURE 8.2 Social scripts for Case 8

Weight of the peer group

As outlined in Chapter 5, over the past 50 years criminologists and sociologists have produced a wealth of evidence demonstrating the particularly 'weighty' influence that peers have over the decisions that individuals make during adolescence – much of which was discussed by Warr in his 2002 book *Companions in Crime: The Social Aspects of Criminal Conduct*. In this publication Warr chronicles the growing evidence about the cultural contexts around the world in which peer influence is at its strongest. He argues that when young people are making social and immediate decisions, as opposed to long-term decisions about careers, for example, the influence of peers generally outweighs that of parents.

Warr was particularly concerned to explore the nature of peer influence on 'delinquent' behaviours and like others (Gardner & Steinberg, 2005) established that individuals are more influenced by peers to engage in 'risky' behaviours during adolescence than during adulthood or the earlier stages of childhood. A reciprocal relationship between individual decision-making and peer group behaviours has been noted about offending in general and peer-on-peer abuse more specifically. As highlighted in Chapter 6, studies into young people who abuse their partners (i.e. Barter, et al., 2009) and/or their peers (i.e. Letourneau, et al., 2013) have evidenced an association between these behaviours and the nature of young people's peer groups. The weight of peer group influence was clearly evident in the nine cases I reviewed. Peer groups were the most likely environment in which the 145 young people featured in my study encountered harm (Table 8.1).

When the role that young people played in the cases is considered, leaders, followers and bystanders had relatively consistent exposure to abusive norms and behaviours within their peer group, whereas those who led abusive incidents were far more likely to be harmed at home than those who followed them (Table 8.2).

Considered together, the consistent exposure to harm within peer groups, coupled with the relatively inconsistent exposure to harm within homes, demonstrates how living in safe homes was an insufficient protective factor for the young people featured in the cases I reviewed. On these occasions, contextual interplay resulted in harmful norms of peer groups disrupting safe norms of the homes (as explored in Chapters 4 and 5 and demonstrated by the experience of James and his family), while the norms of a young person's home had little bearing on those of their peers. The exception to this rule in the cases reviewed appeared to be with leaders who, unfortunately for the parents of followers, transferred the harmful norms to which

TABLE 8.1 'Harmful' social fields by categorisation of young people

	Complainants (n = 9)	Suspects (n = 76)	Witnesses (n = 45)
'Harmful' home	66%	43%	4%
'Harmful' peer group	89%	100%	100%
'Harmful' school	89%	93%	91%
'Harmful' neighbourhood	89%	75%	100%

TABLE 8.2 'Harmful' social fields by roles in the peer network across all files

	Leaders (n = 20)	Followers (n = 52)	Bystander (+) (n = 31)	Bystander (–)(n = 20)
'Harmful' home	70%	39%	16%	10%
'Harmful' peer group	100%	98%	96%	100%
'Harmful' school	90%	94%	90%	90%
'Harmful' neighbourhood	80%	69%	100%	95%

they were exposed at home into their peer group. The process of rule transference from homes into peer groups (via leaders) would benefit from further study, but it was such a relationship between home and peers that we saw emerge in the case study of Melissa that has run throughout this book. What happened within her family was brought into, and reinforced within, every other environment in which she spent her time.

This is not to say that abusive homes carry more influence than those which promote safe social norms. Evidence in the cases I reviewed, coupled with the wider research outlined earlier in this chapter, suggests that young people who lead abusive incidents are also more likely to experience harm at home, and it is their leadership role that ensures the transference of norms from their homes to their peer groups. This pattern has the potential to be a positive intervention in addition to a risk. If a young person who plays a leadership role within their peer group has been exposed to safe social norms at home, then it could be that they have the power to inform the attitudes of their peers in a pro-social manner. Given, however, the somewhat transient nature of leadership and instigation in group offending (Porter, 2013; Warr, 2002), this initial supposition requires further investigation.

Evidencing the weight of peer group influence is important for how we understand both the help-seeking behaviour of bystanders (demonstrated in Chapter 5) and the abusive behaviours of leaders and followers. Warr (2002) notes that fear of isolation, rejection and a loss of status, in addition to a desire for loyalty, goes some way to explaining the significant influence that peers have over young people during adolescence. While research into peer-on-peer abuse, particularly serious youth violence, has evidenced this in terms of the threats to personal safety following 'snitching' to authorities (Anderson, 1999; Pitts, 2008), wider research into peer group dynamics suggests that, beyond safety, simply the sense of belonging and identity can be sufficient for maintaining peer group conformity. Within the cases I reviewed a desire to remain associated with peers, despite their abusive behaviour, was evidenced particularly by the behaviour of bystanders. While young people in two of the murder cases and five of the rape cases tried to intervene when they saw things were escalating (as noted in Chapter 5), no one spoke to an adult. It seems that young people only intervened to the extent that they could remain part of their peer group – they did not want to end up alone.

This book has demonstrated how the drivers of peer group allegiance can serve to undermine environments that are relatively safe for young people. If the weight of peer group influence can usurp parental authority and limit the ability of young people to seek help from adults, then in many cases it should be central to building any kind of social response to peer-on-peer abuse. If peers could be supported to be pro-social and supportive, and in doing so challenge abusive norms, then they could complement, rather than undermine, interventions with families and individuals affected by peer-on-peer abuse. Without such consideration, peers remain at risk of undermining familial interventions – the bread and butter of child protection work – which, as this book has implied, may do very little in isolation to prevent the abuse of young people by their peers.

Highlighting the extent to which peers can reinforce or challenge familial norms also suggests potential limitations of research, policy and practice which has focused on evidencing and addressing the individual and familial characteristics of those who abuse, or have been abused by, their peers. Arguably, familial factors identified in the literature, such as living with domestic abuse or being abused in early childhood, only become vulnerabilities associated with peer-on-peer abuse when the person experiencing them is part of an abusive peer group and assumes a leadership role in this setting. Furthermore, an absence of these factors may mean very little for young people who are in safe homes but abusive peer groups. Far more evidence is required to establish the extent to which this is true through further study of the construction of vulnerability within the interplay between (rather than a listing or counting of) the peer, familial and individual characteristics associated with peer-on-peer abuse.

Sharing 'abusive' spaces

Beyond their peer groups, the extent to which risk escalates when young people share social spaces with those who abuse them also warrants further attention. Previously in this chapter I suggested that the only factor which made Lara vulnerable to peer-on-peer abuse was that she was in the same school and year group as those who abused her. In all likelihood this would be an oversimplified conclusion to draw. Propinquity, while being a key driver of peer associations (Warr, 2002), is not necessarily sufficient to determine risks of abuse. As Chapter 6 demonstrated, risk escalated between Melissa, James and Lara not because they shared a space (their school) but because the culture of that shared environment was one that reconstructed norms conducive with peer-on-peer abuse. Their school was not equipped to manage the impact of Melissa's home environment and James' experiences of the street on their respective behaviours. If it had been, then her school may have been a perfectly safe place for Lara to be. Furthermore, the risk that Lara faced after the incident couldn't be managed simply by ensuring that she had no further contact with James and Melissa. After she was raped she was physically assaulted by other students, and other boys in school started to approach her for sex. A whole-school approach to abuse and bullying, as promoted by scholars such as Cowie (2011) and outlined in Chapter 6, was clearly required. Such an approach could have addressed the abusive cultural context that had emerged in the space these three young people shared and in doing so disrupted some of the norms that facilitated the rape of Lara.

Returning to Figures 8.1 and 8.2 further illustrates this suggestion. It was in the school in Figure 8.1, and in the peer group in Figure 8.2, that young people came into contact with the peers who later went on to abuse them. In both cases the space that was shared was one in which abusive social norms were prevalent. The latter point is an important one. If complainants and suspects had come together in safe social spaces which could adequately challenge abusive norms and behaviours, then it is possible that peer-on-peer abuse may not have occurred. As such it was the presence and dominance of harmful social norms in these environments, and not just that they were shared by a set of young people, which is important.

Multi-way interplay

To further test the idea of shared abusive spaces, one has to consider the ways in which these environments interact with contexts which are safe and supportive. Returning once again to Figures 8.1 and 8.2 to explain the point, in Figure 8.1 the complainant's peers were relatively safe, but on their own could not undermine the abusive norms of the school they were in; neither could the home of the suspect – mirroring the relationship between Lara's peers and their school, and James' family. When environments are considered in isolation from one another, they appear insufficient in undermining the abusive norms that percolate in shared abusive spaces. But what if the adults, professionals and young people in safe shared spaces were better coordinated – would they be collectively equipped to undermine the norms of harmful, and shared, environments with which they interact?

Rather than influencing one another in a linear fashion, the social environments featured in this book appear to interact reflexively and through this process create conditions conducive with peer-on-peer abuse (Letourneau & Borduin, 2008; Losel & Bender, 2006; Warr, 2002). While some contexts, such as peer groups, appear more dominant in the literature and in the cases I reviewed, it does not seem to be the case that any individual context is subjected to the norms of another in a particular order. For example, some young people who are exposed to domestic abuse between parents/carers run away from home as a means of self-protection (as outlined in Chapter 4). In doing so, some spend time on the street – a context in which they can be exposed to physical abuse and harassment (as documented in Chapter 7). To safely navigate their neighbourhood some young people seek the support or protection of peers who embody the harmful rules of that environment and engage in abusive behaviours on the street and in school to achieve status/safety (evidenced in Chapter 5). Some schools fail to challenge harmful norms underpinning peer-on-peer abuse or the unequal gender relations they reproduce, and host abusive peer groups within a reinforcing context (illustrated in Chapter 6). While this sentence structure suggests a linear order to contextual influence, it is important to note in the cases I reviewed much of this reflexivity occurred relatively simultaneously and recurred over an extended period. It was during this on-going reproduction of harmful norms, within environments in which young people were dependent on a range of professionals for their development and protection, that abusive incidents occurred.

Given this multi-way reflexive interaction it is far too simplistic to suggest, as many politicians and social commentators have stated, that 'it all starts with the parents'. While this may be true for some young people, neither the literature nor the cases I reviewed suggest that parental influence is the driving factor for all, or even most, of the behaviours displayed by young people affected by peer-on-peer abuse in England. All environments featured in this book require the attention of researchers, policymakers and practitioners simultaneously, in order to acknowledge and respond to the contextual interplay that is a central feature of peer-on-peer abuse.

Conclusion: location, location, location

Collectively, the chapters that precede this one have illustrated the significance of locations for the nature of peer-on-peer abuse – not any single location, but all of the environments in which young people spend their time. In providing the space to reflect upon all of these spaces, and illustrate their association through case study evidence, the interplay between contexts comes to the fore. In doing so, questions emerge about the capacity of existing safeguarding policy and practice to recognise and engage with interplays between public and private social fields of influence and in particular their ability to accommodate the fact that:

1   Vulnerability is socially constructed in context
2   Peer groups have significant influence over other social environments, including households, in setting social norms for young people
3   The nature of the environments in which young people form relationships can inform the dynamics of those relationships
4   Environments influence one another in multiple directions

The fact that the 145 young people featured in the cases I reviewed didn't share a single individual characteristic, experience or behaviour that could 'predict' the likelihood of them being abused by, or abusing, their peers demonstrates the importance of contextualising vulnerability. Yet the methods adopted to assess vulnerability are largely concerned with young people's individual life stories, behaviours and characteristics, and sometimes their families, abstracted from the environments in which they spend their time. It seems that rather than use individual vulnerabilities as predictors of peer-on-peer abuse, it may be more helpful to consider vulnerabilities (and their absence) with reference to the contexts with which they interact.

Given the weight of peer group influence within these interactions, the absence of reference to young people's peer relationships within safeguarding policy and media accounts of peer-on-peer abuse is also of note. In all of the political critiques levelled at parents there is very little recognition of the influence that young people's friends can have on the capacity of their parents to keep them safe. Furthermore, the potential influence that young people's friends can have in setting social norms could be embraced as a strength through which to safeguard young people rather than only be perceived as a challenge to be overcome through practitioner intervention.

Finally, it is critical that policymakers and practitioners interrogate and respond to the *nature* of the environments in which abuse occurs. After Lara was raped on a school premise she was moved to another school, as were the young people who abused her. But these actions did not address the influence that the school culture itself had on both the abusive incident and the relationship that developed between Lara, Melissa and James. Nor did they acknowledge that boys in Lara's school reacted to the rape by approaching her for sex rather than reporting the incident to teachers. In a case such as this an intervention was required that invoked the sociological imagination of C Wright Mills (1959) and recognised that the abusive incident in the school was an example of a public issue (affected by the social and cultural fabric of the school environment) rather than a private trouble which could be addressed by solely intervening with the individuals involved. Such an intervention would not only address the environmental dynamics of peer-on-peer abuse but it would also bolster the potential impact of any 1:1 intervention put into place. By addressing the social contexts in which abusive norms develop, 1:1 interventions are able to recognise the social dynamics of young people's decisions – and potentially support them to make safer choices in safer spaces: a process which the following chapter considers.

9

A CONTEXTUAL ACCOUNT OF CHOICE

Dominant approaches to the assessment of, and intervention with, young people affected by peer-on-peer abuse has focused upon identifying and changing individual behaviours which 'contribute to' or are 'associated with' their experiences of harm. However, the account of peer-on-peer abuse presented in this book places those behaviours in wider social and public contexts (and the locational interplay presented in the previous chapter). In doing so it asks questions of the relationship between contexts and behaviours and draws us towards a more social account of the choices that young people make.

The opening chapters of this book questioned what it was about individual young people, and their life histories, that took them to a point where they were abused by, or abused, their peers. So disturbing were the accounts of the behaviours involved that it was all too easy to search for a medically diagnosable or morally judgemental explanation of the phenomenon in question. Reaching these conclusions can make the issue of peer-on-peer abuse feel more manageable – fixing or controlling a small number of problematic individuals rather than an embedded social problem. However, they construct behaviours as the consequence of choices abstracted from the contexts in which they take place – and in this sense peer-on-peer abuse can be conceived of as a 'private trouble' caused by the decisions of individuals rather than 'public issues' associated with the social conditions of the societies in which we live (Jenks, 2005; Mills, 1959). However, the evidenced scale (Chapter 2) and environmental dynamics (Chapters 4–7) of the issue signifies that intervening with individuals affected by peer-on-peer abuse may be insufficient. Biological, behavioural or moral accounts of the choices made by young people affected by peer-on-peer abuse are too limited to engage with the social conditions (both limitations and freedoms) in which the issue occurs. They don't help to explain why James raped Lara, why Lara's friends didn't recognise his behaviour as abusive, or why Melissa instigated the process. It was only by considering the interplay between the homes, peer groups, school and neighbourhood in which these three spent their time, and their engagement with these spaces, that the motivation for, and development of their behaviours, came to light.

But what are the practice and policy implications of understanding young people's choices in this way? This chapter considers this question by outlining the legal and policy framework for how 'choice' is constructed by policy and legislation in England and Wales and then critically assessing this construction with reference to the account of peer-on-peer abuse documented in this book. In doing so, it raises questions about how the agency of young people is conceived of by policymakers, practitioners and researchers concerned with violence, abuse and child protection and adds to wider calls which have been made for a social account of the choices made by young people.

Understanding the policy of choice: consent, responsibility and culpability

The choices made by young people who are abused by, or who abuse, their peers can be conceptualised in many ways. For this chapter the terms 'consent', 'responsibility' and 'culpability' are drawn upon to explore how the choices of young people affected by, or involved in, peer-on-peer abuse have been constructed in policy and practice. These three terms all have statutory and legal associations that inform the response of professionals, the media and the public to instances of peer-on-peer abuse, and are drawn upon here in that regard.

In England and Wales, the statutory definition of consent to sexual activity is made up of two parts – the first makes reference to the capacity of an individual to make a choice and the second to their freedom to make that choice:

> Section 74 defines consent as 'if he agrees by choice, and has the freedom and capacity to make that choice'. Prosecutors should consider this in two stages. They are:
>
> • Whether a complainant had the capacity (i.e. the age and understanding) to make a choice about whether or not to take part in the sexual activity at the time in question.
> • Whether he or she was in a position to make that choice freely, and was not constrained in any way. Assuming that the complainant had both the freedom and capacity to consent, the crucial question is whether the complainant agrees to the activity by choice (Crown Prosecution Service, 2003).

This definition of consent is specifically related to sexual activity, and therefore the sexually abusive elements of peer-on-peer abuse. However, the notions of capacity and freedom that it draws upon can also be held in mind for young people's choices more broadly albeit primarily those made by young people who are abused by their peers.

For those young people who abuse peers, notions of both 'responsibility' and 'culpability', in addition to 'capacity', come into play. According to the Oxford English Dictionary an individual is culpable for an act when they are 'deserving of blame' for it. This has been interpreted in policy, practice and legislation through the concept of *mens rea* and factors which may aggravate or mitigate culpability. The term *mens rea* makes reference to the criminal intent – or state of mind – that is required for someone to be considered culpable of a criminal element of an act – for this book, the criminal element of physical, sexual and/or emotional abuse. For young people in England and Wales this becomes relevant once they reach the age of 10 – the current legal age of criminal responsibility. By criminally responsible, the law infers that an individual understands that what they have done is criminal and that they also understand the consequences of their actions, that is, they are 'capable of committing a crime and old enough to stand trial and be convicted of a criminal offence' (NSPCC, 2016). Therefore, from the age of 10 onwards an individual in England and Wales can be considered criminally responsible for abusing a peer, and through the application of *mens rea*, culpable for their abusive behaviours.

It is interesting to note that differing levels of consideration are given to contextual factors within the definitions of consent, criminal responsibility and culpability. It is only the definition of consent that considers the contexts in which individuals make choices. This is achieved with reference to the term 'freedom' which creates a space to consider social, as well as physical, limitations that can affect a person's ability to consent. Whereas, the definition of 'criminal responsibility' is based upon whether an individual understood that what they were doing was wrong (i.e. criminal), and culpability is defined in terms of who was responsible, to blame, for what occurred. It is possible to conclude that an individual is responsible for what they did and/or that they understood that their actions were wrong without considering any contextual limitations that may have restricted the choices available to them in a way that is possible for the definition of consent. Having said this, however, statutory guidance does recognise factors that may aggravate or mitigate the culpability of an individual which provides a route to consider contextual factors associated with their actions. Take the offence of 'Wounding or Inflicting Grievous Bodily Harm with Intent' as an example. Crown Prosecution Service guidelines identify factors that would aggravate or mitigate the culpability of an individual who was responsible for such an offence as outlined in Table 9.1.

Most of the culpability factors considered in Table 9.1 relate to an individual's capacity to harm, or their intention to harm, as opposed to any social factors which may limit their freedom (i.e. agency) within a given set of circumstances. The exception to this is consideration of group roles and hierarchies involved in the commission of an offence – a contextual factor of particular relevance to peer-on-peer abuse. Given the weight of peer group influence on the choices that young people make (as outlined in Chapter 5), the fact that it can be drawn upon as both a mitigating and aggravating factor when assessing culpability is important. However, as is explored later in this chapter, distinguishing mitigating and aggravating factors solely on the grounds of an individual's role within a peer group may be limited.

TABLE 9.1 Wounding or inflicting grievous bodily harm with intent – aggravating and mitigating factors

Statutory aggravating factors	Offence racially or religiously aggravated
	Offence motivated by, or demonstrating, hostility to the victim based on his or her sexual orientation (or presumed sexual orientation)
	Offence motivated by, or demonstrating, hostility to the victim based on the victim's disability (or presumed disability)
Other aggravating factors	A significant degree of premeditation
	Use of weapon or weapon equivalent (for example, shod foot, head-butting, use of acid, use of animal)
	Intention to commit more serious harm than actually resulted from the offence
	Deliberately causes more harm than is necessary for commission of offence
	Deliberate targeting of vulnerable victim
	Leading role in group or gang
	Offence motivated by, or demonstrating, hostility based on the victim's age, sex, gender identity (or presumed gender identity)
Factors indicating lower culpability	Subordinate role in group or gang
	A greater degree of provocation than normally expected
	Lack of premeditation
	Mental disorder or learning disability, where linked to commission of the offence
	Excessive self-defence

Except for considering group roles to assess culpability, in England and Wales we are positioned to explore the culpability and responsibility of those who abuse their peers largely with reference to capacity alone. Whereas, for those who are abused, their freedom, as well as capacity, can be drawn upon to build a more social account of the choices that they make. Holding this legal framework in mind, the remainder of this chapter considers the account of peer-on-peer abuse presented in this book and the implications of it for how policy and practice engage with the choices of young people affected by, or involved in, peer-on-peer abuse with reference to:

- Overlaps between 'victim' and 'perpetrator' identities
- Young people who act in ways to survive or pursue safety in harmful contexts
- The potential to create safe spaces in which those affected by peer-on-peer abuse can make alternative choices

Drawing upon evidence of the contextual interplays associated with peer-on-peer abuse considered in the previous chapter, the legal and policy framework outlined previously, and its practical application, is called into question. A contextual account of peer-on-peer abuse highlights the social lens required to explore 'freedom' as a critical factor to understanding culpability and responsibility as well as consent. In addition, it draws attention to the complexity of group roles which, when explored in isolation as either mitigating or aggravating factors rather than through a social lens, can be oversimplified and misunderstood. Building upon Pearce's social model of consent (2013), the evidence in this chapter indicates that the behaviours of those affected by peer-on-peer abuse are best understood, and responded to, through a social model of choice.

Victim/perpetrator overlap

An extensive international evidence base clearly demonstrates that young people abuse their peers: the picture painted in this book, and illustrated in the cases I reviewed, does not seek to dispute this fact. There is no denying that Melissa and James raped Lara. In fact, in all of the cases I reviewed for this book, along with others I have encountered in my work with local authorities across England since, there is no doubt that some young people have abused their peers. The challenge, and debate, arises when one seeks to attach victim or perpetrator status, in a static fashion, to those involved. When I use the cases featured in this book in training sessions, practitioners often ask me, 'So was Melissa a perpetrator or a victim?' They want to know which of the two labels to apply to Melissa so that they can refer her to an appropriate service – either a justice or welfare intervention. However, such an approach enforces an artificial victim/perpetrator dyad to young people who are both abused and abusive, sometimes simultaneously (Criminal Justice Joint Inspection, 2013). The contextual lens provided by this book affords us an opportunity to explore the limitations of such a challenging binary and consider the implications for how culpability is conceived in policy and practice when we abandon such a rigid approach.

The literature and case view evidence in this book illustrates the contextual life histories of young people affected by peer-on-peer abuse (Anderson, 1999; Catch 22, 2013; Chung, 2005; Letourneau & Borduin, 2008; Messerschmidt, 2012b; Ringrose, et al., 2011; Warr, 2002). These life stories include multi-layered experiences of victimisation that young people encounter and engage in as they move in and out of different social contexts. The nuanced message that emerges about victimisation, instigation and perpetration suggests that narratives of passive victims and predatory perpetrators do not always accurately reflect cases of peer-on-peer abuse – not just the experiences of suspects, but of complainants too (Melrose, 2013; Pitts, 2013).

Let's take James as an example and compare him with other young men who featured in the cases I reviewed. Unlike his co-defendant Melissa, James' home was safe and stable, yet both he and his older brother had abused their peers in gang-associated contexts. Far from fitting the stereotype of 'broken family = broken child', James' family did not provide a source of motivation for his trajectory into abusive behaviours and contexts. However, his family lost control over him in a power struggle with his peers and the influence of the street in a manner documented in a range of studies and in other cases I reviewed as outlined in Chapter 4 (Aisenberg & Herrenkohl, 2008; Catch 22, 2013; Pitts, 2008). Not only was James' family less powerful than his peers, but also so was James who, by virtue of his age and experiences (Chapter 5), was groomed by those who were older than he so that he could offend on their behalf. He was abused repeatedly on the street (Chapter 7), and increasingly so, from the age of 10 – and his peers were both his protection and primary source of harm. The adults around James, both relatives and professionals, failed to, and in some respects were unable to, keep him safe; opportunities were missed to disrupt the escalating risks that he faced and posed to others. In this context James found power in school through the abuse of his peers (Chapter 6). A sense of power enabled him to realise those stereotyped, societal ideals of masculinity that had been undermined when he was abused in his local community. James was not simply a perpetrator – he was a young person, a child, who had been victimised by peers for four years while simultaneously relying on them for protection and increasingly victimising others. This reality does not justify or excuse what he did to Lara, but it demonstrates that there were multiple power imbalances at play at the point of the rape and that preventing it required all of them to be addressed.

James' life narrative reflects accounts of other young people who featured in other cases I reviewed and the wider evidence base. Like James, another young man – who was murdered in Case 7 – had begun associating with gang-involved peers and truanting from school following his experiences of robbery and violence in community contexts. For this young man, however, his association with violent peers, and the fact that he wasn't in school, created the social conditions for his murder – a very different outcome, albeit similar trajectory, to that of James. Do experiences such as these mean that this young man was 'to blame' or 'responsible' for his murder? Firstly, he could have done all of those things and not been murdered – in the same way that James was not. Secondly, he made choices in the build-up to his murder relevant to the risky contexts in which he found himself. While he was not a 'passive victim', a puppet or subject that would have made it easier for us to conceptualise his victimhood, he was still victimised.

The conceptual, strategic and practical challenges of accommodating the victimisation of young people who act in ways that are deemed to increase the likelihood that they will come to harm are documented in serious case reviews and inquiries into young people's experiences of exploitation and violence in England (Berelowitz, et al., 2013; Jay, 2014; Johnson, 2013). In her inquiry into the sexual exploitation of young people in Rotherham, Professor Jay stated:

> Police and children's social care were ineffective and seemed to blame the child. A core assessment was done but could not be traced on the file. An initial assessment accurately described the risks to Child D but appeared to

> blame her for 'placing herself at risk of sexual exploitation and danger'. Other than Risky Business, agencies showed no comprehension that she had been groomed at 13, that she was terrified of the perpetrators, and that her attempts to placate them were themselves a symptom of the serious emotional harm that CSE had caused her.
>
> *(Jay, 2014:39)*

In the struggle to recognise both agency and victimization, some practitioners have held young people, and their 'risky behaviours', as responsible for the abuse that they later experience. Such a position loomed large in the cases I reviewed, with the behaviour of young people, particularly young women who were sexually assaulted and young men who were gang-affiliated, being focused on as the root cause of their abusive experience. For example, investigation files reviewed for cases featured emails and assessments written by practitioners who described young women who had been sexually exploited by their peers as 'sexually aware', 'sexually experienced', 'consenting albeit unwittingly' and 'putting her friends above all others'. All of these phrases served to make central the young person's role, and the role of their agency, in the escalation towards their own abusive experience. Mirroring criticisms levelled at practitioners in serious case reviews, the lack of passivity amongst victims in the cases I reviewed was drawn upon by practitioners to apportion responsibility or to assert that young people in a sense 'chose' to be abused. In late 2015 I was delivering a training session when one frustrated practitioner said to me, 'Well who is to blame then? If you (the practitioner) and their parents have been telling them to stay in and they insist on going out and breaking rules, and then get raped, who is to blame?' Despite public outcry about victim-blaming in the same year (The Guardian, 2015), such attitudes and questions persist amongst some professionals.

Ultimately, a contextual account highlights that while, in cases of peer-on-peer abuse, some young people abuse others, a passive victim/predatory perpetrator label cannot be used to characterise those involved, particularly if this labelling process is intended to inform the professional response to an incident. To prevent James from harming others, both his victimisation and his own abusive behaviours required attention – and most importantly, the harmful contexts in which those experiences and behaviours emerged. Some young people who are abusive have power over the person that they abuse while simultaneously having no power over or within the group with whom they are abusive, and/or are arguably groomed to abuse by the contexts and associations with which they interact. Documenting such experiences leads to a consideration of another aspect of choice – motive.

Motive: acts of survival and pursuits of safety

Research has identified a number of motives for why young people abuse their peers. Pursuits of status and/or safety, trauma from past experiences of abuse, psychological dysfunction, loyalty to peer groups who are abusive and/or fear of isolation from them and normalised experiences of violence are just a few explanations that have been offered – many of which have been explored throughout this book (Gardner & Steinberg, 2005; Hackett, 2014; Losel & Bender, 2006; Messerschmidt, 2012a; Warr, 2002; Woodhams, 2013). Bourdieu, and his theoretical concepts which underpin this book, contends that individuals are motivated to act in pursuit of cultural status (Bourdieu, 1992).

According to Bourdieu's social lens, individuals will reproduce harmful rules when engaging in social fields, even when doing so may reinforce their own subordination, in a bid to climb the status ladder and in the absence of an interaction with a field that affords an individual with an alternative. Bourdieu refers to this behaviour as 'symbolic violence', and it has been used by scholars to explore a range of social issues related to peer-on-peer abuse, including consent (Powell, 2010) and gang association (Pitts, 2013). In keeping with this train of thought, research into gang affiliation, sexual exploitation and serious youth violence routinely suggests that abusive behaviours, and non-disclosure of abusive experiences, can be associated with young people's attempts at surviving or navigating abusive contexts (Beckett, et al., 2013; Young & Hallsworth, 2011; Melrose, 2013). In these instances what may appear an irrational and harmful choice in a safe context can become a rational choice within a context that is unsafe (Cepeda & Valdez, 2003).

Some of the reasons for why young people did what they did in the cases I reviewed will never be known – evidence within investigation files did not always provide an answer or even an indication. However, the information that was available is in keeping with the wider arguments made by Cepeda, Valdez and others that young people act in order to survive in harmful environments and both chimes with and calls into question Bourdieu's social theory. It appears true that young people featured in the cases acted in ways that maintained harmful rules and sustained their subordination in abusive social conditions as Bourdieu contends. However, case review evidence also implied that they did so in an ultimate pursuit of safety rather than to achieve cultural status – contrary to Bourdieu's theory. In this sense young people engaged in harmful behaviours as a means of surviving in harmful spaces – suggesting that safety was a motor of human action. In some instances achieving cultural status was a means to achieving safety, but in other instances securing safety impacted negatively on the cultural status of those involved.

When complainants, suspects and witnesses in the cases I reviewed seemingly engaged in acts of symbolic violence, their behaviours sustained harmful social norms within a range of contexts while supporting them to achieve some sense of safety. Such behaviour created a 'spectrum of safety' for the 145 young people who featured. For example, complainants talked about not saying 'no' during a sexual assault to avoid physical violence. In such examples young women made constrained choices determined by the parameters of their field: they were not consenting to the sexual activity that took place while also seeking protection from physical violence. Likewise, suspects who took part in the murder or rape of their peers verbalised being unable to turn against the peer group for fear of physical violence and/or social isolation. Bystanders failed to intervene during escalation

TABLE 9.2 Melissa's social field summary

Home	Continuous exposure to domestic abuse across all of her father's relationships. Father involved in violent crime. Mother blames Lara for being raped.
Peers	Female peer is being sexually exploited by a local group of boys. Young men she spends her time with are involved in violent crime.
School	Young women are sexually harassed in school corridors. Young men have physically assaulted young women in the playground in view of staff. Responses have been confined to school sanctions (detentions, etc.).
Neighbourhood	She has been approached by young men on the street and harassed.

periods in ways that would have compromised their physical safety – for example, they counselled their friends against abusive behaviours but didn't tell an adult for fear of reprisals or social isolation from their peer network. All of these behaviours sustained unsafe environments in the pursuit of individual (physical) safety.

In the cases I reviewed, this pursuit of safety was particularly evident amongst young people who were not afforded access to a field with an alternative social script. This aspect of Bourdieu's social theory – the reconstruction of harmful social rules in the absence of any engagement of a field that promoted an alternative – was evident in case file material. Taking Melissa as an example – in every social field in which she spent time she encountered harmful gender power relations (Table 9.2).

Each field reinforced one another, chronically limiting Melissa's exposure to that which was alternative – a clear requirement of Bourdieu's theory to enable individuals to generate and engage in new and different rules to that with which they have previously embodied. In the years before the rape, Melissa had witnessed her father emotionally and physically abuse her mother and had lived through her mother's attempted suicide and on-going mental health issues. Instead of providing her with an alternative social script, the peer group, school and neighbourhood locations in which Melissa spent her time also featured the abuse of women and girls, by men and boys, the impact of which was not addressed by being placed on a child protection plan for neglect. Instead, wherever she was Melissa received the message that women were the abused and men were the abuser.

Through this process Melissa made a choice. At home, amongst her peers and on the street she was relatively powerless and experienced little control. In school, Melissa was able to regain control and she did this through the abuse of others. Melissa's choices ultimately reinforced harmful gender relations in her school and amongst her peers. By instigating the rape of Lara she continued the subordination and abuse of young women and arguably used this to establish a sense of power for herself. The rules may not have applied to Melissa, but she drew upon them (while also challenging them) in order to secure safety. It is arguably impossible to conceptualise the motivation for Melissa's choices when they are viewed in isolation of this wider social context. According to Bourdieu, simply demonstrating or telling

Melissa about an alternative course of action (and accompanying set of social rules) would have been insufficient. Melissa needed to engage in an alternative social field in order to embody alternative social rules and safely realise behaviours that were non-abusive.

Creating safe spaces for alternative action

When young people's choices are framed with reference to the social rules in which they are engaged, notions such as culpability become harder to apply. Who/ what was to 'blame' for James' abusive behaviours? What would have contributed to him following a different course of action? According to Bourdieu, and the theoretical framework employed throughout his book, James needed to engage in a social field where an alternative set of rules were in operation in order for him to act differently.

Unlike Melissa, James was living in a safe family – and one could therefore argue that he had a safe space in which to engage in non-abusive behaviours. In keeping with research and case review evidence presented in Chapter 4, many parents/carers seek to provide young people with a field (their home) in which non-abusive social rules are promoted (Aisenberg & Herrenkohl, 2008; Catch 22, 2013; Pitts, 2008; Shuker, 2013a; Thomas, 2015). However, being in a safe family did not necessarily equip James with a space in which to explore alternative peer interactions – for two main reasons. Firstly, the familial environment is not the one in which young people, like James, enter into friendships/intimate relationships, nor is it an environment in which the social norms of peer relationships form (Catch 22, 2013; Chung, 2005; Losel & Bender, 2006). Secondly, the fact that James was in a safe family did not provide him with the cultural, social or economic capital to achieve safety when on the streets – and it was this desire for safety in this social space that motivated his engagement in harmful social rules. The social capital afforded to him by his peer group meant he could achieve some sense of safety on the street, and achieve greater status, and therefore sense of control and safety within school. Young people therefore not only need a safe environment, but also they need a safe environment which is relevant to the process of adolescent socialisation and the forming of peer relationships.

There are two key ways in which policy and practice could afford young people safe environments in which to engage with non-abusive social norms. Practice could focus on disrupting harmful norms in operation on the streets (that informed the choices that James made) – as documented in Chapter 7. Bystander intervention, situational crime prevention and other lessons from community safety intervention and research could all be leveraged to create a sense of safety on the streets in which James would no longer be reliant on the social capital afforded to him by a violent peer group. Such approaches would seek to change the social rules at play on the street in order to change the individual decisions of James. A second option would be to expose James, and young people like Melissa, to an alternative set of peer relationships. The provision of youth services, for example, has the potential to introduce young people to alternative friendships within social fields in which it is safe to engage with peers in a non-abusive way. While this approach wouldn't have ensured that James was safe on the streets, it would have given him an experience of what is was like to have safe peer relationships. Likewise, it would have allowed Melissa to engage in, and witness, friendships in which young women were not abused – a potentially powerful counter-narrative to that which she was experiencing in all the social fields in which she spent her time.

If practice responses to peer-on-peer abuse were to move in the direction just outlined, they would recognise the significance of peer relationships and the importance of creating contexts in which young people can make safer choices. However, the direction of policy in the field of child protection to date has focused on intervening with children's families (Chapter 4) or delivering 1:1 intervention with individual young people who are involved in peer-on-peer abuse. Neither of these approaches to service development is designed to create protective, *relevant* environments in which young people can make safer choices associated with their experiences of peer-on-peer abuse. The current funding landscape appears persistently focused on delivering awareness-raising or behaviour-modification programmes to change the decisions that young people make, in the absence of services which can offer environments in which safe decisions can be practiced. These models of practice are supported by evaluation, policy and legislative frameworks that all promote individualised accounts of choice. Interventions are evaluated as successful when they change the behaviour of individuals – regardless of the contexts in which those behaviours are displayed. Policymakers continue to focus largely on the provision of family intervention rather than authorise consistent safeguarding interventions into community or school contexts. Both of these approaches are consistent with a legislative framework that judges the culpability of those involved in peer-on-peer abuse largely with reference to their individual decisions, understanding and behaviours, rather than the environments in which those behaviours form.

Conclusion: a contextual account of choice

The dynamic and social nature of choice implied by a contextual reading of the peer-on-peer abuse evidence base suggests policy and practice needs to recognise:

- The environmental, social and cultural constraints on choice
- The conditions in which young people exercise agency
- Occasions in which young people experience limited choices as opposed to having no choice at all

As it stands the legislative definition of 'consent' enables a contextual account of choice through recognition of the factors that may compromise the freedom of those who are abused. However, as evidenced in this chapter this definition of consent to sexual activity does not provide a legislative, policy or practice framework capable of engaging with the overlap between victimisation and perpetration; the social conditions in which harmful behaviours can provide a route to safety; or the need to create safe environments in which young people who have been abusive can make alternative choices. This limitation is particularly evident in policy approaches to conceptualising the culpability and responsibility of young people who are abusive and in the 1:1 approach offered to impact the behaviours of young people who have been abused.

Ultimately, a contextual account of peer-on-peer abuse allows for a large area of grey – in which choices are made but social conditions have compromised the freedom and/or capacity of a young person to make a safe choice. The definition of consent to sexual activity goes some way, in theory, towards recognising this dynamic for young people who are sexually abused. However, practice responses have illustrated the individualised interpretation of the decisions that young people make when they are abused by peers. Furthermore, for young people abused in others ways – such as those killed by peers in acts of serious youth violence, and for young people identified as abusive, the contextual nature of their choices is yet to be fully considered in policy and practice. To say that a young person is criminally responsible or culpable for what they did simply tells us that they did those behaviours – it fails to highlight how they could have chosen differently, why they made the choices that they did and what the professional engagement could have been, or was, in both of these regards. If we present a contextual account of choice, we are then required to develop a contextual practice response that appropriately engages with the agency that young people display within contexts that are managed by a wide range of social actors. The following chapter explores the implications of this – particularly for child protection, safeguarding and social care frameworks – and presents a contextualised relationship of dependency between young people affected by peer-on-peer abuse and the professionals, peers and members of the public who shape the nature of the social spaces in which such abuse occurs.

10

AGENCY AND DEPENDENCY

A contextual account of childhood

A social account of choice presented in the previous chapter raises questions about the sufficiency of 1:1 and family interventions for young people affected by peer-on-peer abuse. This chapter explores the way in which child protection and safeguarding policy and practice engages with the choices made by young people who abuse, or are abused by, their peers – when these choices are viewed within the contextual lens presented in this book. In doing so the chapter highlights the dependency that young people and their families have on professionals to create safe extra-familial contexts that both set the stage upon which young people form healthy and non-abusive relationships and impact the nature of their familial environments.

To begin this process, instead of in a school or on the street, consider that Lara was raped in her home when she was 14 and James was victimised in his from the age of 10. If this had happened, professionals would have responded in accordance with traditional child protection procedures. They would have assessed each home environment, and the capacity of the adults who were responsible for it, to keep James and Lara safe while they were there. They would have removed the individuals who had abused Lara and James from their respective homes. It is likely that they would have also considered whether any other children who were living with Lara and James were also at risk of abuse. Following assessment a decision would have been made regarding the level of intervention required with the family involved. Different approaches would have been offered to support the safe carers of Lara and James to prevent them from being harmed at home again. James and Lara would have been removed from their homes as a last resort if all other attempts to make their homes safe had failed. While their parents/carers were being supported, Lara and James may have also received 1:1 intervention to address how these experiences of abuse had affected their well-being and to re-establish a secure relationship with their safe parent or carer.

The foregoing approach recognises Lara and James as dependent upon adults for their safety and identifies parents or carers as the adults responsible for managing/ensuring the safety of Lara and James when they are at home. Acknowledging dependency in this manner does not undermine any recognition of Lara or James as social agents. They would have chosen to eat foods at home at certain times of day, switch on the television, talk to those they lived with, sit with them and play a board game, etc. By making choices to use, and spend time, in their home environment, neither Lara nor James was responsible for any abuse that they experienced within it.

In such a scenario it is highly unlikely that, having been abused at home, Lara and James would have been referred for 1:1 support without any professionals visiting their homes or engaging with the adults who were responsible for their care while they were there. Such a response would have left Lara and James in unsafe home environments, with people who had abused them. The 1:1 intervention they received would have supported them to better understand their experience and recognise how unsafe they were but on its own would not have made their homes safe. It is also improbable that any siblings of Lara and James would have been presumed safe in those homes without proper investigation and, where necessary, intervention.

And yet when we change the location of abuse from home to school or street (and therefore reflect on accounts of peer-on-peer abuse documented in this book), it is these improbable service responses that emerge. Many young people like Lara who are abused by peers are provided 1:1 support to manage the impact of their experiences (or to navigate harmful environments by making 'safer' choices) and if this fails may be relocated to a different school or local authority to get them away from abusive social contexts (Catch 22, 2013; Gadd, et al., 2013; Hackett, 2014; Shuker, 2013a). The schools or streets in which they were abused, and the professionals responsible for managing these localities, are not always the subject of an assessment or intervention as part of the safeguarding response – in the way that parents and homes are. Other young people who use those schools or streets alongside young people like Lara and James are not the subject of assessment in the way that siblings would be. The intervention circles around the individuals affected – and not the environments in which they are abused.

Because peer-on-peer abuse presents a risk of significant harm to young people, many would argue that it is a child protection issue that requires a safeguarding response led by social care. And yet, the child protection procedures that are called upon when young people are abused in their homes appear non-transferable to other contexts in which young people are abused. The account presented in this book has indicated that risks associated with the peer-on-peer abuse exist beyond young people's homes and are primarily located in public and social spaces. In this sense adults, and particularly professionals, who manage and use the extra-familial contexts in which young people encounter abuse have a role to play in keeping young people safe while they are there. From their journeys on public transport, to time spent in schools, parks, youth clubs and shopping centres, young people are dependent upon professionals, peers and adult members of the public (i.e. all those who manage or use those spaces) to keep them safe. Running in tandem with this dependency is the ability of young people to make choices and exercise agency when in those same spaces – in the same way that they would do when at home.

If we want to respond to peer-on-peer abuse as a child protection issue, opportunities to apply, extend, develop or reform child protection procedures to respond to public and social contexts need to be identified. Building on the contextual account of choice outlined in the previous chapter, this chapter discusses this challenge and identifies potential routes to recognise the dependency that young people have on professionals, peers and other adults when they are at risk in environments beyond the influence of their families. By recognising both the contextual nature of young people's agency and the dependency that young people have on a range of social actors to secure their safety, a social response to peer-on-peer abuse is made possible. In particular this chapter explores:

- The ways in which young people are dependent upon adults for setting standards and maintaining order, thereby creating cultures of safety within social contexts
- Young people's dependency upon peers for setting social norms
- Agency as informed by a suite of 'safe' choices within any given social context, and therefore directly informed by dependency on adults responsible for that context

In doing so, the discussion uses the contextual account of peer-on-peer abuse presented in this book to build upon calls that have been made for less individualised (Parton, 2014) and more social (Featherstone, et al., 2016) models of child protection. It articulates the importance of, and opportunity to develop, a reformed approach to safeguarding which better recognises the social nature of the risks posed to young people and is therefore better equipped to keep them safe.

Setting standards, maintaining order: professionals and public space cultures

As Chapters 4 to 7 of this book have highlighted, abuse between young people does not occur in a vacuum but rather within interplays between contexts and individual agency. While these contexts are often beyond the boundaries of young people's homes, they are not beyond the boundaries of all professional and/or adult influence. The normalisation of sexual harassment, bullying and gendered stereotypes in schools identified in Chapter 6 contribute to creating educational contexts conducive with peer-on-peer abuse (Cowie, 2011; EVAW, 2010a; Frosh, et al., 2002; Peguero, 2009; Ringrose, et al., 2011). The same can be said of streets and other public spaces explored in Chapter 7 in which sexual harassment, physical violence and robbery colour young people's experiences of peer socialisation (Bates, 2014; Squires & Goldsmith, 2011). In these contexts, professionals, young people and the general public interact with abusive norms and in doing so collectively fail to set dominant healthy relational standards, suppress violence or maintain order. Whereas when these contexts are safe, and are not ones in which young people encounter violence and abuse, professionals, young people and members of the general public play a role in maintaining order and sustaining healthy social and protective norms in which young people can form safe peer relationships.

At present there is some, albeit limited, policy guidance which recognises the relationship just outlined. Statutory guidance for *Keeping Children Safe in Education* in addition to guidance documents for responding to bullying, gang association and radicalisation (all referenced in Chapter 6) recognise the role professionals play in maintaining order within educational settings. Collectively these documents suggest a relationship between the behaviours of staff and students within schools and the ability of a school environment to safeguard those within it. Likewise, government departments have issued policy, legislation and guidance to advise community safety practices that ensure the well-being of young people in public spaces (Chapter 7). Tools such as anti-social behaviour orders, gang injunctions and other behaviour and dispersal orders have all been provided by the government to respond to risk in public spaces. These tools are designed to equip police forces and councils to disrupt risk from escalating by intervening with individuals or groups who have demonstrated concerning behaviours in local communities. However, the general focus of all of these provisions is the management of individual behaviour rather than the redressing of social norms within harmful contexts. Existing policy frameworks that relate to neighbourhoods and schools do not recognise the role that professionals play in creating, challenging or reinforcing harmful or healthy social norms within the contexts that they manage. In this sense policy and practice is, at this stage, reactive and focused on maintaining order via the disruption of individuals – rather than proactively concerned with creating safe contexts for adolescent socialisation by empowering a range of professionals to recognise the influence that they have in setting social norms of the contexts that they manage.

Research into bystander intervention, referenced on multiple occasions throughout this book, has evidenced the role that leaders play within institutions in creating contexts that enable staff members to intervene when they witness problematic behaviours. Studies suggest that, for individuals to intervene with abusive behaviours, they need to feel like they are acting in accordance with social norms that promote their intervention. Therefore, school leaders have a role to play in creating social norms that enable staff and students to intervene and disrupt abusive behaviours that they may encounter. In the absence of this wider leadership, individuals can still intervene but without the support of adults, professionals and others peers – and potentially put themselves at risk as some young people did in Chapter 5.

Furthermore, existing approaches to intervention and national policy frameworks support professionals to intervene with individual incidents. Harmful behaviours are managed via the disruption of people and the sanctioning of individuals involved in abusive incidents. However, individual case management is not necessarily sufficient to inform cultural norms or to challenge harmful social contexts in which such behaviours occur. In the cases I reviewed, professionals in schools (teachers, learning mentors, pastoral care) and on the streets (police, transport providers, park wardens, housing caretakers) responded to abusive incidents, but struggled to identify, assess and address the cumulative impact of these incidents on the social and cultural norms of those contexts. Responses to individual incidents do contribute to expectations within any given social field – the inability of professionals to respond to harmful sexual behaviours displayed by young people in Lara's school set certain expectations amongst Lara's peers about what behaviour was acceptable and what was not. However, holding individual practices within a wider framework – the whole-school and situational crime-prevention approaches outlined in Chapters 6 and 7 – has the potential to address the cumulative impact of individual incidents and proactively set healthy social standards.

The role that professionals play in setting standards within contexts that they manage is similar to that played by parents/carers in the home. While a range of social actors may engage with the rules of a home (other young people, friends of the parents, wider family members, etc.) child protection assessments are primarily focused on the role of parents in setting standards and maintaining order in that environment. When peer-on-peer abuse occurs in other settings, the national policy landscape doesn't yet allow for similar consideration of the roles played by those who manage school or community contexts, but the evidence in this book suggests an opportunity for it to do so. Social workers, who assess risk within families, are not currently equipped or trained to assess risk in other social spaces or the role of other leaders (beyond families) in creating safety in those spaces. Given that young people encounter peer-on-peer abuse in other social spaces, consideration of how to extend child protection policy in this regard could be helpful. If achieved, it would provide an avenue through which to recognise the role that young people play as social agents within a range of social and public contexts while also noting the dependency that they have on professionals to set standards of behaviour within those settings.

Peer dependency, influence and social norms

While the foregoing characterisation of agency and dependency identifies ways in which professionals engage with, and inform, young people's choices, the evidence presented in this book highlights the role of peer influence in setting social norms, and the peer group as a context in which choices are limited. Unlike schools, buses or parks, peer groups are arguably less controlled by adults or professionals, and therefore present a more challenging proposition to traditional child protection processes. For example, if a young person is harmed in their friendship group rather than their home, school or neighbourhood, identifying the individual/s responsible for the management or safety of that peer group is a less straightforward proposition. And yet, research into peer group norms, peer group behaviours and group-based offending, in addition to studies of peer-on-peer abuse more specifically, indicate that peer social norms can outweigh the influence of homes, and potentially even schools and neighbourhoods, when setting behavioural standards for peer relationships. Therefore, the relationship between agency and peer influence warrants attention.

There are two ways in which the agency/dependency relationship can be explored with reference to peer group dynamics. Firstly, peer groups do not develop in a vacuum. Peer groups are formed within online and offline spaces which are, to differing extents, managed by adults. When young men seek the support of their peers in response to violence and intimidation in their local neighbourhoods, as James did, the nature of the neighbourhoods in which these peer groups form are influenced by the professionals and communities (members of the public) who manage and interact with them. Therefore, while other young people, and not professionals, are on one level responsible for the social norms of their friendship groups, these norms are shaped by environments that are often managed by professionals and wider communities in ways outlined earlier in this chapter. As noted, international literature of bystander intervention (introduced in Chapters 6 and 7) illuminates this relationship by highlighting the influence of institutional cultures in encouraging or discouraging individuals to intervene when they witness problematic or abusive behaviour (Cowie, 2011; Powell, 2011). Therefore, if young people's peers, particularly those who witness or are aware of the abuse experienced by their friends, believe that they can intervene safely they may do so. In the absence of real or perceived safety in environments managed by adults (such as their neighbourhood or school), young people, as illustrated in the cases I reviewed, may stand back and either fail to intervene to safeguard their friends or encourage the abuse they witness so as to avoid being victimised themselves.

Moving beyond the relationship between harmful public contexts and harmful peer norms, there is a second manner in which peer influence can inform the dependency/agency relationship. If professionals are able to garner the engagement and support of other young people, then peers can be seen as partners in safeguarding rather than simply a risk factor requiring control or removal (Warrington, 2013). As evidence on whole-school approaches to bullying and gender equality (Cowie, 2011; EVAW, 2010b) and bystander intervention (Powell, 2011) suggest (Chapter 6), young people can act as a positive source of intervention and support within environments that enable such behaviours. As the cases I reviewed illustrate, young people are willing to, and do attempt to, intervene and disrupt escalations towards peer-on-peer abuse. If these attempts at positive peer intervention are harnessed by professionals, they could provide a contextual, and socially weighty, route to informing the agency of young people. If young people believe their peers will support non-abusive, rather than abusive, behaviours, this could open up an otherwise limited set of available choices.

It is important to consider such peer potential across a spectrum. For example, as outlined in Chapter 6, when Lara told her friends that James was harassing her, they told her to ignore it. Lara sought the support of her peers and did not find safety in this approach; instead, their response normalised sexual harassment. Had Lara's peers recognised James' behaviour as problematic, actively encouraged her to seek protection/advice from professionals, and not isolated her for being a 'snitch', they would have provided Lara with a route to safety. In such a situation Lara's peers were not abusive, but they still required support to be protective. This is different from a situation such as James' where his peers, even though they didn't ultimately take part in the rape with him, drew upon abusive social norms and used other forms of violence to secure safety for James and themselves in their local neighbourhood. If all young people in his peer group had supported James to feel safe, without the use of violence and aggression in their local community, then professionals could have worked with his peers to play a disruptive rather than encouraging role in the escalation towards the rape of Lara.

The foregoing examples utilise the agency of young people and the influence they hold over the decisions and beliefs of their peers. However, to achieve these outcomes young people remain dependent on professionals to recognise and maximise the potential of peer influence within safeguarding practices. Consider Lara's peers: where could they engage with social norms that promoted and enabled healthy relationships? As a peer group they were dependent on others to provide them with these opportunities. They may have accessed messages from their families, but their ability to practice safe peer relationships was informed by factors beyond their homes. They didn't form peer relationships at home – they did so online, at school and in their local communities. They were therefore dependent upon those who managed those environments to give them the space to engage in healthy peer relationships. In the case example the school environment failed to provide Lara's peers with that space. While this would have been ideal, it was not the only option. A local youth service or other voluntary provider could have engaged with Lara's peers and provided them with the physical, social and cultural space to develop healthy attitudes and behaviours towards relationships and intimacy.

Such an intervention does not seek to control or sanction young people into making pro-social choices. Rather, they offer a context which enables safe choices – as called for in the previous chapter. A current tension in this regard is the ways in which young people use the online space. References to online contexts have been interwoven throughout this book, and purposefully so. In all of my conversations with young people to date, they have not described online spaces as separate from the offline communities in which they are engaged – rather the two are connected and sometimes interwoven. I am at a party – I take a picture at that party and post it online – the same experience is shared offline and online almost simultaneously; made even more possible through the introduction of live video streaming. Or I am gang-affiliated in my local neighbourhood – I post music videos online to elevate my status, boast and threaten others, with an intention to make offline impact. The direction of UK policy at present is to work with internet providers to restrict young people's access to web content that promotes problematic ideas or images about sex and relationships. There have also been calls to educate and equip parents to safeguard young people from the influences of online content – through parental controls on internet settings and raising parents' awareness about the violent nature of the imagery that young people can access online. These approaches once again rely heavily on parents to control and influence how young people behave. Work with internet providers goes some way to engaging those responsible for an environment in making it safe for young people to use. However, given peer influence one might argue a more effective strategy to intervention would be to support young people to recognise and challenge harmful content to which they and their peers may have been exposed. In the absence of consistent sex and relationships education (Chapter 6) or other informal education provision, such as through youth work, young people have limited access to social spaces in which they can discuss and challenge the ideas they have been exposed to online. Investment in these approaches has the potential to utilise peer dynamics and peer influence in conversations about relationships, sex and harmful behaviours – as opposed to parenting interventions which may each target an individual child but won't necessarily inform the wider attitudes held by the peer group of which that child may be a part.

A dependency on peers for status, belonging and arguably safety, therefore, presents an opportunity for professionals to utilise, rather than control, agency. Were child protection processes to incorporate peer dynamics into assessments and intervention plans, they may be able to identify: where peer relationships pose a risk to the young person they are concerned about; where peer relationships may be a protective factor; and opportunities for professionals to engage with and influence both of these dynamics. The agency of individual young people and their peers then becomes an asset, and the dependency that peer cultures have on other services becomes a route to influence individual and group behaviour. By utilising the relationship between young people's agency and their dependency of those who manage public and social spaces, intervention has the potential to create a menu of safe or unsafe choices associated with young people's experiences of peer-on-peer abuse.

The suite of safe choices: linking agency and dependency in public spaces

Chapters throughout this book have demonstrated that as individuals move through the period of adolescent development they become increasingly dependent for their development, both socially and culturally, on environments that go well beyond their family home. Young people experience safety, or a lack of it, in all of these spaces and are dependent on a range of people – teachers, police officers, park wardens, members of the public, housing officers and their peers, to name but a few – to ensure that these environments are safe. Therefore, while they are social agents, the behaviours that young people display are informed by these two dependencies. If the rules within a given social field, and the other actors who are engaged in that field, provide a social-cultural context of safety, then they enable young people to engage in safe actions. If, however, the social field in which young people spend their time promotes harmful social norms, and the other actors within that field adhere to, promote or fail to challenge those norms, then young people's opportunity to realise safety is restricted.

Consider the neighbourhood in which James, Lara and Melissa spent their time. This was the context in which James was victimised from the age of 10 in his local park; Lara was assaulted once she reported the rape; and Melissa was exposed to sexual exploitation and gang association amongst her peers. Unfortunately, and to differing extents, these experiences coloured the ways in which James, Lara and Melissa interacted with one another, their local neighbourhood, their school and their families. The risks that all three experienced in their local neighbourhood demonstrated perceived and real limitations to their agency and their ability to make safe choices.

James encountered harm in his local park when his bike was stolen from him, and from that point onwards he did not perceive the park as a context in which he would be safe. For Melissa, the behaviours she encountered in her local neighbourhood did little to challenge the harmful social norms about the abuse of women and girls that she had been exposed to at home and in school. The reciprocity between the norms in her school, home and neighbourhood constricted the ability of Melissa to identify an avenue for acting in non-abusive ways while avoiding being abused. Finally, for Lara the safety she had experienced in the neighbourhood diminished when the norms and relationships she engaged with in school increased risks that she faced on the street. Lara ended up leaving her local neighbourhood to avoid these risks because she was unable to travel to school safely once she sought help after her rape. Figure 10.1 illustrates the different dynamics of these three scenarios.

In James' scenario, risk within his neighbourhood, before the rape, created a need for a violent peer group and impacted negatively on school. This was the opposite to Lara whose experiences of school negatively impacted her experience of the neighbourhood. Finally, Melissa experienced equally harmful norms across all social contexts in which she spent her time. All three routes of direction-influence, however, constrained the safety, and therefore choices, of James, Melissa and Lara in their local neighbourhood. All three were social agents and used their agency to engage with the social rules at play in both the neighbourhood and in the interplays between the neighbourhood and other social contexts. James made choices to engage in crime and violence in order to engage with these social rules. Melissa enabled the abuse of young women in her school while engaging with harmful

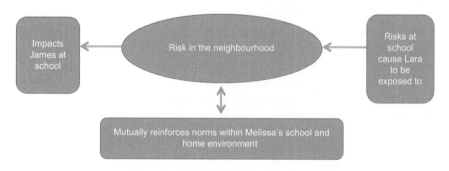

FIGURE 10.1 Contextual interplay and suites of choices

norms that were reinforced across all the social spaces (including her neighbour-hood) in which she formed relationships. Lara left the social field completely.

There were, however, ways that professionals could have supported James, Melissa and Lara to make alternative choices. In the case of James, he was unsafe in the park. Therefore, professionals who were responsible for the park could have engaged in this space to make it safer for James to spend his time there – from using detached workers to engage young people in the park in safe activities, to ensur-ing that park wardens were equipped to identify concerning behaviours and refer them to safeguarding partnerships. Being alert to the risks faced by James in the park could have been disrupted through intervention with the older people who were grooming James into violent behaviour, for example, through police enforce-ment. Similarly, if Melissa had witnessed that professionals were seeking to disrupt the sexual exploitation of her peers in her local neighbourhood, this space could have become an environment which challenged the abusive social norms to which she had become accustomed. Lara was relocated by professionals who felt unable to keep her safe in her local neighbourhood. However, if professionals had intervened with the physical violence and sexual exploitation on the streets as outlined previ-ously, this may have also had an impact on Lara's ability to safely travel to and from school. Melissa, Lara and James were dependent on professionals to change the nature of the neighbourhood in which they experienced harm. Successful interven-tion in this space could have enabled all three to safely engage as active agents in the neighbourhood – and herein lies the relationship between agency and dependency in the safeguarding of adolescents from peer-on-peer abuse.

The contextual experiences of James, Melissa and Lara documented throughout this book, and the limited suite of safe choices available to them, did not determine the rape that occurred. However, they did create a pessimistic scenario (Lawler, 2004) in which opportunities to act alternatively were constricted and in which their dependency on others for their safety in particular social contexts remained an unmet need. The decisions of young people who are abused by, or who abuse, their peers are not in the control of their parents/carers, friends or professionals they encounter. But these individuals contribute to the nature of the social spaces in which those decisions are made. In this manner all young people affected by peer-on-peer abuse are dependent agents – simultaneously acting while being informed by other individuals and environments when they do so.

Conclusion: dependent agents

This chapter has explored the opportunities to engage with, and maximise the potential of, young people's agency when safeguarding them from peer-on-peer abuse. While it is true that from a very early biological age individuals demon-strate agency, research has also noted that during the period of adolescent devel-opment the opportunities in which young people act as social agents outside of familial influences changes and develops (Coleman, 2011; Losel & Bender, 2006; Warr, 2002). Whether it is travelling to school on their own or socialising without parental supervision, young people begin to make decisions and act in ways that form or break relationships in social-cultural contexts demarcated as ones in which 'teenagers' hang out.

Whether it is the park, the bus stop, the shopping centre or the school, these so-called sites of adolescent socialisation are ones in which there is minimal, if any, parental influence. Instead, parents/carers hand over safeguarding responsibilities to the professionals who manage those spaces, that is, teachers, transport providers and park wardens, and to young people themselves. Young people are encouraged to make decisions which will keep them safe, and to varying extents the media, politicians and the public recognise responsibilities amongst professionals to contribute to this process.

And yet, as the evidence presented in this book has demonstrated, recognising both the agency of young people and their dependency on others for protection is not so easily practiced with child protection processes. When James' behaviour began to escalate, interventions to support him, or enforce against him, were intended to change his behaviour in isolation of any wider contextual change. The risks that James experienced in his neighbourhood or peer group were not subject to intervention; the dependency that James had on those who managed or engaged in those spaces was not the focus of concern; and as a result it was James' agency and not his dependency on others that was associated with his abusive behaviour.

Much of the foregoing is informed by a cultural professional context in which 1:1 intervention is prioritised. It feels more manageable to change an individual's behaviour rather than the wider social context with which this behaviour is associated. However, this chapter has demonstrated a relationship between the agency that is challenged by intervention and a dependency on contexts, and professionals who manage them, to offer or constrain available choices. In a sense it isn't possible to accurately assess, intervene with and shift the choices that young people make without also considering the contexts, and professional contextual management, that inform those choices. And yet, professionals who operate in a child protection system that locates risk with individual and familial behaviours are not equipped to identify or change the social-cultural nature of peer group, school, park or transport hubs. The three sections in this chapter have identified opportunities for professionals to impact the contextual dynamics of peer-on-peer abuse. Professionals will be better placed to build a relevant response to peer-on-peer abuse when they recognise: their contribution to the norms and values of extra-familial contexts; opportunities to shape safe and supportive peer relationships; and the relationship between young people's agency and their dependency on others to create spaces in which there are safe choices available. In doing so, young people can be viewed as dependent agents, afforded safe places in which to make safer choices and become partners in their own safeguarding and that of their peers (Warrington, 2013).

Such recognition would begin to address the limitations of individualised child protection responses that have been identified by a range of social work and safeguarding specialists (i.e. Parton, 2014). Considered alongside the social account of choice and the exploration of location interplay presented in the previous two chapters, this chapter provides the final component of the foundations for developing a contextual model of safeguarding – a theoretical framework that the final chapter of this book presents.

11

CONCLUSION

Towards contextual safeguarding

The contextual account of abuse between young people presented in this book suggests that the phenomenon:

- Largely occurs within, and is influenced by, peer groups, schools and neighbourhoods in which young people spend their time – social contexts that are sites of adolescent socialisation whose rules often outweigh familial norms
- Is informed by reflexive interplays between individual young people and the homes, peer groups, schools and neighbourhoods in which they spend their time – a process through which young people's choices are opened up or constrained
- Involves physical, sexual and emotional abuse, cutting across the definitional silos of child sexual exploitation, serious youth violence, harmful sexual behaviour and intimate partner abuse

Such an account has significant implications for existing approaches to safeguarding young people in England (and other Western countries that share similar social-cultural dynamics and social work practices) which warrant further investigation. Currently, child protection and safeguarding practices:

- Are largely built upon processes designed to respond to a risk of significant harm posed by the adults in young people's familial network
- Seek to change the behaviour of young people, and sometimes that of their families, as means of reducing risk
- Have been built to provide distinct responses to particular manifestations of peer-on-peer abuse, including sexual exploitation, serious youth violence, young people with harmful sexual behaviour and teenage relationship abuse

Exploring each of these challenges in turn highlights potential directions for advancing research, policy and practice concerned with safeguarding young people affected by peer-on-peer abuse. In doing so this concluding chapter uses the contextual account presented in this book to propose a cultural shift in how peer-on-peer abuse, other extra-familial risks that undermine the well-being of young people, and the safeguarding of adolescents' agenda are understood.

Child protection in public spaces

The nature of peer-on-peer abuse, as outlined in this book, indisputably presents a risk of significant harm to young people in the UK and internationally. Involving a spectrum of physically, sexually and emotionally abusive behaviours, the phenomenon clearly impairs young people's development or health and is therefore accommodated by definition of significant harm in English child protection policy:

> Where the question of whether harm suffered by a child is significant turns on the child's health and development, his health or development shall be compared with that which could reasonably be expected of a similar child.

- 'Harm' means ill-treatment or the impairment of health or development (including, for example, impairment suffered from seeing or hearing the ill-treatment of another);
- 'Development' means physical, intellectual, emotional, social or behavioural development;
- 'Health' means physical or mental health; and
- 'Ill-treatment' includes sexual abuse and forms of ill-treatment which are not physical.

Children Act 1989, Section 31(9) and 10

Despite this definitional fit, the contextual nature of peer-on-peer abuse is far from comfortably accommodated within the practical and strategic parameters of child protection policy in England – and a number of other Western social care contexts – as highlighted in the previous three chapters.

As introduced in Chapter 4, from a historical perspective the child protection system, and the definition of significant harm upon which it is implemented, was established in UK policy to safeguard children from abuse within a familial context and/or to work with families to keep young people safe (Corby, et al., 2012; Parton, 2014). For example, according to Working Together 2015, the purpose of a child protection plan, drawn up to prevent significant harm, is to:

- Ensure the child is safe from harm and prevent him or her from suffering further harm;
- Promote the child's health and development; and
- Support the family and wider family members to safeguard and promote the welfare of their child, provided it is in the best interests of the child.

(HM Government, 2015:45)

Planning intervention in this policy framework locates safety with the behaviour of individual young people and their family members in isolation of wider social factors. This narrow focus on the family has been embedded through wider national policy initiatives such as the Troubled Families programme, which locates social harm within the family environment and in particular the relationship between children and their parents.

Yet, the contextual account of peer-on-peer abuse presented in this book not only highlights the risks posed to young people within environments beyond their homes, but it also recognises the interplay between familial and extra-familial contexts. A parent's capacity to keep young people safe can be undermined by factors beyond their control – such as the influence of young people's peers or the violence they encounter at school or on the street. In these instances, what happens in public spaces affects the capacity of parents whose domain is safety in the private space of their home. Reflecting upon the remit of the child protection plan, for example, supporting families and wider family members will not necessarily reduce the risk that young people will encounter significant harm on the streets or in their peer groups.

As young people spend increasing amounts of time in public and social spaces independently of parental supervision, other adults and young people who are engaged in those spaces also have a role in safeguarding (as outlined in Chapter 10). As argued in Chapter 10, dependency during adolescence expands to bus drivers, park wardens, teachers and young people's peers, who all influence the nature of the social spaces in which young people spend their time. By expanding an account of peer-on-peer abuse to consider the peer groups, schools and neighbourhoods associated with the phenomenon, experiences of significant harm beyond familial settings are brought into focus, as well as the roles of adults who have a responsibility to safeguard young people in public spaces. To accommodate these dynamics a child protection plan may need to explicitly consider contributions from a range of individuals and agencies, beyond social workers and the police, who manage public spaces where norms either pose a risk to young people's safety or serve to undermine the capacity of parents to keep young people safe. Developing child protection plans in this direction will only be possible if the assessments that inform them and the interventions that can be offered as part of them are also contextual. If families and young people are the only subjects of assessment, then it won't be possible to include individuals and agencies responsible for other social contexts within the plan itself – risks in those spaces will not be considered in assessment. Likewise, if the only interventions available in response to peer-on-peer abuse focus on supporting young people and their families, then social workers will be unable to source routes to address the contextual risks identified within their assessment and plan. To realise child protection responses to risk in public spaces, the individualised nature of intervention and assessment requires consideration.

The limitations of 1:1 assessment and intervention

When a young person goes missing from school, arms themselves with a knife or threatens to share a sexually explicit image of a peer, I all too often hear them described by practitioners, academics and policymakers as making 'risky choices'. To an extent such an assessment is true – carrying a knife is said to make it more likely that a young person will be stabbed. When a young person is not in school at times when they should be, they are often unsupervised and more likely to be on the streets with other vulnerable young people or adults where they can experience harm. And if a young person shares an explicit image of anyone, even themselves, they are currently committing a criminal offence. On occasions such as this practitioners in England, in both voluntary and statutory sectors, are tasked with changing such behaviours in a bid to reduce the risk that a young person will be abused by, and/or abuse, their peers. Assessing the extent to which young people are demonstrating behaviours or attitudes that increase their risk of peer-on-peer abuse, and then intervening, is thought in turn to safeguard them from significant harm.

And yet – what if a young person who is missing from school is truanting to avoid peer-abuse, as Lara was? Surely the decision not to attend school could be assessed as a protective, rather than risky, behaviour – an attempt at survival discussed in Chapter 9. We can only really assess the behaviours displayed by young people if they are considered in relation to the social contexts in which they formed. For young people who are truanting from school to avoid bullying and abusive behaviours (Centre for Social Justice, 2016), assessments may need to consider the nature of their school environment, actions taken to date to make it a safe place by school leadership and other staff members, and the ability of those professionals to keep that young person safe at school in the future. However, the current policy landscape holds young people, and their families, responsible for school attendance – including authorising the fining of parents who fail to get their young people to attend. This position is maintained even when young people don't attend school as a result of bullying and only requires an assessment of the family's capacity to get a young person to attend school rather than the capacity of school professionals to ensure that a young person is safe while in their care. Ultimately, a young person always has a choice to attend school, but the extent to which this choice is free is determined by the reflexive interplays between their individual agency and the contextual risk/safety at school that is documented in this book – it is not determined by their parents. An assessment of the processes which open up or constrain young people's choices will enable professionals to consider them when concluding if young people are culpable for, or consenting to, the behaviours in which they partake; and to identify the required response. For example, did the process of street-based victimisation constrain the extent to which James could choose to socialise with safe and non-abusive peers? Or was it the lack of a protective response to that experience which ultimately constrained the choices that were available to him?

When moving from assessment to intervention, traditional child protection processes in England and Wales promote multi-agency planning (MAP) and strategy meetings/conferences to discuss concerns about young people's behaviours and the capacity of their parents to keep them safe from harm. However, these mechanisms won't create *safe* spaces for young people to make alternative choices if they are only concerned with changing the behaviours of families and individual young people. Information about the contexts in which young people abuse, or are abused by, their peers need to inform decision-making in these meetings. Without this information, interventions could be designed with the aim of increasing a young person's attendance at school even if such an outcome could actually increase the likelihood that they would engage in, or experience, abuse.

Familial and 1:1 interventions may build resilience amongst some young people and their families (Hackett, 2006) and build awareness of behaviours and issues that will compromise their safety. For some young people this will be sufficient to change behaviours associated with peer-on-peer abuse. However, for other young people, solely teaching them about safer choices and behaviours that are different to theirs is not enough. In keeping with Bourdieu's social theory, some young people need to actively engage in that which is different in order to act in an alternative way. Young people who encounter violence on their way to school may need to travel to school on a bus route where they feel safe, and where their possessions won't be stolen, in order to feel that they no longer need to associate with a violent peer group to keep safe. Interventions are therefore required which seek to create safer contexts in order to affect young people's choices.

But who is responsible for delivering interventions which shift the nature of contexts that are associated with peer-on-peer abuse? As indicated in the previous chapter, beyond social workers, the police and young people's families, there is a network of other agencies and professionals who could play a role at multi-agency planning and strategy meetings, who should feature in care plans, and who could be held to account at child protection conferences. If young people are at risk in the park, or at school, then individuals who manage those spaces, and the people within those spaces who pose a risk to young people, should be the concern of child protection processes. While this may already happen in some local areas in an ad hoc fashion, an explicit recommendation for such an approach is absent from policy documents that provide the foundation of child protection practices such as *Working Together*. Although some attention has been made to violence within schools and communities (Chapters 6 and 7), the policy framework in place to address these is significantly less developed, and largely divorced from, child protection processes.

To extend the current reach of child protection intervention and sufficiently develop procedures which accommodate the opportunities for contextual practice introduced in the previous chapter, two questions require attention. Should professionals be assessing individuals who navigate harmful spaces and/or the spaces themselves? Should professional seek to change the behaviour of individual young people in harmful spaces and/or the spaces themselves? At present the system is best equipped to assess, and seek to change, the behaviour of individuals who navigate harmful spaces. Yet the contextual account of peer-on-peer abuse presented in this book can only be addressed by systems that can assess, and intervene with the rules of, harmful social spaces.

Beyond issues

Throughout my research into peer-on-peer abuse I have often been pressed by practitioners, academics and policymakers to specify what 'issue' I am actually concerned with: is it youth violence, domestic abuse or sexual exploitation that I am trying to understand and address? Surely the differences between the issues are so stark that considering them together in one book or one training session only serves to conflate or simplify how peer-on-peer abuse is understood or even confuse those seeking to protect young people. It is easy to see why so many people automatically reach for siloed definitions of abuse and associated practice boundaries. It can feel more manageable, from the perspective of research, policy and practice, if we can maintain distinctive lines between different manifestations of abuse. Furthermore, at different points in time particular presentations of abuse have required specific attention. For example, introducing a definition of child sexual exploitation (DCSF, 2009) was helpful in challenging practice responses in which exploitative exchanges were perceived as consensual decisions to engage in sexual activity. At times like this, researchers and campaigners have championed the need to improve how particular dynamics of abuse are understood in order to ensure that young people who experience that 'type' of abuse are appropriately safeguarded.

Beyond research and campaign priorities, political pressures have generated a focus on narrow manifestations of abuse at different points in time. In 2008 it was gun crime that topped the policy agenda, by 2009 it was knife crime, and by 2011 political discourse was largely focused on child sexual exploitation. Fast forward to 2015 and the radicalisation of young people had everyone scratching their heads. Sometimes just one case, or a series of cases which imply an escalation of an issue, can be enough to shift the attention of the media and politicians to prioritise one form of abuse above others. These shifts in prioritisation are often followed by grants to develop research and services, thematic inspections of practice across the country and the introduction of new strategic documents designed to offer a more effective response to that specific issue. I have worked through, and sometimes moved with, the crests of these political waves. In 2009 I was championing the voices of gang-affected young women, a cohort of young people who were yet to be recognised in UK policy. By 2011 it was teenage relationship abuse that occupied my conversations with policymakers and the press.

And yet when we move beyond these silos, the account offered by this book demonstrates what different forms of peer-on-peer abuse have in common – both the nature of the phenomenon and the challenges faced by parents, practitioners and policymakers in building a response to it. The contextual dynamics of different forms of peer-on-peer abuse and the escalation towards incidents that were reviewed all featured:

- A demise of parental or carer capacity to safeguard young people from harm – all too often described as a loss of control
- Harmful, influential peer norms that encouraged, or at least failed to challenge, abusive behaviours
- Choices constrained by contexts that reinforced gendered stereotypes, exposed young people to a lack of safety and required them to source survival routes to avoid victimisation
- Young people who made disclosures that they were being abused by peers through changes in their behaviour. These behaviours were then interpreted by practitioners as them acting in risky ways and/or posing a risk to others rather than as signs of vulnerability
- Norms and expectations within local neighbourhoods, schools and peer networks which facilitated harm in public spaces

If policy and practice frameworks provided a safeguarding response to these thematic characteristics of peer-on-peer abuse, they would enable a more effective response to the issue regardless of the siloed definition used to describe it. Central to such a framework would be: assessments capable of recognising behaviours that were the consequence of a young person being abused by peers; interventions capable of disrupting public and social environments where risk of abuse was escalating; approaches which recognised and utilised young people's dependency on adults in public as well as private spaces; services equipped to engage with peer influence as a means of safeguarding individual young people; and organisational cultures and professional partnerships which support parents whose ability to keep their children safe was being undermined by factors beyond both their control and their front door.

With the provision of such a framework, practitioners would be better placed to safeguard young people from extra-familial forms of significant harm – regardless of whether that issue was called sexual exploitation, serious youth violence or something else. Yes, the cases I reviewed had an initial heading – rape or murder. And beyond those headings the incidents under investigation could be labelled as serious youth violence, or sexual exploitation or teenage relationship abuse and so on. But the contextual review methodology that I utilised (Chapter 3) identified that some young people involved in murders had also sexually harmed peers or physically abused, or been abused by, their partners. Young people who were sexually exploiting peers had been robbed for their mobile phones and been involved in robbery against others. The incident that came to the attention of the police, and was ultimately subject to case review, may have been siloed. But the escalation towards each incident certainly didn't sit neatly in a single strategic government document, area of service delivery or research agenda.

Building upon publications that have offered holistic accounts of different forms of peer violence (Barter & Berridge, 2011), this book evidences how different manifestations of peer-on-peer abuse present similar challenges to the current policy and practice landscape that warrant joint attention. Recommending a shift towards holistic accounts of, and responses to, peer-on-peer abuse is not intended to dismiss the definitions, siloed research areas, services or strategies upon which this book has been built. Rather it is a proposal that seeks to recognise that which may unite these relatively discrete areas of work to provide an overarching response to all instances where young people are abused by, and/or abuse, their peers.

Final thoughts: towards contextual safeguarding

Ultimately, a contextual account of peer-on-peer abuse requires a contextual approach to safeguarding, that is, an approach to the phenomenon which seeks to identify and assess and, where appropriate, intervene with *all* of the social spaces associated with young people's experiences of harm. To a certain extent we are not that far off realising this vision. Ecological and systemic models of working have been established within social work, youth work and youth justice provisions for many years (National Children's Bureau, 2006; Youth Justice Board, 2004). A number of assessment frameworks recognise the individual, family and so-called 'environmental' factors that may protect, or pose a risk to, young people. The evidence in this book furthers that practice agenda and suggests that to realise a truly contextual safeguarding framework the recognition of environmental factors needs to both broaden and deepen.

Firstly, there are many contexts that require consideration that are currently defined under the 'environmental' label in current assessment and intervention frameworks, including school, community and peer social spaces. Conflating them under one heading – environment – suggests that taken together they are as weighty in influence as the family. However, peer group influence may override that of families, and that is before schools or other public settings are considered. Stipulating all potential social environments independently of, and then interplaying with, one another, *broadens* this category of 'environmental' factors so that they can be given the attention that they warrant.

Secondly, when environmental factors are brought to the fore in the way they that they have been in this book, the extent to which they are addressed, and expected to change, requires *in-depth* consideration. When reviewing cases I read care plans, minutes taken at strategy meetings, plans to reduce re-offending and so on. To differing extents these plans recognised strengths and risk factors within contexts beyond a young person's home. The challenge across most cases appeared to be in the identification of actions to address these contextual risks. A contextual safeguarding approach not only recognises environmental risk factors but also seeks to address them – largely by engaging those agencies or individuals who are responsible for those environments. Within the proposed framework, attempts to change contexts would be recorded in individual care plans as part of the agreed multi-agency response to an identified risk of peer-on-peer abuse.

At the close of this book, contextual safeguarding is largely a theoretical approach. As I have been writing up my research, 11 local multi-agency partnerships have begun to implement the principles of a contextual approach to building their response to peer-on-peer abuse. Some of these sites are applying the theory of contextual safeguarding presented in this final chapter to conduct root-and-branch reform of their local child protection processes, illuminating the ways in which such an approach may be possible and, more importantly, if it is effective. The findings of this pilot implementation will be published over the next two years and create an evidence base through which to inform national and international policy. To sustain contextual approaches, and ensure the principles of such a theory are consistently understood across England, national policymakers need to incorporate principles of contextuality into key safeguarding and child protection documentation. Furthermore, sectors which are not primarily established for safeguarding, such as housing, transport and education, all require policy frameworks that explicitly encourage their involvement in child protection processes from a contextual safeguarding perspective. We are, therefore, at the very start of this journey. However, the approach is built upon decades of research that have questioned individualised accounts of abuse, indicated environmental risks, and called for holistic approaches to promoting the welfare of adolescence. In this sense much has already been achieved.

Historically, child protection and safeguarding practice has been critiqued for a lack of multi-agency working. Now agencies meet together regularly, breaking down sector silos, but they do so to discuss individuals who are experiencing what are perceived to be siloed issues – be that sexual exploitation, domestic abuse or gang affiliation and so on. No longer separated by sector, we are now separated by abuse type and remain focused on individuals. This book signifies a need to work across agencies and across issues to identify individuals, families and social-cultural contexts in which vulnerability, risk, resilience and strength interplay during escalations towards peer-on-peer abuse. A holistic approach to safeguarding adolescents in this regard is long overdue.

REFERENCES

Adamson, J. & Templeton, L., 2012. *Silent Voices: Supporting Children and Young People Affected by Parental Alcohol Misuse.* London: OCC.

Aisenberg, E. & Herrenkohl, T., 2008. Community Violence in Context: Risk and Resilience in Children and Famililes. *Journal of Interpersonal Violence,* 23(3), pp. 296–315.

Aldridge, J., Shute, J., Ralphs, R. & Medina, J., 2011. Blame the Parents? Challenges for Parent-Focused Programmes for Families of Gang-Involved Young People. *Children and Society,* 25, pp. 371–381.

Allen, K. K., 2011. Guilt by (More Than) Association: The Case for Spectator Liability in Gang Rapes. *Georgetown Law Journal,* 99, pp. 837–867.

Allenye, E., Fernandes, I. & Pritchard, E., 2014. Denying Humanness to Victims: How Gang Members Justify Violent Behavior. *Group Processes and Inter-Group Relations,* 17(6), pp. 750–762.

Anderson, E., 1999. *Code of the Street: Decency, Violence, and the Moral Life of the Inner City.* New York: WW Norton.

Anti-Bullying Alliance, 2005. *Bystanders and Bullying: A Summary of Research for Anti-Bullying Week.* [Online] Available at: www.anti-bullyingalliance.org.uk/media/1050/bystanders_and_bullying.pdf [Accessed 03. 12. 2015].

Ashurst, L. & McAlinden, A. M., 2015. Young People, Peer-to-Peer Grooming and Sexual Offending: Understanding and Responding to Harmful Sexual Behaviour within a Social Media Society. *Probation Journal,* 62(4), pp. 374–388.

AVA, 2016. *Prevention Platform.* [Online] Available at: www.preventionplatform.co.uk/?page_id=2291 [Accessed 15. 01. 2016].

Aynsley, C., Davies, H., Girling, S., Hammond, R. & Hughes, T. 2016. *'Sexting' in Schools: Advice and Support around Self-Generated Images: What to Do and How to Handle It.* s.l.: Compass Community.

Barnardo's, 2011a. *An Assessment of the Potential Savings from Barnardo's Interventions for Young People Who Have Been Sexually Exploited.* Barkingside: Barnardo's.

Barnardo's, 2011b. *Puppet on a String: The Urgent Need to Cut Children Free from Sexual Exploitation.* Barkingside: Barnardo's.

Barnardo's, 2013. *The Tangled Web: How Child Sexual Exploitation Is Becoming More Complex.* Barkingside: Barnardo's.

Barnes, A., Cross, D., Lester, L., Hearn, L., Epstein, M. & Monks, H. 2012. The Invisibility of Covert Bullying among Students: Challenges for School Intervention. *Australian Journal of Guidance and Counselling*, 22(2), pp. 206–226.

Barter, C., 2006. Discourses of Blame: Deconstructing (Hetero) Sexuality, Peer Sexual Violence and Residential Children's Homes. *Child and Family Social Work*, 11(4), pp. 346–356.

Barter, C., 2009. In the Name of Love: Partner Abuse and Violence in Teenage Relationships. *British Journal of Social Work*, 39, pp. 211–233.

Barter, C., 2014. *Briefing Paper 2: Incidence Rates and Impact of Experiencing Interpersonal Violence and Abuse in Young People's Relationships*. [Online] Available at: http://stiritup.eu/wp-content/uploads/2015/06/STIR-Briefing-Paper-2-English-final.pdf [Accessed 20. 05. 2015].

Barter, C., 2015. *Briefing Paper 2: Incidence Rates and Impact of Experiencing Interpersonal Violence and Abuse in Young People's Relationships*. [Online] Available at: http://stiritup.eu/wp-content/uploads/2015/06/STIR-Briefing-Paper-2-English-final.pdf [Accessed 22. 09. 2015].

Barter, C. & Berridge, D., 2011. *Children Behaving Badly? Peer Violence between Children and Young People*. West Sussex: John Wiley and Sons Ltd.

Barter, C., McCarry, M., Berridge, D. & Evans, K., 2009. *Partner Exploitation and Violence in Teenage Intimate Relationships*. London: NSPCC.

Bates, L., 2014. *Everyday Sexism*. London: Simon & Schuster.

BBC, 2008. *Teenage Rapper Jailed for Killing*. [Online] Available at: http://news.bbc.co.uk/1/hi/england/london/7758574.stm [Accessed 01. 12. 2015].

BBC, 2010. *Man Jailed for Life for Killing Girlfriend Aliza Mirza*. [Online] Available at: www.bbc.co.uk/news/uk-england-london-11512831 [Accessed 01. 12. 2015].

BBC, 2011. *East Dulwich Bus Murder Victim 'Stabbed 24 Times'*. [Online] Available at: www.bbc.co.uk/news/uk-england-london-12370018 [Accessed 03. 12. 2015].

BBC, 2013. *Gang Murdered Boy During Rush Hour at Victoria Station*. [Online] Available at: www.bbc.co.uk/news/uk-15310015 [Accessed 03. 12. 2015].

BBC, 2015a. *Boy, 15, Stabbed on Top Deck of Birmingham Bus*. [Online] Available at: www.bbc.co.uk/news/uk-england-birmingham-34867042 [Accessed 03. 12. 2015].

BBC, 2015b. *Children in England 'among Unhappiest in World'*. [Online] Available at: www.bbc.co.uk/news/education-33984082 [Accessed 03. 12. 2015].

BBC, 2015c. *Rotherham Abuse Scandal: Key Dates*. [Online] Available at: www.bbc.co.uk/news/uk-28955170 [Accessed 03. 12. 2015].

BBC, 2015d. *School Sex Crime Reports in UK Top 5,500 in Three Years*. [Online] Available at: www.bbc.co.uk/news/education-34138287 [Accessed 03. 12. 2015].

BBC, 2015e. *Offending Rates Among Children in Care Investigated*. [Online] Available at: http://www.bbc.co.uk/news/uk-33221247 [Accessed 02.12.2016].

Beckett, H., 2011. *Not a World Away: The Sexual Exploitation of Children and Young People in Northern Ireland*. Belfast: Barnardo's NI.

Beckett, H., 2013. Looked after Young People and CSE: A View from Northern Ireland. In: M. Melrose, & J. Pearce, eds. *Critical Perspectives on Child Sexual Exploitation and Related Trafficking*. Basingstoke: Palgrave Macmillan, pp. 69–82.

Beckett, H., Brodie, I., Factor, F., Melrose, M., Pearce, J., Pitts, J. & Warrington, C. 2013. *It's Wrong But You Get Used to It: A Qualitative Study of Gang-Associated Sexual Violence towards, and Sexual Exploitation of, Young People in England*. London: Office of the Children's Commissioner.

Beckett, H., Firmin, C., Hynes, P. & Pearce, J., 2014. *Tackling Child Sexual Exploitation: A Study of Current Practice in London Full Report*. London: London Councils.

Beckett, R. & Gerhold, C., 2003. Treatment of Adolescents Who Rape and Sexually Assault Peers and Adult Women. *13th Annual NOTA conference: 'Working towards Working Together. Sharing What We Know'*. Edinburgh: Herriot-Watt University.

Benton, C. J., 2014. The Profession Feminism Left Behind: Heterosexism in Schooling and the Teaching Profession. *Wagad*, 12(14), pp. 173–203.

Berelowitz, S., Clifton, J., Firmin, C., Gulyurtlu, S. & Edwards, G. 2013. *If Only Someone Had Listened: Office of the Children's Commissioner's Inquiry into Child Sexual Exploitation in Gangs and Groups*. London: Office of the Children's Commissioner.

Berelowitz, S., Firmin, C., Edwards, G. & Gulyurtlu, S., 2012. *I Thought I Was the Only One, the Only One in the World: The Office of the Children's Commissioner's Inquiry into Child Sexual Exploitation in Gangs and Groups Interim Report*. London: Office of the Chidren's Commissioner.

Bijleveld, C. & Hendriks, J., 2003. Juvenile Sex Offenders: Differences Between Group and Solo Offenders. *Psychology, Crime and Law*, Volume 9, pp. 237–245.

Bijleveld, C., Weerman, F. M., Looije, D. & Hendriks, J., 2007. Group Sex Offending by Juveniles: Coercive Sex as a Group Activity. *European Journal of Criminology*, Volume 4, pp. 5–31.

Boswell, G., 2006. Implications of Different Residential Treatments for Young People Who Commit Serious Crimes. In: A. Hagell & R. Jeyarajah-Dent, eds. *Children Who Committ Acts of Serious Interpersonal Violence*. London: Jessica Kingsley, pp. 129–144.

Bourdieu, P., 1967. Systems of Education and Systems of Thought. *International Social Science Journal*, 19, pp. 192–193.

Bourdieu, P., 1992. *An Invitation to Reflexive Sociology*. Chicago: University of Chicago Press.

Bourdieu, P., 2001. *Masculine Domination*. Stanford: Stanford University Press.

Bourgois, P., 1995. *In Search of Respect: Selling Crack in El Barrio*. Cambridge: Cambridge University Press.

The Bristol Ideal, 2012. *Guidance: Taking a 'Whole School Approach'*. [Online] Available at: www.bristolideal.org.uk/wp-content/uploads/2014/03/Guidance-Whole-School-Approach.pdf [Accessed 03. 12. 2015].

Brodie, I., 2013. Young People, Trafficking and Sexual Exploitation: A View from Scotland. In: M. Melrose, & J. Pearce, eds. *Critical Perspectives on Child Sexual Exploitation and Related Trafficking*. Basingstoke: Palgrave Macmillan, pp. 83–95.

Butler, J., 1990. *Gender Trouble: Feminism and the Subversion of Identity*. New York: Routledge.

Butler, J., 1999. *Excitable Speech: A Politics of the Performative*. New York: Routledge.

Cassidy, J. & Shaver, P. R., 2008. *Handbook of Attachment, Second Edition: Theory, Research, and Clinical Applications*. New York: Guilford Press.

Catch 22, 2013. *The Role of the Family in Facilitating Gang Membership, Criminality and Exit*. London: Catch 22.

Centre for Social Justice, 2009. *Dying to Belong: An In-Depth Review of Street Gangs in Britain*. London: Centre for Social Justice.

Centre for Social Justice, 2016. *Bullying and Self-Exclusion: Who Cares?* London: CSJ.

Cepeda, A. & Valdez, A., 2003. Risk Behaviours among Young Mexican-American Gang-Associated Females: Sexual Relations, Partying, Substance Use, and Crime. *Journal of Adolescent Research*, 8, pp. 90–106.

Chambers, D., van Loon, J. & Tinckn, E., 2010. Teachers' Views of Teenage Sexual Morality. *British Journal of Sociology of Education*, 25(5), pp. 563–576.

Channel 4, 2013. *Parents 'Blamed' for Child Sexual Exploitation*. [Online] Available at: https://www.channel4.com/news/grooming-child-sex-exploitation-parents-blame [Accessed 12. 09. 2016].

Chung, D., 2005. Violence, Control, Romance and Gender Inequality: Young Women and Heterosexual Relationships. *Women's Studies International Forum*, 28, pp. 445–455.

Cialdini, R. B. & Trost, M. R., 1998. Social Influence: Social Norms, Conformity, and Compliance. In: D. Gilbert, S. Fiske & G. Lindzey, eds. *The Handbook of Social Psychology.* New York: McGraw-Hill, pp. 151–192.

Citizen's Report, 2016. *Mapping the Location and Victim Profile of Teenage Murders in London from 2005 to 2015.* [Online] Available at: www.citizensreportuk.org/reports/teenage-murder-london.html [Accessed 17. 01. 2016].

Cockbain, E., Brayley, H. & Ashby, M., 2014. *Not Just a Girl Thing: A Large-Scale Comparison of Male and Female Users of Child Sexual Exploitation Services in the UK.* London: UCL, Barnardo's and NatCen.

Coffey, A., 2014. *Real Voices: Child Sexual Exploitation in Great Manchester, an Independent Report by Ann Coffey MP.* Manchester: GMP.

Coleman, J., 2011. *The Nature of Adolescence*, 4th Edition. Howe, East Sussex: Routledge.

Community Care, 2015. *Social Workers 'Lacking Professional Curiosity' Failed to Identify Child Sexual Exploitation.* [Online] Available at: www.communitycare.co.uk/2015/03/03/social-workers-lacking-professional-curiosity-failed-identify-child-sexual-exploitation-oxfordshire/ [Accessed 03. 12. 2015].

Condry, R., 2016. *The Needs of the Adolescent in Adolescent to Parent Violence.* London: University of Bedfordshire.

Connell, R. & Messerschmidt, J., 2005. Hegemonic Masculinity: Rethinking the Concept. *Gender & Society*, 19(6), pp. 829–859.

Connolly, J., Papler, D., Craig, W. & Taradash, A., 2000. Dating Experiences of Bullies in Early Adolescence. *Child Maltreatment*, 5(4), pp. 229–310.

Corby, B., Shemmings, D. & Wilkins, D., 2012. *Child Abuse: An Evidence Base for Confident Practice*, 4th Edition. Berkshire: Open University Press.

Corr, M. L., Gadd, D., Butler, I. & Fox, C. L., 2012. *From Boys to Men: Phase Two Findings.* Manchester: University of Manchester School of Law.

Cossar, J., Brandon, M., Bailey, S., Belderson, P. & Biggart, L. 2013. *'It Takes a Lot to Build Trust': Recognition and Telling: Developing Earlier Routes to Help for Children and Young People.* London: Office of the Children's Commissioner.

Cowie, H., 2011. Understanding Why Children and Young People Engage in Bullying at School. In: C. Barter & D. Berridge, eds. *Children Children Behaving Badly? Peer Violence between Children and Young People.* West Sussex: John Wiley and Sons Ltd, pp. 33–47.

Cowie, H. & Hutson, N., 2005. Peer Support: A Strategy to Help Bystanders Challenge School Bullying. *Pastoral Care*, 23(2), pp. 40–45.

Cowie, H., Hutson, N. & Jennifer, D., 2008. Taking Stock of Violence in U.K. Schools: Risk, Regulation, and Responsibility. *Education and Urban Society*, 40(4), pp. 494–505.

Cowie, H. & Oztug, O., 2008. Pupils' Perceptions of Safety at School. *Pastoral Care in Education*, 26(2), pp. 59–67.

Coy, M., 2009. Moved around Like Bags of Rubbish Nobody Wants: How Multiple Placement Moves Can Make Young Women Vulnerable to Sexual Exploitation. *Child Abuse Review*, 18, pp. 254–266.

Coy, M., Kelly, L., Elvines, F., Garner, M. & Kanyeredzi, A. 2013. *'Sex without Consent, I Suppose That Is Rape': How Young People in England Understand Sexual Consent.* London: Office of the Children's Commissioner.

Coy, M., Thiara, R. & Kelly, L., 2011. *Boys Think Girls Are Toys?: An Evaluation of the Nia Project Prevention Programme on Sexual Exploitation.* London: CWASU London Metropolitan University.

Criminal Justice Joint Inspection, 2013. *Examining Multi-Agency Responses to Children and Young People Who Sexually Offend: A Joint Inspection of the Effectiveness of Multi-Agency Work with Children and Young People in England and Wales Who Have Committed Sexual Offences and Were Supervised in the community.* London: HM Inspectorate of Probation.

Cross, D., Epstein, M., Hearnl, L., Slee, P., Shaw, T. & Monks, H. 2011. National Safe Schools Framework: Policy and Practice to Reduce Bullying in Australian Schools. *International Journal of Behavioral Development*, 35(5), pp. 398–404.

Crown Prosecution Service, 2003. *Rape and Sexual Offences: Chapter 2: Sexual Offences Act 2003 - Principal Offences, and Sexual Offences Act 1956 - Most commonly charged offences.* [Online] Available at: http://www.cps.gov.uk/legal/p_to_r/rape_and_sexual_offences/soa_2003_and_soa_1956 [Accessed 04.02.2017].

Crown Prosecution Service, 2012. *CPS Guidance on: Joint Enterprise Decisions.* London: CPS.

Crown Prosecution Service, 2014. *Crown Prosecution Service Offers Clear Guidance for Prosecutors on 'Revenge Pornography'.* [Online] Available at: www.cps.gov.uk/news/latest_news/crown_prosecution_service_offers_clear_guidance_for_prosecutors_on_revenge_pornography/ [Accessed 03. 12. 2015].

Crown Prosecution Service, 2017. *Anti-Social Behaviour Orders on Conviction (ASBOs).* [Online] Available at: http://www.cps.gov.uk/legal/a_to_c/anti_social_behaviour_guidance/ [Accessed 02. 04 .2017].

D'Arcy, K., Dhaliwal, S. & Thomas, R., 2015. *Families and Communities against Child Sexual Exploitation (FCASE).* Luton: University of Bedfordshire.

D'Arcy, K. & Thomas, R., 2016. *Nightwatch: CSE in Plain Sight.* Luton: University of Bedfordshire.

DCSF, 2009. *Safeguarding Children and Young People from Sexual Exploitation: Supplementary Guidance to Working Together to Safeguard Children.* London: DSCF.

DCSF, 2010. *Safeguarding Children and Young People Affected by Gang Activity.* [Online] Available at: www.gov.uk/government/uploads/system/uploads/attachment_data/file/288804/Safeguarding_children_Gang_activity.pdf [Accessed 03. 12. 2015].

Decker, S. & Van Winkle, B., 1996. *Life in the Gang.* Cambridge: Cambridge University Press.

De La Rue, L., Polanin, J. R., Espelagel, D. L. & Piggot, T. D., 2014. *School-Based Interventions to Reduce Dating and Sexual Violence: A Systematic Review.* s.l.: Campbell Systematic Reviews.

Department for Education, 2016. *Keeping Children Safe in Education: Proposed Changes.* [Online] Available at: www.gov.uk/government/consultations/keeping-children-safe-in-education-proposed-changes [Accessed 10. 01. 2016].

DfE, 2014. *Preventing and Tackling Bullying Advice for Headteachers, Staff and Governing Bodies.* London: Crown Copyright.

DfE, 2015a. *Keeping Children Safe in Education: Proposed Changes.* [Online] Available at: www.gov.uk/government/consultations/keeping-children-safe-in-education-proposed-changes [Accessed 04. 01. 2016].

DfE, 2015b. *The Prevent Duty: Departmental Advice for Schools and Childcare Providers.* [Online] Available at: www.gov.uk/government/uploads/system/uploads/attachment_data/file/439598/prevent-duty-departmental-advice-v6.pdf [Accessed 03. 12. 2015].

DfE, 2016. *Keeping Children Safe in Education Statutory Guidance for Schools and Colleges.* London: Crown Copyright.

DfE, 2017. *Child Sexual Exploitation Definition and a Guide for Practitioners, Local Leaders and Decision Makers Working to Protect Children from Child Sexual Exploitation.* London: Crown Copyright.

Dobash, E., Dobash, R. & Noaks, L., 1995. *Gender and Crime*. 1st Edition. Cardiff: University of Wales Press.

EDC, 2013. *Promote Prevent: Prevent Bullying*. [Online] Available at: http://preventingbullying. promoteprevent.org/school-and-community-prevention-and-intervention [Accessed 03. 12. 2015].

EVAW, 2010a. *Almost a Third of Girls Experience Unwanted Sexual Touching in UK Schools: New YouGov Poll*. [Online] Available at: www.endviolenceagainstwomen.org.uk/2010-poll-on-sexual-harassment-in-schools [Accessed 08. 2013].

EVAW, 2010b. *A Whole School Approach: A Template Model for Education Establishments to Prevent Violence and Abuse of Girls*. [Online] Available at: www.endviolenceagainstwomen. org.uk/data/files/Whole_School_Approach.pdf [Accessed 03. 12. 2015].

Evening Standard, 2012. *Absent Fathers Are Key Cause of Knife Crime, Says David Lammy*. [Online] Available at: https://www.standard.co.uk/news/absent-fathers-are-key-cause-of-knife-crime-says-david-lammy-8193990.html [Accessed 10.10.2016].

Evening Standard, 2017. *Head of Scotland Yard's Murder Squad: It's Up to Parents to Tell Their Children to Stop Carrying Knives*. [Online] Available at: www.standard.co.uk/news/crime/top-detective-its-up-to-parents-to-help-children-stop-carrying-knives-in-london-a3471031. html [Accessed 22. 02. 2017].

Farmer, E. & Pollock, S., 2003. Managing Sexually Abused and/or Abusing Children in Substitute Care. *Child and Family Social Work*, 8, pp. 101–112.

Featherstone, B., Gupta, A., Morris, K. & Warner, J., 2016. Let's Stop Feeding the Risk Monster: Towards a Social Model of 'Child Protection'. *Families, Relationships and Societies*. DOI: https://doi.org/10.1332/204674316X14552878034622

Finkelhor, D., Ormrod, R. & Chaffin, M., 2009. *Juveniles Who Commit Sex Offences against Minors*. s.l. Office of Juvenile Justice and Delinquency Prevention, US Department of Justice.

Firmin, C., 2008. *Building Bridges Project: A Study into Weapon Use in London*. London: ROTA.

Firmin, C., 2011. *This Is It: This Is My Life . . . Female Voice in Violence Final Report*. London: ROTA.

Firmin, C., 2013. Something Old or Something New: Do Pre-Existing Conceptualisations of Abuse Enabe a Sufficient Response to Abuse in Young People's Relationships and Peer Groups? In: M. Melrose, & J. Pearce, *Critical Perspectives on Child Sexual Exploitation and Related Trafficking*. Hampshire: Palgrave Macmillan, pp. 38–51.

Firmin, C. 2017. From Genograms to Peer-Group Mapping: Introducing Peer Relationships into Social Work Assessment and Intervention. *Families, Relationships and Societies* (Accepted). DOI: https://doi.org/10.1332/204674317X15088482907590

Firmin, C. & Curtis, G., 2015. *Practitioner Briefing #1: What Is Peer-on-Peer Abuse*. [Online] Available at: www.msunderstood.org.uk/assets/templates/msunderstood/style/documents/ MSUPB01.pdf [Accessed 10. 2015].

Firmin, C., Warrington, C. & Pearce, J., 2016. Sexual Exploitation and Its Impact on Developing Sexualities and Sexual Relationships: The Need for Contextual Social Work Interventions. *British Journal of Social Work*, 46(8), pp. 2318–2337.

Flyvbjerg, B., 2006. Five Misunderstandings About Case Study Research. *Qualitative Inquiry*, 12(2), pp. 215-249.

Foshee, V. A., McNaughton Reyes, H. L., Ennett, S. T., Suchindran, C., Mathias, J. P., Karriker-Jaffe, K. J., Bauman K.E. & Benefield, T. S., 2011. Risk and Protective Factors Distinguishing Profiles of Adolescent Peer and Dating Violence Perpetration. *Journal of Adolescent Health*, 48(4), pp. 344–350.

Fox, C. L., Corr, M. L., Gadd, D. & Butler, I., 2013. *From Boys to Men: Phase One Findings.* Manchester: University of Manchester School of Law.

Franklin, K., 2004. Enacting Masculinity: Antigay Violence and Group Rape as Participatory Theatre. *Sexuality Research and Social Policy*, 1, pp. 25–40.

Franklin, K., 2013. Masculinity, Status, and Power: Implicit Messages in Western Media Discourse on High-Profile Cases of Multiple Perpetrator Rape. In: M. A. Horvath & J. Woodhams, eds. *Handbook on the Study of Multiple Perpetrator Rape: A Multidisciplinary Respnse to an International Problem.* Oxon: Routledge, pp. 37–66.

Frosh, S., Phoenix, A. & Pattman, R., 2002. *Young Masculinities: Understanding Boys in Contemporary Society.* Basingstoke: Palgrave Macmillan.

Futures Without Violence, 2009. *The Facts on Domestic, Dating and Sexual Violence.* [Online] Available at: www.futureswithoutviolence.org/userfiles/file/Children_and_Families/DomesticViolence.pdf

Gadd, D., Corr, M. L., Fox, C. L. & Butler, I., 2013. *From Boys to Men: Phase Three Key Findings.* Manchester: University of Manchester School of Law.

Gardner, M. & Steinberg, L., 2005. Peer Influence on Risk Taking, Risk Preference, and Risky Decision Making in Adolescence and Adulthood: An Experimental Study. *Developmental Psychology*, 41, pp. 635–635.

GirlGuiding UK, 2014. *Girls' Attitudes Survey 2014.* [Online] Available at: http://new.girlguiding.org.uk/girls-attitudes-survey-2014 [Accessed 03. 12. 2015].

Glover, D., Gough, G., Johnson, M. & Cartwright, N., 2010. Bullying in 25 Secondary Schools: Incidence, Impact and Intervention. *Educational Research*, 42(2), pp. 141–156.

The Guardian, 2008. *Youth Crime: Greedy, Rude Adults 'Fuelling Teen Violence'.* [Online] Available at: *https://www.theguardian.com/education/2008/jul/11/schools.uk* [Accessed 12. 09. 2016].

The Guardian, 2009. *Girl, 15, Sentenced to Eight Years Over Bullying Death of Rosimeiri Boxall.* [Online] Available at: www.theguardian.com/uk/2009/dec/15/hatice-can-sentenced-bullying-death [Accessed 03. 10. 2015].

The Guardian, 2012. *Jealous Teenager Who Stabbed Girlfriend 60 Times Jailed for Life.* [Online] Available at: www.theguardian.com/uk/2012/sep/07/teenager-stabbed-girlfriend-jailed-life [Accessed 03. 12. 2015].

The Guardian, 2015. *Professionals Blamed Oxfordshire Girls for Their Sexual Abuse, Report Finds.* [Online] Available at: www.theguardian.com/society/2015/mar/03/professionals-blamed-oxfordshire-girls-for-their-sexual-abuse-report-finds [Accessed 03. 12. 2015].

Guilty By Association. 2014. [Film] Directed by Fran Robertson. UK: Fran Robertson.

Hackett, S., 2006. Towards a Resilience-Based Intervention Model for Young People with Harmful Sexual Behaviours. In: M. Erooga & H. Masson, eds. *Children and Young People Who Sexually Abuse Others: Current Developments and Practice Responses*, 2nd Edition. Oxon: Routledge. pp. 103-115

Hackett, S., 2014. *Children and Young People with Harmful Sexual Behaviours.* Dartington: Research in Practice.

Hackett, S., Balfe, M., Masson, H. & Phillips, J., 2014. Family Responses to Young Poeple Who Have Sexually Abused: Anger, Ambivalence and Acceptance. *Children and Society*, 28(2), pp. 128–139.

Hackett, S., Phillips, J., Masson, H. & Balfe, M., 2013. Individual, Family and Abuse Characteristics of 700 British Child and Adolescent Sexual Abusers. *Child Abuse Review*, 22(4), pp. 232–245.

Hagell, A. & Jeyarajah-Dent, R., 2006. *Children Who Committ Acts of Serious Interpersonal Violence.* London: Jessica Kingsley.

Hall, A., 2015. *Ofsted Inspections and Safeguarding from Sept, 2015.* [Online] Available at: www. safeguardinginschools.co.uk/wp-content/uploads/2015/06/Ofsted-Inspection-and-Safeguarding-from-September-2015-FINAL.pdf [Accessed 03. 12. 2015].

Halpern, C. T. et al., 2001. Partner Violence Among Adolescents in Opposite-Sex Romantic Relationships: Findings From the National Longitudinal Study of Adolescent Health. *American Journal of Public Health,* 91(10), pp. 1679–1685.

Hanson, E. & Holmes, D., 2015. *The Difficult Age: Developing a More Effective Response to Risk in Adolescence.* Darlington: Research in Practice.

Harber, C. & Sakade, N., 2009. Schooling for Violence and Peace: How Does Peace Education Differ from 'Normal' Schooling? *Journal of Peace Education,* 6(2), pp. 171–187.

Harding, S., 2012. *The Role and Significance of Social Capital and Street Capital in the Social Field of the Violent Youth Gangs in Central Lambeth.* Bedfordshire: University of Bedfordshire.

Henggeler, S., Letourneau, E., Chapman, J., Bourdin, C., Charles, M., Schewe, P. & McCart, M. 2009. Mediators of Change for Multisystemic Therapy with Juvenile Sexual Offenders. *Journal of Consulting and Clinical Psychology,* 77(3), pp. 451–462.

Henry, S., 2008. *Bullying as a Social Pathology: A Peer Group Analysis.* New York: Edwin Mellen Press.

Herald Express, 2013. *Inquest Hears 'Bullied' Brixham Student Izzy Dix Hanged Herself.* [Online] Available at: www.torquayheraldexpress.co.uk/Inquest-hears-bullied-Brixham-student-Izzy-Dix/story-20315950-detail/story.html [Accessed 03. 12. 2015].

Herrera, V. M. & Stuewig, J., 2011. Impact of Child Maltreatment and Domestic Abuse. In: C. Barter & D. Berridge, eds. *Children Behaving Badly? Peer Violence between Children and Young People.* West Sussex: John Wiley and Sons Ltd, pp. 155–166.

Hickman, L., Jaycox, L. & Aronoff, J., 2004. Dating Violence among Adolescents: Prevalence, Genderdistribution and Prevention Program Effectiveness. *Trauma, Violence and Abuse,* 5(2), pp. 123–142.

HM Government, 2015. *Working Together to Safeguard Children: A Guide to Inter-Agency Working to Safeguard and Promote the Welfare of Children,* London: Department for Education (DfE).

HM Government, 2016. *Ending Gang Violence and Exploitation.* London: The Stationary Office.

Holland, J., Ramazanoglu, C., Sharpe, S. & Thomson, R., 1998. *The Male in the Head: Young People, Heterosexuality and Power.* London: The Tufnell Press.

Home Office, 2011. *Ending Gang and Youth Violence: A Cross Government Report Including Further Evidence and Good Practice Cases.* London: The Stationary Office.

Home Office, 2013. *Information for Local Areas on the Change to the Definition of Domestic Violence and Abuse.* London: Crown Copyright.

Horvath, M. A. H., Alys, L., Massey, K., Pina, A., Scally, M. & Adler, J. R., 2013. *Basically Porn Is Everywhere: A Rapid Evidence Assessment on the Effect That Access and Exposure to Pornography Has on Children and Young People.* London: Office of the Children's Commissioner.

Horvath, M. A. H. & Kelly, L., 2009. Multiple Perpetrator Rape: Naming an Offence and Initial Research Findings. *Journal of Sexual Aggression,* 15, pp. 83–96.

Horvath, M. A. H. & Woodhams, J., 2013. *Handbook on the Study of Multiple Perpetrator Rape.* Oxon: Routledge.

House of Commons Education Committee, 2012. *Children First: The Child Protection System in England.* London: The Stationary Office.

Hughes-Jones, L. & Roberts, S., 2015. Closing the Gap: Confronting the Problem of Hotels as Venues for Child Sexual Exploitation. *The Howard Journal of Criminal Justice,* 54(4), pp. 336–351.

IICSA, 2016. *Independent Inquiry into Child Sexual Abuse.* [Online] Available at: www.iicsa. org.uk/ [Accessed 01. 12. 2016].

Institute of Physics, 2015. *Opening Doors: A Guide to Good Practice in Countering Gender Stereotyping in Schools.* London: IOE.

Jay, A., 2014. *Independent Inquiry into Child Sexual Exploitation in Rotherham (1997–2013).* Rotherham: s.n.

Jenks, C., 2005. *Childhood,* 2nd Edition. Oxon: Routledge.

Johnson, F., 2013. *Redacted Overview Report on the Serious Case Review Relating to Tom and Vic.* Kingston: Kingston LSCB.

JTAI, 2016. *'Time to Listen': A Joined Up Response to Child Sexual Exploitation and Missing Children.* London: Ofsted.

Kendrick, A., 2011. Peer Violence in Provision for Children in Care. In: C. Barter & D. Berridge, eds. *Children Behaving Badly? Peer Violence between Children and Young People.* West Sussex: John Wiley and Sons Ltd, pp. 71–84.

Kenyon, J. & Rookwood, J., 2010. 'One Eye in Toxteth, One Eye in Croxteth': Examining Youth Perspectives of Racist and Anti-Social Behaviour, Identity and the Value of Sport as an Integrative Enclave in Liverpool. *International Journal of Arts and Sciences,* 3(8), pp. 296–519.

Khan, L., Brice, H., Saunders, A. & Plumtree, A., 2013. *A Need to Belong: What Leads Girls to Join Gangs.* London: Centre for Mental Health.

Latchford, L., Firmin, C., Fritz, D. & Hackett, S. 2016. *Young People Who Sexually Harm Peers in Groups: A Rapid Evidence Assessment of International Literature.* Luton: University of Bedfordshire.

Lambine, M., 2013. Numbers Matter: Characteristic Differences between Lone, Duo and 3+ Group Rapes. In: M. A. Horvath & J. Woodhams, eds. *Handbook on the Study of Multiple Perpetrator Rape: A Multidisciplinary Response to an International Problem.* Oxon: Routledge, pp. 67–81.

Larasi, L., 2015. *Local Responses to Peer-on-Peer Abuse: Applications for Support.* [Online] http://www.msunderstood.org.uk/assets/templates/msunderstood/style/documents/ MSUTB02.pdf [Accessed 10. 12. 2015].

Lawler, S., 2004. Rules of Engagement: Habitus, Power and Resistance. *Sociological Review,* 52(s2), pp. 110–128.

Letourneau, E. & Borduin, C., 2008. The Effective Treatment of Juveniles Who Sexually Offend: An Ethical Imperative. *Ethics and Behavior,* 18(2–3), pp. 286–306.

Letourneau, E., Henggeler, S., McCart, M., Borduin, C. & Schewe, P., 2013. Two-Year Follow-Up of a Randomized Effectiveness Trial Evaluating MST for Juveniles Who Sexually Offend. *Journal of Family Psychology,* 27(6), pp. 978–985.

Light, R., 2007. Re-Examining Hegemonic Masculinity. *Quest,* 59(3), pp. 323–338.

Losel, F. & Bender, D., 2006. Risk Factors for Serious and Violence Antisocial Behaviour in Children and Youth. In: A. Hagell & R. Jeyarajah-Dent, eds. *Children Who Commit Acts of Serious Interpersonal Violence: Messages for Best Practice.* London: Jessica Kingsley, pp. 42–73.

Mail Online, 2008. *Pathetic Posturing Won't Stop Knife Crime.* [Online] Available at: *http:// www.dailymail.co.uk/news/article-1023215/Pathetic-posturing-wont-stop-knife-crime.html* [Accessed 04. 12. 2015].

Mail Online, 2013. *Teenager, 16, Stabbed Schoolboy on Bus Full of Horrified Passengers on the Victim's 16th Birthday.* [Online] Available at: www.dailymail.co.uk/news/article-2493080/ Teenager-16-stabbed-schoolboy-bus-horrified-passengers-victims-16th-birthday.html [Accessed 03. 12. 2015].

Mail Online, 2015. *Bad parenting made young white girls an easy target for 'grotesque' exploitation at the hands of Asian sex gangs, says Judge.* [Online] Available at: http://www.dailymail.co.uk/news/article-3225226/Six-members-Asian-child-sex-abuse-gang-jailed-total-82-years-grooming-white-girls-sex-exchange-milkshake-McDonald-s.html [Accessed 02. 10. 2016].

Mail Online, 2015a. *'I Cannot Watch Him Suffer Anymore': Mother Wins Global Support After She Reveals Her Heartbreaking Decision to Take Teen Son Out of School Amid Relentless Violent Bullying.* [Online] Available at: www.dailymail.co.uk/news/article-3328329/Mother-wins-worldwide-support-takes-teenage-son-school-amid-violent-bullying.html [Accessed 03. 12. 2015].

Mail Online, 2015b. *Teenage Girl Tragically Killed Herself after Bullies Flooded Her Social Media Accounts with Horrible Messages . . . as Her Parents Call for Action Against the Two Boys Responsible.* [Online] Available at: www.dailymail.co.uk/news/article-3043651/Parents-teen-committed-suicide-suffering-vicious-bullying-Facebook-demand-greater-protection-kids-online.html [Accessed 03. 12. 2015].

Maxwell, C. & Aggleton, P., 2010. Agency in Action: Young Women and Their Sexual Relationships in a Private School. *Gender and Education*, 22(3), pp. 327–343.

McNay, L., 2004. Agency and Experience: Gender as a Lived Relation. *Sociologial Review*, 52(s2), pp. 175–90.

McNaughton Nicholls, C. et al., 2014. *Research on the Sexual Exploitation of Boys and Young Men: A UK Scoping Study, a Summary of the Findings.* Barkingside: Barnardo's.

McRobbie, A., 2004. Notes on 'What Not To Wear' and Post-Feminist Symbolic Violence. *Sociological Review*, 52(s2), pp. 97–109.

Melrose, M., 2013. Young People and Sexual Exploitation: A Critical Discourse Analysis. In: M. Melrose & J. Pearce, eds. *Critical Perspectives on Child Sexual Exploitation and Related Trafficking.* Hampshire: Palgrave Macmillan, pp. 9–22.

Melrose, M. & Pearce, J., 2013. *Critical Perspectives on Child Sexual Exploitation and Related Trafficking.* Basingstoke: Palgrave Macmillan.

Mentors in Violence Prevention, 2016. *Mentors in Violence Prevention.* [Online] Available at: http://mvpscotland.org.uk/MVPabout.html [Accessed 01. 12. 2016].

Messerschmidt, J. W., 1994. Schooling, Masculinities and Youth Crime by White Boys. In: T. Newburn & E. A. Stanko, eds. *Just Boys Doing Business?* London: Routlegde, pp. 81–99.

Messerschmidt, J. W., 2012a. Engendering Gendered Knowledge: Assessing the Academic Appropriation of Hegemonic Masculinity. *Men and Masculinities*, 15(1), pp. 56–76.

Messerschmidt, J. W., 2012b. *Gender, Heterosexuality, and Youth Violence: The Struggle for Recognition.* Plymouth: Rowman and Littefield Publishers, Inc.

Miller, J., 2001. *One of the Guys: Girls, Gangs, and Gender.* New York: Oxford University Press.

Mills, C. W., 1959. *The Sociological Imagination.* New York: Oxford University Press.

Mirror, 2016. *Boy, 16, Stabbed to Death at London Playing Field after Attending Friend's 16th Birthday Party.* [Online] Available at: www.mirror.co.uk/news/uk-news/boy-16-dies-after-stabbing-7150882 [Accessed 17. 01. 2016].

Mohr, A., 2006. Family Variables Associated with Peer Victimization: Does Family Violence Enhance the Probability of Being Victimized by Peers? *Swiss Journal of Psychology*, 65(2), pp. 107–116.

Moore, J., 1991. *Going Down to the Barrio: Homeboys and Homegirls in Change.* Philadelphia: Temple University Press.

MOPAC, 2015. *MOPAC Challenge – Child Sexual Exploitation.* [Online] Available at: https://www.london.gov.uk/sites/default/files/gla_migrate_files_destination/MOPAC%20Challenge%20CSE%20June%2010%202015%20-%20Transcript.pdf [Accessed 20. 01. 2016].

Muelle, A., James, W., Abrutyn, S. & Levin, M., 2015. Suicide Ideation and Bullying among US Adolescents: Examining the Intersections of Sexual Orientation, Gender, and Race/Ethnicity. *American Journal of Public Health*, 105(5), pp. 980–985.

Murder Games: The Life and Death of Breck Bednar, 2016. [Film] Directed by Katharine English, UK: Rare Day Limited.

National Children's Bureau, 2006. *The Ecological Approach to the Assessment of Asylum Seeking and Refugee Children*. [Online] Available at: www.ncb.org.uk/media/963289/arc_1_1 ecologicalapproach.pdf [Accessed 03. 12. 2015].

Naylor, P. B., Petch, L. & Williams, J. V., 2011. Sibling Abuse and Bullying in Childhood and Adolescence: Knowns and Unknowns. In: C. Barter & D. Berridge, eds. *Children Behaving Badly? Peer Violence between Children and Young People*. West Sussex: John Wiley and Son's Ltd, pp. 47–58.

NICE, 2016. *Harmful Sexual Behaviour among Children and Young People*. s.l.: NICE.

Nieuwbeerta, P. & van der Laan, P. H., 2006. Minors Involved in Murder and Manslaughter: An Exploration of the Situation in the Netherlands. In: A. Hagell & R. Jeyarajah-Den, eds. *Children Who Commit Acts of Serious Interpersonal Violence: Messages for Best Practice*. London: Jessica Kingsley, pp. 92–108.

NSPCC, 2016. *A Child's Legal Rights: Legal Definitions*. [Online] Available at: www.nspcc.org.uk/preventing-abuse/child-protection-system/legal-definition-child-rights-law/legal-definitions/ [Accessed 16. 01. 2016].

O'Brien, C., 2011. Young People's Comparisons of Cross-Gender and Same-Gender Bullying in British Secondary Schools. *Educational Research*, 53(3), pp. 257–301.

O'Brien, K., Daffern, M., Meng Chu, C. & Thomas, S. D. M., 2013. Youth Gang Affiliation, Violence, and Criminal Activities: A Review of Motivational, Risk, and Protective Factors. *Aggression and Violent Behavior*, 18(4), pp. 417–425.

The Observer, 2008. *The Killing of Kodjo*. [Online] Available at: www.theguardian.com/uk/2008/nov/16/kodjo-yenga-knife-stabbing-teenage [Accessed 03. 12. 2015].

OCC, 2012. *Briefing for the Rt Hon Michael Gove MP, Secretary of State for Education, on the Emerging Findings of the Office of the Children's Commissioner's Inquiry into Child Sexual Exploitation in Gangs and Groups, with a Special Focus on Children in Care*, London: Office of the Children's Commissioner.

Office of National Statistics, 2013. *Crime in England and Wales, Year Ending March 2013*. [Online] Available at: www.ons.gov.uk/ons/rel/crime-stats/crime-statistics/period-ending-march-2013/stb-crime–period-ending-march-2013.html#tab-Crime-experienced-by-children-aged-10-to-15 [Accessed 03. 12. 2015].

Ofsted, 2011. *Ages of Concern: Learning Lessons from Serious Case Reviews*. London: Ofsted.

Ofsted, 2012. *Not Yet Good Enough: Personal, Social, Health and Economic Education in Schools*. London: Ofsted.

ONS, 2015. *Chapter 4: Violent Crime and Sexual Offences: Intimate Personal Violence and Serious Sexual Assault*. [Online] Available at: www.ons.gov.uk/ons/dcp171776_394500.pdf [Accessed 03. 12. 2015].

Our Watch, 2016. *Respectful Relationships Education in Schools: The Beginnings of Change*. Victoria: Our Watch and Victoria State Government.

Palmer, S. & Pitts, J., 2006. Othering' the Brothers: Black Youth, Racial Solidarity and Gun Crime. *Youth and Policy*, 91, pp. 5–22.

Parton, N., 2014. *The Politics of Child Protection*. London: Palgrave.

Pearce, J., 2013. A Social Model of 'Abused Consent'. In: M. Melrose & J. Pearce, eds. *Critical Perspectives on Child Sexual Exploitation and Related Trafficking*. Hampshire: Palgrave Macmillan, pp. 52–68.

Pearce, J. & Pitts, J., 2011. *Youth Gangs, Sexual Violence and Sexual Exploitation: A Scoping Exercise for the Office of the Children's Commissioner for England.* London: Office of the Children's Commissioner.

Pedersen, M. L., 2014. Gang Joining in Denmark: Prevalence and Correlates of Street Gang Membership. *Journal of Scandinavian Studies in Criminology and Crime Prevention,* 15, pp. 55–72.

Peguero, A. A., 2009. Opportunity, Involvement, and Student Exposure to School Violence. *Youth Violence and Juvenile Justice,* 7(4), pp. 299–312.

Pitts, J., 2008. *Reluctant Gangsters: The Changing Shape of Youth Crime.* Exeter: Willan Publishing.

Pitts, J., 2013. Drifting into Trouble: Sexual Exploitation and Gang Affiliation. In: M. Melrose & J. Pearce, eds. *Critical Perspectives on Child Sexual Exploitation and Related Trafficking.* Basingstoke: Palgrave Macmillan, pp. 23–37.

Polk, K., 1994. Masulinity, Honour and Confrontational Homicide. In: T. Newburn & E. A. Stanko, eds. *Just Boys Doing Business?* London: Routledge, pp. 166–188.

Porter, L. E., 2013. Leadership and Role-Taking in Multiple Perpetrator Rape. In: M. A. Horvath & J. Woodhams, eds. *Handbook on the Study of Multiple Perpetrator Rape.* Oxon: Routledge, pp. 160–181.

Porter, L. E. & Alison, L. J., 2001. A Partially Ordered Scale of Influence in Violent Group Behaviour: An Example from Gang Rape. *Small Group Research,* Volume 32, pp. 475–497.

Porter, L. E. & Alison, L. J., 2006. Examining Group Rape: A Descriptive Analysis of Offender and Victim Behaviour. *European Journal of Criminology,* 3, pp. 357–381.

Powell, A., 2008. Amor Fati? Gender Habitus and Young People's Negotiation of (Hetero) Sexual Consent. *Journal of Sociology,* 44(2), pp. 167–84.

Powell, A., 2010. *Sex, Power and Consent: Youth Culture and the Unwritten Rules.* Cambridge: Cambridge University Press.

Powell, A., 2011. *Review of Bystander Approaches in Support of Preventing Violence against Women.* Carlton, Victoria: Victorian Health Promotion Foundation.

Prange, A. & Neher, C., 2014. *Brazilians Believe Victims Deserved Sexual Assault, Study Finds.* [Online] Available at: *http://www.dw.com/en/brazilians-believe-victims-deserved-sexual-assault-study-finds/a-17536234* [Accessed 03. 12. 2015].

Prime Minister's Office, 2015. *PM Unveils Tough New Measures to Tackle Child Sexual Exploitation.* [Online] Available at: www.gov.uk/government/news/pm-unveils-tough-new-measures-to-tackle-child-sexual-exploitation [Accessed 03. 12. 2015].

Radford, L., Corral, S., Bradley, C., Fisher, H., Bassett, C., Howat, N. & Collishaw, S. 2011. *Child Abuse and Neglect in the UK Today.* London: NSPCC.

Ralphs, R., Medina, J. & Aldridge, J., 2009. Who Needs Enemies with Friends Like These? The Importance of Place for Young People Living in Known Gang Areas. *Journal of Youth Studies,* 12(5), pp. 483–500.

Rewind&Reframe, 2014. *Rewind&Reframe: Challenging Sexist and Racist Music Videos.* [Online] Available at: www.rewindreframe.org/ [Accessed 04. 2014].

Rigby, K. & Johnson, B., 2005. Student Bystanders in Australian Schools. *Pastoral Care,* 23(2), pp. 10–16.

Ringrose, J., Gill, R., Livingstone, S. & Harvey, L., 2011. *A Qualitative Study of Children, Young People and 'Sexting'.* London: NSPCC.

Ringrose, J. & Renold, E., 2011. Boys, Girls and Performing Normative Violence in Schools: A Gendered Critique of Bully Discourses. In: C. Barter & D. Berridge, eds. *Children Behaving Badly? Peer Violence between Children and Young People.* West Sussex: John Wiley and Sons Ltd, pp. 181–196.

Root, T., 2005. Student/Teacher Partnerships Can Be the Key to Combat Bullying. *Education*, 7(92). p. 7.

Royal Commission, 2016. *Royal Commission into Institutional Responses to Child Seuxal Abuse.* [Online] Available at: www.childabuseroyalcommission.gov.au/ [Accessed 01. 12. 2016].

SafeLives, 2015. *Safe Lives Dash Risk Checklist.* [Online] Available at: www.safelives.org.uk/sites/default/files/resources/Dash%20with%20guidance%20FINAL.pdf [Accessed 03. 12. 2015].

Sharp, N., 2013. Missing from Discourse: South Asian Young Women and Sexual Exploitation. In: M. Melrose & J. Pearce, eds. *Critical Perspectives on Child Sexual Exploitation and Related Trafficking.* Basingstoke: Palgrave Macmillan, pp. 96–109.

Shuker, L., 2013a. Constructs of Safety for Children in Care Affected by Sexual Exploitation. In: M. Melrose & J. Pearce, eds. *Critical Perspectives on Child Sexual Exploitation and Related Trafficking.* Basingstoke: Palgrave Macmillan, pp. 125–138.

Shuker, L., 2013b. *Safe Accommodation Need to Complete.* Barkingside: Barnardo's.

Skelton, T. & Valentine, G., 1998. *Cool Places: Geographies of Youth Cultures.* London: Routledge.

Smallbone, S., Rayment-Mchugh, S. & Smith, D., 2012. Youth Sexual Offending: Context, Good-Enough Lives, and Engaging With a Wider Prevention Agenda. *International Journal of Behvaioural Consultation and Therapy*, 8(3–4), pp. 49–54.

Smith, J., 2007. 'Ye've Got to 'Ave Balls to Play This Game Sir!' Boys, Peers and Fears: The Negative Influence of School-Based Cultural Accomplices in Constructing Hegemonic Masculinities. *Gender and Education*, 19(2), pp. 179–198.

Spindler, A. & Bouchard, M., 2011. Structure of Behaviour? Revisiting Gang Typologies. *International Criminal Justice Review*, 21, pp. 263–282.

Squires, P. & Goldsmith, C., 2011. Bullets, Blades and Mean Streets: Youth Violence and Criminal Justice Failure. In: C. Barter & D. Berridge, eds. *Children Behaving Badly? Peer Violence between Children and Young People.* West Sussex: John Wiley and Sons Ltd, pp. 199–216.

Stanko, E. A., 1994. Challenging the Problem of Men's Individual Violence. In: T. Newburn & E. A. Stanko, eds. *Just Boys Doing Business?* London: Routledge, pp. 32–45.

The Stylist, 2014. *Teen Girl Learns of Her Rape When Pictures Are Posted Online.* [Online] Available at: www.stylist.co.uk/life/outrage-over-a-teenage-girls-rape-that-went-viral-on-social-media [Accessed 03. 12. 2015].

Talbot, K. & Quayle, M., 2010. The Perils of Being a Nice Guy: Contextual Variation in Five Young Women's Constructions of Acceptable Hegemonic and Alternative Masculinities. *Men and Masculinities*, 13, pp. 255–278.

Teisl, M. & Cicchetti, D., 2008. Physical Abuse, Cognitive and Emotional Processes, and Agressive/Disruptive Behaviour Problems. *Social Development*, 70, pp. 797–809.

The Telegraph, 2008. *Gordon Brown Says Parents to Blame for Teenage Knife Crime.* [Online] Available at: http://www.telegraph.co.uk/news/politics/labour/2403766/Gordon-Brown-says-parents-to-blame-for-teenage-knife-crime.html [Accessed 04. 10. 2015].

Thomas, R., 2015. *CSE Research Briefings Film Parents as partners in safeguarding children from sexual exploitation* [Online]. https://www.youtube.com/watch?time_continue=8&v=HCeNqXuQKrI [Accessed 02.02.2016].

Thomson, P. & Gunter, H., 2008. Researching Bullying with Students: A Lens on Everyday Life in an 'Innovative School'. *International Journal of Inclusive Education*, 12(2), pp. 185–200.

Transport Select Committee, 2014. *Transport Committee - Fifth Report: Security on the Railway,* London: Stationary Office.

Tremblay, R. E., Nagin, D. S. & Seguin, J. R., 2004. Physical Aggression During Early Childhood. *Peadiatrics*, 114(1), pp. 43–50.

Trotter, J., 2006. Violent Crimes? Young People's Experiences of Homophobia and Misogyny in Secondary Schools. *Practice*, 18(4), pp. 291–302.

UN Broadband Commission, 2015. *Cyber Violence against Women and Girls: A Worldwide Wake-Up Call*. [Online] Available at: www.unwomen.org/~/media/headquarters/attachments/sections/library/publications/2015/cyber_violence_gender%20report.pdf [Accessed 03. 12. 2015].

UNICEF, 2014. *Global Statistics on Children's Protection from Violence, Exploitation and Abuse*. New York: UNICEF.

UNGEI, 2015. *School-Related Gender-Based Violence Is Preventing the Achievement of Quality Education for All*. [Online] Available at: www.ungei.org/resources/files/232107E.pdf [Accessed 03. 12. 2015].

United Nations, 2015. *CRC Call for Submissions on Its General Comment on the Rights of Adolescents*. [Online] Available at: www.ohchr.org/EN/HRBodies/CRC/Pages/CallRightsofAdolescents.aspx [Accessed 01. 04. 2016].

UN Women, 2015. *Facts and Figures: Ending Violence against Women*. [Online] Available at: www.unwomen.org/en/what-we-do/ending-violence-against-women/facts-and-figures [Accessed 03. 12. 2015].

Vivolo-Kantor, A. M., O Malley Olsen, E. & Bacon, S., 2016. Associations of Teen Dating Violence Victimization with School Violence and Bullying among US High School Students. *Journal of School Health*, 86(8), pp. 620–627.

Vizard, E., 2006. Children with Sexually Abusive Behaviours: A Special Subgroup. In: A. Hagell & R. Jeyarajah-Dent, eds. *Children Who Commit Acts of Serious Interpersonal Violence: Messages for Best Practice*. London: Jessica Kingsley, pp. 73–91.

Vizard, E., Hickey, N., French, L. & McCrory, E., 2007. Children and Adolescents Who Present with Sexually Abusive Behaviour: A UK Descriptive Study. *Journal of Forensic Psychiatry and Psychology*, 18(1), pp. 59–73.

Wales Online, 2014. *Crimewatch Appeal after Teenager Was Raped Twice by a Gang of Six Youths in Cardiff Park*. [Online] Available at: www.walesonline.co.uk/news/wales-news/crimewatch-appeal-after-teenager-raped-8221077 [Accessed 03. 12. 2015].

Walters, N., 2011. *Living Dolls: The Return of Sexism*. London: Virago.

Warr, M., 2002. *Companions in Crime: The Social Aspects of Criminal Conduct*. Cambridge: Cambridge University Press.

Warrington, C., 2013. Partners in Care? Sexually Exploited Young People's Inclusion and Exclusion from Decision Making about Safeguarding. In: M. Melrose & J. Pearce, eds. *Critical Perspectives on Child Sexual Exploitation and Related Trafficking*. Basingstoke: Palgrave Macmillan, pp. 110–124.

Weerman, F. M., Bernasco, W., Bruinsma, G. J. N. & Pauwels, L. J. R., 2013. When Is Spending Time with Peers Related to Delinquency? The Importance of Where, What, and With Whom. *Crime & Delinquency*, 20(10), pp. 1–28.

Widom, C. S., 1989. The Cycle of Violence. *Science*, 14(244), pp. 160–6.

Wikström, P. O., Oberwittler, D., Treiber, K. & Hardie, B., 2012. *Breaking Rules: The Social and Situational Dynamics of Young People's Urban Crime*. Oxford: Oxford University Press.

Women's Aid, 2007. *Cycle of Violence*. [Online] Available at: http://www.womensaid.org.uk/domestic-violence-articles.asp [Accessed 02. 12. 2016].

Women and Equalities Committee, 2016a. *Sexual Harassment and Sexual Violence in Schools*. London: Parliamentary Copyright.

Women and Equalities Committee, 2016b. *Sexual Harassment and Sexual Violence in Schools: Government Response to the Committee's Third Report of Session 2016–17*. London: Crown Copyright.

Wood, M., Barter, C. & Berridge, D., 2011. '*Standing on My Own Two Feet': Disadvantaged Teenagers, Intimate Partner Violence and Coercive Control*. London: NSPCC.

Woodhams, J., 2013. Offender Aggression and Violence in Multiple Perpetrator Rape. In: M. A. Horvath & J. Woodhams, eds. *Handbook on the Study of Multiple Perpetrator Rape*. Oxon: Routledge, pp. 182–197.

World Health Organisation, 2002. *World Report on Violence and Health*. Geneva: World Health Organisation.

World Health Organisation, 2014. *Inspire: Seven Strategies for Ending Violence against Children*. s.l.: WHO.

Young, T. & Hallsworth, S., 2011. Young People, Gangs and Street-Based Violence. In: C. Barter, & D. Berridge, eds. *Children Behaving Badly? Peer Violence between Children and Young People*. West Sussex: John Wiley & Sons Publishing, pp. 59–71.

Youth Justice Board, 2004. *Evaluation of the AIM Framework for the Assessment of Adolescents Who Display Sexually Harmful Behaviour*. London: Youth Justice Board.

Zimring, F. E., 1998. *American Youth Violence*. Oxford, England: Oxford University Press.

APPENDIX

Case file data collection template

CODE NAME

SITE CODE

Template for collection of case study material

Section 1: The offence/case

Section 2: The young people and their social fields

Section 3: Response by professionals

Section 1: The offence/case

1.1 *Details presented:*

Unique reference:

Type of case (CSE, DV, SYV)

1.2 *Case overview*

Please provide a synopsis of the case:

Time:

Date:

Individual's age/gender:

Case outline:

1.3 *The nature of the violence involved in the case:*

What do the case notes tell us about the forms of violence used?

Violence	
Physical	
Emotional	
Sexual	
Financial	
Cyber	
Weapons used?	

Details:

Is the offence a 'one-off' incident or did it take place over more than 24 hours?

Were any particular control tactics, such as videoing, threats, grooming evident in the case notes?

What is known about the motive for the offence?

What were the roles played by young people during the offence?

Section 2: The young people and their social fields

2.1 *The individual young people:*

Code	Age	Gender	Ethni-city	Gang-associated individual	Gang-associated family	Gang-associated peers	Gang-associated school	Gang-associated neighbourhood

For each young person involved in the case, do the case notes indicate whether they were known to any of the following services/sectors:

Code								
Children's services								
Police								
Youth offending								
School								
Pupil referral unit								
Sexual health								
CAMHS								
Housing								
VCS other								

Why did these services have a relationship with the young people in the case?

Of the young people involved in the case, were any known to go missing of own accord or abducted?

Was the referral after a period of going missing from the initial place of safety?

Did the young person return to the place of safety after a period of going missing? Why?

What did they say about the intervening period?

What were the living arrangements of the young people involved in the case?

Child's name/code								
Living with parents								
Other relative								
Homeless								
Residential unit – open								
Residential unit – secure								
Private fostering								
Local authority fostering								
Bed & breakfast								
Semi-independent living								
YOIs								
Other								

Sequential account of accommodation:

Reasons for leaving accommodation:

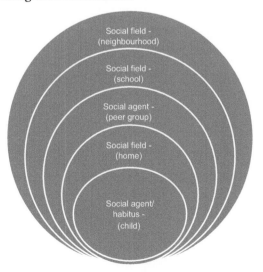

2.2 *Young people's social fields*

Overview of the individual young people: what is recorded about their individual behaviours and characteristics?

In terms of:
a   Abusive behaviours in relation to the categories used in Section 1
b   Criminality
c   Gendered norms
d   Protective and supportive behaviours

- What is recorded about the homes/families from which the young people have come and where they were living at the time of the incident?

- What is recorded about the peer groups to which the young people are associated?

- What is recorded about any intimate relationships in which the individual young people in the case were involved?

- What is recorded about the schools attended by the young people in the case file?

- What is recorded about the neighbourhood from where the young people originated or lived at the time of the incident?

Section 3: Response by professionals

3.1 *Identification*

Who first identified the offence?

Agency	
Police	
Mental health professional	
Sexual health professional	
Physical health professional	
Accident and Emergency	
Children's services	
Social worker	
School	
Parent	
Residential worker	
Foster carer	
Other young person	
Community organisation	
Faith group	
Youth Offending Team	
Other – peer	
Police	

Was the offence identified following a disclosure/complaint or by some other means/behaviour (explain)?

Outline the initial response of agencies and the process by which it came to police attention and recorded.

Stress on **qualitative account** of the circumstances around identification, including: what indicated there had been an offence? What evidence was noted? What were the 'warning signs'?

3.2 *Referral and assessment*

To where did the person who identified the young people in the case refer them? Who else was notified?

Agency	
Immigration	
Children's services	
Police	
Accident and Emergency	
Childline helpline	
Other voluntary agencies	
Solicitors	
Mental health assessment	
Sexual health assessment	
Physical health assessment	
Educational assessment	
School	
Parent	
Social worker	
Residential worker	
Foster carer	
Other young person	
Community organisation	
Faith group	
Youth Offending Team	
Other	

Were any particular assessments conducted on the young people before or following the identification of the offence (Assessment, Intervention, Moving on (AIM) framework, Common Assessment Framework, Domestic Abuse, Stalking and Honour-Based Violence (DASH), child sexual exploitation assessment, gang matrix, etc.)?

3.3 *Multi-agency working*

Which multi-agency structure, if any, had oversight of the case and the young people involved:

Multi-Agency Risk Assessment Conference (MARAC)	
child sexual exploitation (sub-group) of the local safeguarding children's board (LSCB)	
Multi-agency safeguarding hub (MASH)	
Child Protection Conference	
Multi-Agency Public Protection Arrangements (MAPPA)	
Multi-agency gang groups	
Police Gold Group	

Comments:

3.4 *Investigation process*

Following the initial report of the offence, which part/branch/unit of the police force led the investigation (Child Abuse, Sexual Offences, Domestic Abuse, Public Protection, CID, etc.)?

How long did the investigation process take (including up until charge, and between charge and prosecution)?

Were other agencies (outside of the police) involved in the investigation? Did any provide evidence, for example?

Who was interviewed as part of the investigation?

What other forms of evidence were collected and used in the case (phone records, forensics, CCTV footage, etc.)?

Did any of the offenders offer a guilty plea (explain)?

Did the investigation identify leaders/followers within the group of offenders?

Were all suspects charged (explain)?

Were all suspected victims formal complainants (explain)?

What was the complainant's account of the offence (explain)?

What was the suspect's account of the offence (explain)?

Were any suspects considered to have been coerced into offending during the investigation process (explain)?

Where any of the complainants also offenders and, if so, how was this managed (explain)?

What were the Crown Prosecution Service views on the case (if available)?

3.5 *Services*

What services were provided prior to the investigation?

Service									
Children's social care									
Witness protection									
Health – physical									
Health – sexual									
Health – mental/emotional									
Education									
Youth offending									
Housing/accommodation									
Rape crisis									
Sexual Assault Referral Centre									
Recreational/social activities									
Legal									
Domestic Violence									
Child Sexual Exploitation									
Other									

What services were provided during the investigation?

Service									
Children's social care									
Witness protection									
Health – physical									
Health – sexual									
Health – mental/emotional									
Education									
Youth offending									
Housing/accommodation									
Rape crisis									
Sexual Assault Referral Centre									
Recreational/social activities									
Legal									
Domestic Violence									
Child Sexual Exploitation									
Other									

What services were provided following the investigation?

Service									
Children's social care									
Witness protection									
Health – physical									
Health – sexual									
Health – mental/ emotional									
Education									
Youth offending									
Housing/accommodation									
Rape crisis									
SARC									
Recreational/social activities									
Legal									
DV									
CSE									
Other									

Was work undertaken with the family, peer group, school or neighbourhood following charging?

What needs beyond those related to the case had to be met in relation to all of the young people involved?

Were any additional services (specifically related to the offence) provided to the young people in custody?

3.6 *Outcomes*

Were any young people convicted as a result of the investigation?

Were any young people placed on safeguarding or child protection arrangements as a result of the investigation?

Were any children moved or relocated as a result of the investigation?

Were any children secured in custody as a result of the investigation or trial?

Did any children require ongoing mental or sexual health support following the investigation?

Was there any loss of life or further instances of harm to the young people involved in the case following the investigation?

Was a review of the case undertaken, what type and by whom (Domestic Homicide Review, Serious Case Review, etc.)?

Have there been any changes to local practice, strategic planning or service commissioning following the case?

Other relevant details of the case not covered by the previous questions?

INDEX

Note: **Boldface** page references indicate tables. *Italic* references indicate figures and boxed text.